G581001

P 3364 sw

Denver Public Library

NOTE

The Library may have other copies of this title which can be checked out. **Please ask a librarian for assistance.**

DPL 1 (Rev. 7-72)

R01236 92178

Agnes Leslie

THE SWORD OF DUNDEE

A tale of "Bonnie Prince Charlie"

BY
THEODORA PECK
AUTHOR OF "HESTER OF THE GRANTS"

PICTURES BY JOHN RAE

NEW YORK
DUFFIELD & COMPANY
1908

G581001

R01236 92178

Copyright, 1908, by
Duffield & Company

To
The Immortal Memory of
" The Gallant Highlanders
Who Fought For
Scotland and Prince Charlie."

✱   ✱   ✱   ✱   ✱

From the Inscription
On the Cairn at Culloden.

" A wonderful star broke forth,
New-born, in the skies of the North,
To shine on an Old Year's Night.
And a bud on the dear White Rose
Flowered, in the season of snows,
To bloom for an hour's delight.
Lost is the Star from the night,
And the Rose of an hour's delight
Went—where the roses go;
But the fragrance and light from afar,
Born of the Rose and the Star,
Live through the years and the snow."

"Right or wrong, good or bad, weak or wicked, by some strong fascination the unfortunate Stuarts hold the hearts of mankind. Bonnie, sunny-haired Prince Charlie is too picturesque a figure to be speedily blotted from the page of history. Peace to his ashes, and long may the purple bells of the heather ring their soft chimes above the dust of his unforgotten braves!"

"THE FLOWER OF ENGLAND'S FACE."
BY MRS. JULIA C. R. DORR.

CONTENTS

CHAPTER		PAGE
I.	"The News Frae Moidart"	1
II.	"There'll Never be Peace Till Jamie Comes Hame!"	8
III.	"White Roses Under the Moon"	17
IV.	"O Saw Ye Bonnie Lesley as She Gaed Owre the Border?"	31
V.	"Awa, Whigs, Awa!"	41
VI.	"Sae Noble a Look, Sae Princely an Air!"	50
VII.	"Wha'll be King but Charlie?"	59
VIII.	"All Plaided and Plumed in their Tartan Array"	65
IX.	"Dusky Shadows of the Cairngorms"	73
X.	"Glory of Life, Glory of Soul"	79
XI.	"To See Her is to Love Her"	89
XII.	"O'er Highland Hearts Secure He Reigns"	99
XIII.	"Gallant Young Donald"	109
XIV.	"Thou Art a Queen, Fair Lesley"	118
XV.	"The Brightest Jewel in My Crown"	125
XVI.	"The Rose Sae Like the Snaw"	133
XVII.	"I'll to Lochiel and Appin, and Kneel to Them"	141
XVIII.	"Hey! Johnnie Cope, Are Ye Waukin' Yet?"	150
XIX.	"Wi' a Hundred Pipers, an' a', an' a'!"	159
XX.	"The Broken Heart, it Kens Nae Second Spring Again"	167
XXI.	"There are Hills Beyond Pentland, and Lands Beyond Forth"	177

CONTENTS

CHAPTER		PAGE
XXII.	"Locheil, Locheil! Beware of the Day!"	185
XXIII.	"The Field of the Dead"	197
XXIV.	"The Helmet is Cleft on the Brow of the Brave"	208
XXV.	"When the Sun in His Glory has Look'd on Our Sorrow"	216
XXVI.	"Behold, Where He Flies on His Desolate Path!"	226
XXVII.	"Over the Sea to Skye"	233
XXVIII.	"With the Bloodhounds that Bark for Thy Fugitive King"	242
XXIX.	"To Draw the Sword for Scotland's Lord"	250
XXX.	"On Hills that are by Right His Ain"	258
XXXI.	"There Grew in Bonnie Scotland a Thistle and a Brier"	263
XXXII.	"We Watch'd Thee in the Gloamin' Hour"	271
XXXIII.	"Lone Places of the Deer"	279
XXXIV.	"The Bonnie, the Brave, the Dear"	289
XXXV.	"The Crown of Thy Fathers is Torn from Thy Brow!"	300
XXXVI.	"There's Nought Left but Sorrow for Scotland and Me!"	310
XXXVII.	"Rise, Spirits of Yore!"	320
XXXVIII.	"Now Wae to Thee, Thou Cruel Lord!"	326
XXXIX.	"When Tyranny Revelled in the Blood of the True"	336
XL.	"Better Lo'ed Ye Canna Be"	347
XLI.	"Our Hand is on the Broad Claymore"	357
XLII.	"Red Roses Under the Sun"	366
XLIII.	"Mony a Heart will Break in Twa"	379
XLIV.	"The Sun Shines on the Heather"	385
XLV.	"Who Fought and Died for Charlie"	392

LIST OF ILLUSTRATIONS

"Agnes Leslie" . . . . *Frontispiece*

FACING PAGE

"She was Conscious of Nothing Save the Wild, Sweet Witchery of the Moment" 84

"'Are You Mad, that You Seek to Kill the King?'" 142

"'Tell Me no More—O God!—no More—of Donald Cameron!'" 182

"'Your Grace,' the Countess Cried, 'This is no Man!'" 328

"'And the Lad of the Oak-leaves Walks between Armed Men'" 374

"And Looking up, She saw Him Coming toward Her through the Heather" 386

THE SWORD OF DUNDEE

CHAPTER I

"THE NEWS FRAE MOIDART."

"The news frae Moidart cam' yestreen,
  Will soon gang mony ferlie" (much further).

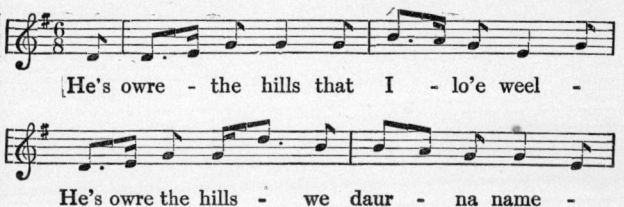

He's owre - the hills that I - lo'e weel -

He's owre the hills - we daur - na name -

"He's owre the hills that I lo'e weel,
He's owre the hills we daur na name,
He's owre the hills ayont Dunblane,
Wha soon will get his welcome hame."

THE voice that sang was thrillingly sweet, and although discreetly hushed, was pulsing through and through with a jubilant undertone that speedily threatened to conquer all restraint, and break into rapturous warbling. It was accompanied by quick dancing steps, so light they could hardly be heard across the wide hall, and the next instant a girl tripped from the gloom of a doorway, and running swiftly to the staircase, leaned warily over the banisters, now hushing her singing long enough to listen for sounds below, now catching up her interrupted song, with a mischievous flash of her lovely brown eyes. She was about one-and-twenty, graceful as a bluebell in her swaying poise, and fair-faced as a rose, with a bewitching blending of sweetness and defiance in her dancing eyes, in her haughty head, its fair curls bound by a white snood, and in the sensitive red lips that hid determination behind their saucy curves.

For several minutes she lingered there, listening breathlessly. At length, reassured by the stillness, she began to descend, observing the precaution, however, of halting on every third step or so to hearken intently. But upon reaching the stair-foot she dismissed prudence, and sped down the long hall and into the great parlour, with quick, confident steps. She swept one glance around the room, gave a saucy pirouette, and exclaimed rapturously, "Thank fate, I am free at last! I maun sing, I maun dance, or I canna live for joy!"

The next instant she had sprung in front of the tall mirror, and was whirling through the reel of Tulloch.

The great parlour, looking eastward on the grey turrets of Holyrood, and northward upon the tall mansions of the Canongate, was peculiarly dark and sombre, and all the radiance of late summer, entering at the windows, served only to emphasise the gloom. The girl herself flashed like a sunbeam through shadows as she flitted here and yonder in the lively dance. She wore a bright plaid wound gaily over her dark-blue dress, the rich folds streaming free with her every motion; the great mirror gave back vivid gleams from the warm sheen of her hair, and the brilliant hues of her tartan. Pausing at last for breath, she glanced again over her shoulder, and drew from beneath her plaid a slip of white bark upon which was written in Gaelic, " Thàinig mo Righ air tir am Muidart." (" My King has landed at Moidart.")

There was neither name nor initial to reveal the sender, and apparently it was not necessary; the message had flashed from heart to heart. She regarded the bark missive as if it were some mighty talisman,—her bosom heaving, her eyes brightening, in a strange ecstasy. She returned it slowly to its hiding-place, then, shaking off her sudden reverie, began to dance more blithely than before, as if her pent-up joy compelled her to wild motion. Her mind had leaped so far beyond her flying feet, that now she neither looked nor listened, and when, in the midst of her maddest whirl, the hall-door opened to admit a figure, she turned with a low cry that was almost terror.

"So I startled you, Agnes?" said the intruder, smiling. He was a young man of twenty-six, tall and stately, with a certain haughtiness in his lofty bearing, and simply yet richly dressed in dark broadcloth. His hair was black; his eyes, too, were dark, and very searching and serious. They had ceased to smile, and regarded the girl's gay attire with grave surprise.

"Why do you wear this festive costume?" he inquired.

She gave her head a half-defiant toss. "To celebrate my freedom, an' you will. Sir Hugh's awa, and the bird is through the bars. On ither days I canna sing because the Whigs object; I canna dance since the Presbyterians disapprove. Oh, Kenneth, ye little ken the feeling. I' the Highlands I was free as a lark on the hills; here I am but a prisoner!"

Kenneth became deeply solicitous. "Are you really unhappy, Agnes?" he said earnestly. "Will love never reconcile you for leaving Auchnacarry?"

Agnes's face quickly showed her dislike of the subject, and she glanced furtively about in an evident desire to escape from the interview. Kenneth gave her no opportunity.

"I do not wonder that you love the Highlands, Agnes;—never shall I cease to love them, for never can I forget that 'twas there I first saw you;—*you*, the loveliest maid that ever eyes beheld. Your hair shone like gold in the moonlight, you wore your plaid as you wear it now, and the picture that you made,—did you think I could ever forget it?" He spoke with unmistakable passion, but the words only stirred the girl to provoking gaiety. Her eyes shot laughing scorn, and it was impatient mockery that curled her scarlet lips.

"Now spare me a' that page o' compliments, Sir Kenneth, for ye maun ken I've heard them a' before. But indeed you gentlemen of Edinbro' find your time of little value, and your brains of little use, since you do naught at all but utter love-speeches in the ears of every maid ye meet. Can you find no better employment? Or do you really think us anxious for such idle praises?"

And she flung him a winning smile, instantly destructive of all her sage advice. Lured by it, Kenneth advanced with the manifest purpose of taking her hand, and compelling her to listen. But she evaded him by a sprightly turn, and finally poised herself on the wide window-ledge, her fringed plaid fluttering just beyond his reach.

"Agnes, have you no heart?" he exclaimed despairingly.

"Oh, indeed, sir, that I have, and one that throbs quite warmly upon occasion. Dinna ye ken the saying: 'True heart aye beats 'neath tartan'? Do ye no' think it beats beneath mine?"

But Kenneth's eyes dwelt gloomily on the bright scarlet hues of her plaid.

"But why the Cameron tartan?" he demanded.

"Why not the Cameron?" she retorted. "Is't no' my adopted clan? An' does it no' become me unco weel?" She had a curious fashion, when excited, of mixing Scotch and English. "Besides, I have made a vow——" she paused abruptly, dangerously near self-betrayal. Her eyes shone again with that bright rapture; her heart was stirred by a joy in which the present had no part.

"Why do you never wear the Campbell?" he said, and his face clouded.

"But I was not brought up among the Campbells; I havena the right to wear their tartan," she rejoined, and then regretted that she had given him a loop-hole for advance.

"But I will give you the right, Agnes!" he cried ardently, "if only you will become——"

"I winna hear another word!" cried Agnes, cutting short his passionate entreaty. "Tak' your love-making elsewhere, Kenneth Campbell! A sad pair we should make, we, wha canna speak twa words in peace,—and small wonder, since *your* ancestor murdered *mine*. I have told you a score o' times I will marry none but a Jacobite!

> And alack, as a Whig ye aye maun be,
> I vow that a Whig shall ne'er wed wi' me!

Will ye no' praise my poetry? 'Tis a fitting theme!"

Suddenly she ceased her raillery, and for a moment gazed full into his face. Whether from what she discerned there, or from some vagary of her own, her merry, teasing tone vanished instantly, and she spoke with a grave sincerity.

"Oh, Kenneth, why will ye trouble me? There's no love in my heart of the kind ye seek. There's love o' kindred, and love o' king, and that's just a'!"

They stood side by side, and he had possessed himself of her hands. He gazed at her beseechingly, looking the words he did not speak, and her eyes were as grave as his as she added:

"Would it be honourable, think ye, to speak ye fair, and gi'e ye promises, when a' the time I lo'ed ye not?"

"Ah!" he cried, "have you forgotten that June evening, four long years ago, and how you saved my life, and took my heart in payment?"

"Kenneth," she interrupted earnestly, " how often have I told ye that 'twas naught I did,—that I had done it a' for ony ither stranger,—but if you do feel there's aught owing, then, as ye bear me friendship, entreat me nae mair!"

And with that she gently drew her hands away, tripped across the room, and flitted through the doorway like some bright-plumaged bird.

When she entered her chamber, and had closed the door, all the mirth and exultation of her earlier mood had disappeared, and her face wore only a sweet seriousness. The ponderous antique furniture, black with age, gave an almost weird effect to the stately chamber, and this was still further increased by the heavy hangings of sombre crimson at bed and window, and the dim light that filtered through the small, diamond-shaped panes. But Agnes's eyes passed by all these details to rest wistfully upon one object. This was an old broadsword which hung aslant upon the wall, its straight, broad blade and curious basket-hilt marking it distinctly from the weapons of other lands,—proclaiming it the sword of Scotland, the claymore of the clans! Just below the hilt was fastened a knot of faded satin ribbon, once stainlessly white. Agnes, kneeling upon a chair, took the sword in reverent hands, touching it softly as if it were a sacred thing! And with a sudden passion of tenderness she stooped and kissed the faded ribbon!

CHAPTER II

"THERE'LL NEVER BE PEACE TILL JAMIE COMES
HAME!"

"The church is in ruins, the state is in jars,
Delusions, oppressions, and murderous wars;
We darena weel say't, but we ken wha's to blame—
There'll never be peace till Jamie comes hame!"

ON an early June evening of the year 1741, Kenneth Campbell, journeying northward through the Highlands, drew rein beside a wooded river-bank, and gazed in perplexity at the road ahead. It was nine o'clock, but the late northern twilight, now at its longest, contended so successfully with the coming darkness that in the open the light was hardly dimmer than that of a cloudy day, though in the woods, through which his pathway led, the dusk was falling fast. He caught a glimpse through an opening in the trees of the sun setting in crimson glory behind hills richly green with heather. Embosomed deep among them, like an opal rimmed by emeralds, gleamed the limpid waters of a mountain-tarn, that caught and mirrored in its placid breast the thousand colours of the sunset. Over it eagles hovered upon wide-spread wings, outlined athwart the burning sky like onyx against amber. A few miles below, a tiny river, whose course the eye could trace by a winding ribbon of green, mingled its slender current with the still expanse. At its outlet, a little isle lay dark upon the iridescent lake, moored like a shadowy bark upon a sea of flame.

But to this scene of beauty he was wholly insensible, and he turned on it the gaze of the unseeing. For he was in Lochaber, the very country he most wished to avoid, and with no hope, apparently, of reaching Argyllshire that night. His ideas of the Highlands were extremely vague, and he had wandered often from his path. Knowing himself to be in the heart of the hostile clans, and remembering the papers in his coat, and the money in his saddle-pockets, he thought his mission a mad one, and wished himself many miles south of the Highland line.

A lovely mountain-river, flowing between deeply shaded banks, had been his companion for some distance, and he watched it idly, wondering whither its course would lead him. But as this aimless musing in no wise helped his difficulty, he at length gathered up his loosened bridle-rein, and resumed his uncertain way. For several miles he rode in undisturbed tranquillity, and yet he viewed with growing apprehension the dangerous mission with which he had been entrusted. Why, in the name of reason, had it not been bestowed on some one fitted to discharge it!

Dusk gathered quickly as he pondered; the shadowy glade grew eerie with faint moonbeams and swaying branches. Kenneth was no coward; but his fancy, vagrant like himself, fashioned warrior-shapes from every mossy boulder and fallen tree. Even his horse partook of the feeling, and snorted at every scurrying rabbit or rustling leaf. The vague foreboding gathered form at last. Out of the darkening woods before him, as from the very shadows at his feet, sprang a number of hostile figures, dimly discernible in that grey light, yet unmistakably declared,—by kilt and plaid and bonnet,—to be the Highland sentries he had dreaded. The foremost unsheathed his broadsword, and with a grimly threatening gesture, commanded the traveller to dismount. Kenneth was armed with gun and pistol, but he knew better than attempt to use them at such close range, when confronted by the lightning agility of a dirk in the hand of a Highlander. He must practise persuasion, his last defence.

"Why do you detain me?" he inquired of the aggressor, who, with firm hold on the bridle, was watching every movement.

"There are good reasons," was the terse reply in clear English.

"If it is money you want, I will give it, rather than delay my journey. You can certainly have no other object in stopping me. Besides, I travel with the authority of—" here he leaned over and whispered the rest of the sentence into the clansman's ear.

A startling result followed. The Highlander's eyes dilated, his muscles swelled, and he seemed to grow in height and breadth before Kenneth's astonished gaze. He shrieked a command in Gaelic to his followers. Bristling with equal rage, they sprang forward like panthers, till the frightened horse reared backward from the uplifted dirks.

Kenneth swept one glance around. There was no way of escape save the river, whose dark waves rippled only a few feet away. He could barely see their dull gleam in the fast-fading moonlight, for the sky, with one of the rapid changes peculiar to the Highlands, was already deeply overcast. But he had forded the same river without difficulty several miles above, and he could not pause to think of peril now, with these dangerous foes confronting him. He simply wrenched his bridle free, wheeled his horse out of the road, and plunged down the steep bank into the shadowy stream. The next instant horse and man were struggling in the headlong current.

But swift as Kenneth's act had been, his assailants were hardly less rapid, and before his horse, snorting and terrified, had gained mid-stream, his bridle was seized by the same Highlander who had relinquished it a minute before. Two others swam closely after, and thereupon commenced a furious struggle. The leader, keeping himself afloat the while, held his raised dirk in one hand, while with the other he tore savagely at Kenneth's coat, with the frantic determination of securing the prize beneath. Kenneth, bending this way and that to escape the clutch of his infuriated foe, strove desperately to guard the papers, and to prevent himself being swept from the saddle by the force of the current, which every moment threatened to engulf both horse and rider.

The crisis came quickly. He felt the horse sink under him, saw the water surge above the saddle-bow; the desperate clutch upon his breast grew stronger, and the uplifted dirk threatened to descend. At that moment a rider galloped up the bank, and a girl's voice called commandingly in Gaelic. The effect was instantaneous. Kenneth's antagonists loosed their hold, and swam off shoreward, leaving him to drown or swim, as it pleased him. Dire, indeed, was his peril, for his feet were so entangled in the stirrups that ere he could free himself from his floundering steed he sank to his neck in the swirling current. At this fateful moment, a log, hurled with dexterous aim, fell splashing into his very grasp, and the same clear voice cried, " Cling to this! I will bring aid! Donald! Donald Cameron! Come hither! There is some one drowning in the river!"

In answer to her cry a young man sprang down the bank, and casting off his coat and plaid, began to swim in Kenneth's direction. He seized the plunging horse, gained the saddle, and turned the animal's head down-stream. Kenneth, almost helpless, felt himself lifted by a strong hand to a seat behind his rescuer, who cried gaily, " As well hang as drown, though indeed there's no danger of either!" and proceeded to guide the snorting steed ashore.

To Kenneth, dripping and almost dazed, the roar of the water still in his ears, the scene that met his eyes was weirdly unreal. The little glen, in its setting of sombre pines, seemed a magic spot; the Highlanders, with their flickering torches and wildly picturesque costumes, were the beings of enchantment, and in their midst, like the fairy of the spell, where moonbeams and red torchlight mingled, he first beheld the girl who had saved him from death.

He saw her then, as he saw her in later years till his life ended,—a maid of seventeen, with eyes of brilliant hazel,—brown eyes that could yet go black with anger,—an exquisite fair skin, delicate lips,

"Never be Peace Till Jamie Comes Hame!" 13

firmly set in a dauntless curve, and a mass of yellow curls tumbling over her shoulders and kindled by the torchlight into ruddy gold.

Her tam-o'-shanter, adorned by an eagle's plume, was saucily poised on the fair head; a claymore hung at her side, secured by a sword-belt buckled round her waist. Over her simple dress she wore a plaid of a dark, rich tartan, crossed over the breast, and fastened upon the left shoulder, after the fashion of a Highland chieftain, by a brooch whose brilliant cairngorm shed an orange flame, one fringed end falling to the knee, the other flowing gracefully backward. Kenneth stood entranced, with eyes for naught but her.

She came quickly forward. "I hope you are not greatly injured, sir," she said with sweet solicitude.

"Oh, no, I am none the worse," he responded hurriedly, and then with passionate gratitude, "I owe you my life! How can I ever repay you!"

"You need not feel it a personal debt, sir," she returned, smiling. "Remember I was quite unaware of your identity at the time. I saved you as I would have saved any mortal. In truth, I did not think of you," she added with a saucy glance. "Donald and I raced from the bridge, and the Prince won,"—she touched the neck of her handsome white horse,— "that is why I saw you first.

"And now, Angus," she cried, addressing Kenneth's assailant, "why did you disobey me, and leave this gentleman to drown?"

Angus, a tall, fair-haired young Highlander, respectfully removed his bonnet.

"Ye maun remember, your ladyship, that ye bid me let the gentleman be, an' your ladyship canna say I didna do't," he said artfully.

To the canny Highlander a foe drowned served the same purpose as a foe captured.

The maiden stamped her foot with displeasure. "You shall not accompany me again, Angus, if you behave thus!" she exclaimed. "But we must set out for Auchnacarry immediately. I can see, sir," she continued to Kenneth, "that you are chilled in spite of Donald's plaid."

And there was nothing left for Kenneth but to accept the proffered hospitality with the best possible grace.

It was not till they were winding along the torch-lit mountain road that his fair preserver, who rode between him and Donald Cameron, said inquiringly:

"And now, sir, tell me why Angus yonder was so anxious to dispute your journey?"

"In truth I am at a loss to say," he answered. "I gave him what I thought a pass-word through these Highlands, and the next I knew, his dirk was at my breast. I had thought the name of Argyle a surety of safety."

"Argyle!" she cried. "You are no Jacobite, then," she continued coldly, "I surmised as much. Yet I think you Highland-born despite your speech. If you wore the tartan I could name you quickly enough; as it is, I might guess your clan."

"I am a Campbell," he said instantly, "and close kin to Argyle."

It was well the torchlight was uncertain, and that

Kenneth could not see the look on the girl's face and how she shrank from him at his last words. But she mastered her antipathy,—whatever it was,—and hardly betrayed it save in her increased reserve of tone and bearing.

"I am Agnes Leslie, the foster-daughter of Lochiel," she presently vouchsafed, "'Agnes of Auchnacarry,' they call me. And this,"—she turned to her companion,—" is Donald Cameron, Master of Lochiel!"

The youth bowed gracefully. Kenneth, with eyes for Agnes alone, saw only that he was handsome and yellow-haired, and that his Highland dress became him to perfection. The girl's witchery absorbed all his vision.

They were now in the very heart of Lochiel's country where the noble Scotch firs grew tall, and rowen and ash throve luxuriantly, and the heather that brushed their saddles was the height of a man's head.

They had been winding up a wooded valley, still following the course of the impetuous river; suddenly before them opened a straight, broad avenue, densely roofed by a black arch of trees, so thickly interlaced that even at noon no beam could penetrate. At the end of the vista the moon shone upon a grey stone pile, which, as they drew near, assumed the outlines of an ancient castle, whose lofty turrets and proud battlements slept softly beneath the spell of the wizard moonshine. Behind and half around it the mountains curved their dark protecting ramparts, now mistily illumed by the moon.

The travellers dismounted in front of the wide

portal, and Donald Cameron conducted Kenneth to a room, and himself assisted in removing the stranger's wet clothing.

"You must wear the Highland dress," he exclaimed, eying his guest in laughing perplexity. "And a Cameron's at that! There are no Lowland costumes here." And he proceeded to enlighten Kenneth in the mysteries of plaid and philabeg. Thus arrayed in dry garments, and further warmed by a drink of usquebaugh, Kenneth followed his companion down a great stairway, and found Agnes awaiting them at the foot.

The girl stole noiselessly along the hall to a door at one end, and knocked softly thereupon. The next instant it swung open, and revealed to the astonished stranger a spacious chamber, decked as for a banquet, and blazing with festive lights.

CHAPTER III

"WHITE ROSES UNDER THE MOON"

"White roses under the moon,
  For the King without lands to give;
But he reigns with the reign of June,
With his rose and his blackbird's tune,
  And he lives while faith may live!"

IT was a great, wide, oak-raftered hall, whose warlike ornaments were antlers and Highland shields, set round with dirks and broadswords, and here and there a faded tapestry, adorned with battle-scenes. The grey walls were now gay with masses of green heather and golden broom, and a wreath of heather encircled the bowl of white roses on the banqueting-table. A few logs glowed red-golden in the great fire-place, dispelling the chill of the mountain air; above, on opposite sides of the massive chimney-piece, two elaborately carved crests of different designs were cut into the stone. The floor was of polished oak, entirely bare. Around the massive table, lit by many-branched bronze candelabra, were gathered a group of Highland gentlemen, who instantly cut short their low-toned conversation, and rose, one and all, as the stranger entered.

Agnes, having swept them a courtesy worthy a maid-of-honour, ran to a sad-faced, handsome gentleman, who kissed her tenderly. She then addressed a tall and stately chieftain upon whose splendid figure the beauty of the Highland costume showed to most graceful advantage. His kinship to Donald Cameron was unmistakable. The same frank, tender, brave blue eyes, the same lofty grace of bearing, the same gentleness of speech, that marked the son, distinguished the father. His hair, which in youth had been fair as Donald's, had grown darker with years, and was now a rich shade of light brown. So noble was his bearing, so gentle and winning his face, that he seemed, like the great Montrose, a perfect model of the heroes of antiquity. It was this courtly demeanour, joined to his faultless character as a man, no less than as a chieftain, which made him known throughout the Highlands by the name of "the gentle Locheil,"—a name to be enshrined in loving memory for all the years to come.

"Cousin Donald," said the girl, "I have brought you a guest, who, though he wears your tartan, is not of Clan Cameron."

Young Donald now recounted their meeting with Kenneth, saying nothing, however, of his own part in the rescue, or of the stranger's dubious errand. Locheil, with polished courtesy, presented Kenneth to the company—among them Lord George Murray, grave and commanding, with a dark, sternly noble face; MacDonald of Keppoch, alert and ardent, and Alexander MacGillivray of Drumnaglass, superbly tall and straight, and the most dexterous swordsman in the Highlands.

But of them all, none was more conspicuous than Norman Leslie. He had a slender, finely propor-

ioned figure, stooping slightly as if from constant
reverie, long, waving brown hair, and pale, clear-cut
features upon which much suffering had marked the
lines of melancholy. The eyes were especially
noticeable,—large, darkly blue, and mournful with
past sorrows. Face and figure alike proclaimed him
of noble birth, gentleman to the core,—a man to
whom ideals were dearer than reality, and memory
sweeter than hope.

The meeting, held for whatever purpose, being
ended, most of the gentlemen dispersed into the courtyard, leaving the principal actors of the scene still
gathered about the great hearthstone.

Agnes stood in the full glow of the firelight, affording Kenneth an entrancing picture. She wore
a green kilted skirt that reached half-way below the
knee, showing the pretty ankles, and feet that were
light and dainty in their low-heeled Highland shoes;
and a close-fitting green bodice, laced in back with a
scarlet ribbon, and worn over a white under-bodice
which left only the throat bare. She had thrown
aside her tam-o'-shanter, and her tumbled yellow
curls fell freely to her waist, bound only by a white
ribbon or snood, worn in Scotland by all maidens.

Norman Leslie, standing in the light from the
great fire-place, glanced first at the girl before him,
and then at a picture he held in his hand. This was
a miniature of a youth about eighteen, with a handsome, spirited face, lighted by large brown eyes, and
shaded by yellow curls which softened the gay boyish
features to almost feminine beauty,—an effect increased by the girlishly fair skin, and bright red lips.

Ardour and daring shone in the dancing eyes, determination was graven upon the handsome, wayward mouth, but, moreover, the face was frank and generous and winning, with a strangely touching charm—a suggestion, almost, of melancholy, about its mischievous beauty.

From the picture he turned to Agnes. Her hazel eyes were dancing in the firelight, the golden hair was tossed away from her face, and there was something of defiance in the back-flung head and erect figure. The wonder deepened in Norman Leslie's face; his hand closed over the miniature. "Strange," he murmured, "strange! There is the same look!"

His musing was interrupted by Kenneth, who touched by the generosity that forebore to question him, now addressed Locheil.

"You should know I come an enemy into your midst. I am a Campbell by name, and a bearer of secret papers to the Duke of Argyle. I lost my way in the Highlands, and owe my life to Mistress Leslie and to your son."

"Perhaps you are not an enemy after all," replied Locheil cordially. "We have friends among the Campbells. If you are of kin to Sir James of Auchinbreck, you can never be a foe!"

"I cannot claim that privilege; I am a Campbell of Breadalbane, and I was born in Glenlyon."

As the name of Argyle had aroused the fiery Angus, so did that of Breadalbane astound the listeners. They all started, but the indignant colour sprang to Agnes's face, and her eyes blazed with positive hatred.

"Do you hear?" she cried fiercely. "He is a Glenlyon Campbell,—a son of the murderers of Glencoe! No wonder Angus MacDonald sought to kill him! I am half-sorry I saved his life!"

"Hush, lassie!" Norman Leslie interposed gently; "remember this young man is not to blame for what his fathers did!"

But the girl's wrath was unallayed. "Will you forget the 13th of February,* and the curse of Glencoe?" she challenged angrily.

Kenneth, however, was unable to account for her fury.

"Glencoe?" he repeated, "Glencoe? Do you refer to the trouble there in King William's time?"

"Trouble?" she echoed bitterly, "aye, trouble, indeed, that shall haunt the Campbells to the last!"

Kenneth surveyed her with incredulous wonder. "But why should the fate of these MacDonalds, half-a-century dead, affect you, Mistress Leslie? Were they kinsmen of yours?"

"No, not at all!" she answered proudly. "But our clans are brothers none the less. We have fought side by side so often in the cause of the King!"

Her voice had grown strangely soft; her wrath was half-forgotten. Kenneth seized the advantage.

"It is through no fault of mine I have incurred your enmity," he said in low, almost pleading tones, "yet you shall see that even a hated Campbell may be generous!

---

* The massacre of Glencoe, which occurred February 13, 1692, was instigated by the Earl of Breadalbane and executed by Campbell of Glenlyon.

"What is your pleasure with me?" he inquired of the rest. "I am virtually your prisoner, for you know my secret. I ask only that you send a message to Argyle to explain my failure to discharge my trust, and one to Sir Hugh Campbell at Edinburgh to apprise him of my fortune."

Locheil listened with pained surprise. "There is no reason why you should not continue your journey to-night, if your condition admits, and necessity requires. Since you will not remain longer as our guest, know that you are as free, here, at this moment, as you were in Edinburgh, and that the papers, whatever their contents, will never be read by me!"

Kenneth stood motionless, stunned by this unexpected magnanimity. Then he grasped Locheil's hands, exclaiming, "I will ride to-night to Edinburgh, not to Inverary, the home of Argyle. Never will I bear tidings unfavourable to such generous foes, who shall be foes no longer. It is slender payment for a gift of life!"

So saying, he tore the disturbing papers from his coat, and flung them upon the glowing logs. They leaped to flame, blazed high, and died in golden ashes.

Agnes broke silence first. "I am not sorry that I saved you," she said softly. "A Campbell *can* be generous!" and her pretty hand touched his in token of forgiveness.

And Kenneth knew that with that one chivalrous act he had sealed the bond of friendship between him and these warm Highland hearts.

Presently Agnes observed that she must arrange

her roses, and flitted away. Norman Leslie's sad eyes followed her through the doorway, and he exclaimed, half to himself, half to Kenneth:

"She comes o' proud blood, bonnie Agnes Leslie. Her mother was a Graham of Claverhouse, niece to the Viscount Dundee, and great-granddaughter to the Marquis Montrose; and her father, William Leslie, was by right of birth the Duke of Rothes, had he not lost his coronet by his devotion to King James the Eighth. She has the look o' 'Bonnie Dundee,' they say; 'the devil with the angel's face,' his foemen called him, so dreadful was he in war, so beautiful in person."

The conversation was here interrupted by Donald Cameron, who announced that supper awaited Kenneth in an adjoining room; and Norman Leslie was left alone by the hearth.

The door had scarcely shut upon the stranger when Agnes entered eagerly.

"Ah, now he's awa, ye may tell the tale, and I may listen, laddie. I feared lest he shouldna go, an' ye wouldna speak when he was by, to one who loved not the cause."

Norman Leslie, lost in thought, looked up questioningly.

"Ye'll no' forget the night, laddie, and the tale it brings?" she whispered softly.

"How oft have I told it, lassie?"

"For seven years," said Agnes gravely. "Ye told it first when I was ten, and begged for a tale o' love and war. Ye've ne'er missed ance in a' the years."

Norman Leslie gazed silently at the ardent face.

His own was pale and grave. It was quite a minute before he spoke.

" It will be the tale of William Leslie, your father, and my brother, and the bravest, bonniest lad that e'er drew sword in the north country!" he said at last in a low, tremulous voice, still gazing into the girl's lovely face. " Oh, lassie, ye are like him!—his hair was golden as yours, his eyes as bright, his laugh as clear and mirthful once,—but that was lang, lang syne!"

" 'Twas in ' the '15 '," murmured Agnes, " when the Earl of Mar raised the standard of the Stuarts, and Sheriffmuir was fought."

Her face had grown rapt and dreamy; her voice sank low as his had done.

" Your mother was an Agnes Leslie, too. Her eyes were hazel, her hair was brown,—that was the Graham beauty,—so looked the great Dundee; the Leslies were blue-eyed, and 'tis from them comes your golden hair.

" And Agnes Graham,—she was but seventeen when Sheriffmuir was fought, but sorrow made her a woman before her years. When her father fell fighting for his King, and her lover was mortally wounded, she showed the loftiest courage in her woe. They bore your father to France, dying, as 'twas thought, while she, perforce, remained in Scotland with her mother. For long there were hopes that his wound might heal in that warm climate, and they waited—in what anguish Heaven alone can tell—in the confidence that fate might spare him.

" But when six years had passed, and he knew

he could never recover, then at last he sent for her, or she had written saying she could bear the separation no longer. So they were wed in France; and for a year thereafter it seemed as if hope and vigour were restored to him. But even love could not hold back the shadow of death which had followed him so long, and at last, with its fatal gloom upon him, the anguished longing to see Scotland returned in fourfold strength. 'I am dying, Norman,' he said to me, 'and even my spirit will not rest, I think, if I die in France. Were I but in Scotland, death would be joy to me; I would sleep beneath the heather like a child on its mother's breast. Oh, let me go back! Let me go back!'

"And so, on a wild March day of the year 1723, we set sail for Scotland. A stormy voyage we had, but 'twas upon a sunny April morning that we sighted the shores of our beloved land. And when he saw the hills all green with heather, and proud Ben Nevis crowned with snow, a little colour tinged his pallid cheek, and the tears sprang to his eyes for joy. Yea, though his lands were forfeited, and his title lost, and a price was set on even his life itself!

"But he had friends true as the broadsword's blade, and it was the brave Lochiel who welcomed him to Auchnacarry, and carved the Leslie crest with that of Cameron upon the chimney here in token that this house should be henceforth his home. There are the buckles which Bartholf of Leslie added after he had saved Queen Margaret from drowning at the ford. When she slipped from the pillion behind him, she caught at the single buckle of his belt, and he cried to her, 'Grip fast!'—the very words you see carved there above the griffins and the coronet of Rothes. And 'tis a motto the Leslies merit, for they have ever 'gripped fast' the right. And fitting, too, is that of the Camerons cut beside it,—'For king and country.'

"Alas, it was not long before William Leslie's eyes were closed forever upon all earthly scenes!

"Yet for five months he lived in a state of rapture,—a paradise begun on earth,—and smiled in the face of death. And all his thought was for the child he should never see. At sunset of a fair September day his spirit parted. Just before, he called to me, and I raised him in my arms. The sword you wear now lay beside him,—the sword of Dundee, which had passed to Agnes Graham as the last of her family.

"The story of that sword you know by heart. A few months before Claverhouse rode forth to raise the clans, and to die for the King at Killiecrankie, James VII. had created him Viscount of Dundee. 'Twas at that time that the King fastened there below the hilt the knot of satin ribbon which you see, and bade him wear it for his sovereign's sake. How he kept that promise you know well, and how his kinsmen kept it, for never has that ribbon left the hilt in all the years of battle that have passed since then."

"The sword of Dundee,—and my father's sword," the girl murmured; "I wear it every 10th of June because of him, and the birthday of James VIII."

"'Norman,' he whispered, 'when my son is grown

put this sword in his hand,—*tell him to fight for the King!*' Those were his last words."

The girl's radiant eyes had overshadowed; now they brimmed with tears.

"'Tis hard to have been a mistake from the beginning," said Agnes mournfully. "'Twas for a lad he longed,—a son to bear his sword and uphold his name!" And her wistful eyes sought the fire.

Norman Leslie paused in his walk to stroke the bright bowed head. "Dinna greet, lassie, dinna greet," he said in his kindly Scotch. "He only spoke thus because o' the King,—'tis he would ha'e been the proudest of a bonnie lass, and there's nae man could wish to change a thing so fair as ye for ony lad alive. So dinna fash your pretty head wi' thinking o't.

"And when our King comes hame, 'tis like a smile from your bonnie een will please him mair than the drawing of bare steel in his service.

"So he died of that cruel wound,—a soldier's death, though not upon the battlefield! The hills he loved were purple with the heather when we laid him in his grave. And then for his wife I feared, lest she should die of grief, for few hearts loved like theirs. But she was brave as she had ever been, and she lived for the child alone.

"You were born on an Old Year's Night,—the third birthday of our bonnie young Prince, as ye know. And when the heather was green again they who loved were re-united. There were left only you and I, lassie,—of them all, only you and I!"

Agnes drew a quick breath like a sob. "They

all died for the King," she said tremulously, "they all died for the King! The great Montrose on the scaffold, and Dundee at Killiecrankie, and then my father! And if the King comes again, there are still lives to lay at his feet!"

"Aye," Leslie answered, "so long as true hearts throb!"

She laid her cheek against his arm, and he pressed her to him in a passion of love almost fatherly. And with the shadow of the past upon their faces,—the one so grave and mournful, the other so fair and radiant,—they passed out into the wide courtyard.

The great fountain in the centre sparkled through a mist of blossoms and green boughs, a bonfire was dancing heavenward in golden flames, and torches flung their crimson gleams athwart the stern grey walls.

Just as Kenneth's horse was led out, saddled, and he prepared to mount, every man of that gay company swung his wine-glass high, held it above the fountain's flowery brim, and cried in ringing accents: "God save King James!"

Kenneth left moonlit Auchnacarry with Donald Cameron walking by his side.

When they were beyond hearing of the Castle, Kenneth turned to the young Gael, saying gravely, "What was the curse of Glencoe?"

"The curse," Donald answered, "was that all who had aught to do with the crime should die childless. See how strangely it has been fulfilled: King William, who signed the order for the massacre, died childless; and Lord Stair, the instigator; and Campbell of Glen-

yon, who perpetrated the outrage. That curse is
the most dreadful we of the Highlands can invoke;
to have no son to bear our name,—no daughter to
love and cherish,—to be like some lightning-blasted
tree, which adds no atom to the greenness around it;
a living death from which no acorn ever springs to
fill the land with shade and beauty!"

He spoke with the unconscious imagery of the Gael,
and Kenneth listened with a shadowy face.

At the end of the avenue rose the castle-gate, a
massive structure of wrought and gilded iron, and
beside it Kenneth drew rein, expecting his companion
to produce a key.

Instead, Donald faced him gravely. "The way
lies yonder," he explained, pointing along the road.
"This gate has never been opened since King James
passed through in ' the '15,' nor will it ever again
unclose save to *a Prince of the Stuart line!*"

. . . . .

Having bade his guest godspeed, Donald wended
his way homeward by a foot-path winding around a
wooded hill not far from the Castle. At its base he
paused beneath a wide-spreading tree, for he saw
Agnes kneeling in the moonlight beside a low green
mound, and as he looked she laid upon it a wreath of
snow-white roses, murmuring low, "For the sake of
him I never saw! I will wear the sword in honour,
lass though I am!" And her tears fell among the
flowers.

"White roses under the moon!" Sad memories in
the mournful moonlight,—the fading roses of a lost

cause! They lay there in the dust like the fallen hopes of this brave, chivalrous people, whose high courage, and tried loyalty, and pure devotion to their exiled King, though trampled in the dust of defeat, were white and stainless roses that would never die!

CHAPTER IV

"O SAW YE BONNIE LESLEY AS SHE GA'ED OWRE THE BORDER?"

> "O saw ye bonnie Lesley
>   As she ga'ed owre the border?
> She's gane, like Alexander,
>   To spread her conquests farther."

KENNETH'S return to Edinburgh with the tale of his adventures wrought sad havoc in the mind of his uncle, Sir Hugh Campbell, who considered the loss of the papers unimportant,—for he had copies, and the delay involved was trivial,—but deemed the effect upon Kenneth far more dangerous. He had brought up his orphan nephew in the strictest Presbyterian fashion, and here the lad had come home with his mind full of a mischievous Highland beauty, and Heaven knew how many wild Tory notions besides.

Sir Hugh was of middle age and middle height, with cold grey eyes and a face sown with the wrinkles of a stern, unloving life; a man quick to resent, keen to cherish hatred, who never forgot, and rarely forgave. Naturally austere, he had been still more embittered by disappointment, and since his greatest wish,—for a son to succeed him,—had been denied, he looked out upon the world with hostile eyes. His wife was an elder sister of that Agnes Graham who had died so long ago, and often had poor Mistress

Catherine longed to see the child, of whom she knew nothing beyond the bare fact of its existence. For from the day that William Leslie drew sword for King James, Sir Hugh had had no intercourse with the family, toward whom he felt the contempt he bestowed on all Jacobites; and Mistress Campbell no more thought of crossing his will than she would of burning the roof above her head. The one would certainly have matched the other in terrifying consequences.

But upon discovery that the daughter of the hated William Leslie had saved his nephew's life, stern justice, one of Sir Hugh's icy virtues, compelled his reluctant obedience. After duly pondering Kenneth's recital, Sir Hugh took out ten pounds, counted them carefully, considered their value keenly, and finally despatched them to Norman Leslie at Auchnacarry with a reluctant sigh, for although due reward for Kenneth's life, he mourned that such good Whig money should be stained by the touch of Jacobites, and even shuddered lest some of it should reach the exiled King. His fears were needless, however, for only six days later a wild-eyed Highlander appeared at his door and presented him with the selfsame packet he had so generously despatched northward. Among the notes was a slip of paper upon which was written: "We weigh not lives by money!" And Sir Hugh, divided between rage at the insult, and joy at the recovery of his treasure, made no further attempt to reach these proud-spirited benefactors.

Of this high-minded act Kenneth knew nothing, for two days after his arrival in Edinburgh, he left,

at Sir Hugh's persuasion, to resume his studies on
the Continent, carrying with him some sweet, disturbing memories. It was not till his home-coming
three years later that capricious Fate ensnared him
afresh, and brought fair Agnes Leslie again across
his path.

Kenneth had lived so much of his life abroad that
his own land seemed foreign to him. He had been educated at Eton and Cambridge, owing to Sir Hugh's
belief that the University of Edinburgh was largely
Jacobite in sentiment; and upon completing college
had spent several years in Germany, where his uncle's
influence at the court of George II. had given him
every advantage. With the exception of the brief
visit to Edinburgh three years earlier, and that ever-memorable journey through the Highlands, he had
been far removed from that " hot-bed of Tory sentiment," as the Whigs called Scotland. Having arrived, however, at the grave and judicial age of
twenty-five, Kenneth was warmly welcomed to Edinburgh, but his own joy was by no means wholly due
to the pleasure of revisiting his old home. Three
years had no more dimmed his memory of Agnes than
a passing cloud dims the beauty of a mountain lake,
when the sun shines once more upon it. His mind
drew the picture as clearly as the lake mirrors the
mountain.

How well he remembered her as she came forward
into the light of the torches, a haughty little figure,
a plaid of the Leslie tartan flung gracefully from one
shoulder, and one hand grasping an old broadsword,
in whose curious hilt the wrought steel formed the

letter S—the letter S, for Stuart, was one of the secret symbols the Jacobites engraved upon their swords—and from which hung a worn knot of faded ribbon that had once been white. There was haughty grace in the poise of the golden head,—the haughty grace of her kinsman, Dundee; and the sword she held in her hand was the sword the dying Claverhouse had borne at Killiecrankie. And though this exquisite picture of her was graven forever on his mind, in after years it was joined to another so terrible he could hardly bear to recall it,—a picture burned upon his memory by the lightning-flash of one fearful moment!

Kenneth ardently proposed to his uncle that, considering the connection of the families, Sir Hugh might show his gratitude to Norman Leslie by inviting Agnes to become a member of the household in Edinburgh, thus affording the young lady better opportunities of completing her education. It was artfully suggested, and, strangely enough, met with favour, for Sir Hugh, iron toward all others, became softer metal in Kenneth's hands. And so it happened that a second missive was despatched to Auchnacarry.

The evening of its arrival found Agnes gaily employed. "The gentle Locheil" had just returned from a visit to his father in France, bringing for Agnes the most wonderful riding-dress to be found in all Paris. It was a deep shade of blue, the coat made of velvet, the long skirt of fine broadcloth; both richly laced with silver. The hat was a jaunty three-cornered cockade, also edged with silvery lace; and

"O Saw Ye Bonnie Lesley"

the effect of the whole was bewitching, as the great Venetian mirror at Auchnacarry bore witness.

Agnes was surveying the exquisite image of herself with undisguised delight, when a servant entered to announce a visitor, and the next moment Sir Duncan Forbes of Culloden, President of the Court of Sessions, and a revered friend of Norman Leslie's, was shown into the room.

"So 'tis you, fair Mistress Agnes; how fine ye are!" he said, his grave face changing to a smile.

Agnes favoured him with a gay courtesy. "Cousin Lochiel's from home, but sit ye down, while I call Addie."

And she caught up her trailing skirt, and fluttered away, like some bright spirit, leaving him alone in the deepening August twilight. He heard her go tripping merrily up the stairs with her candle, and the mellow tones of her voice floated back to him in that lithe rallying-song of "the '15":

> "Little wat ye wha's coming!
> Little wat ye wha's coming!
> Little wat ye wha's coming!
> Ilka Duinnewassal's coming!"

And before the song had ended, Norman Leslie entered the room.

The two friends faced each other in grave understanding. Duncan Forbes grasped Leslie's hand.

"Ye know for what I've come, Norman, and we both know of the stir across the water, and what it soon will mean. Norman, set my mind at rest; tell me ye've no part in it!"

"And that's what I winna do!" cried Leslie
friendly but emphatic tones. "Am I so fickle ye k
na where to find me?"

"Aye, Norman, the lassie's song answers i
'Little wat ye wha's coming!' Ye're asteer for ru
as lightly as the lass sings that old ballad! For yo
ain sake, Norman, and for the sake o' William Le
lie, my boyhood's dearest friend, tak' heed to yo
course, and shift rudder while there's yet time!"

Norman Leslie's face had grown very pale, as usu
with him when any reference was made to his brothe
He trembled visibly, and it required all his force
will to listen with forbearance. Sir Duncan, mista
ing his silence for acquiescence, continued with add
persuasiveness.

"Here's this young Prince, not twenty-fo
crazed already wi' that mad longing to regain t
throne which James VII. forfeited, and the Old Chev
lier failed to win. And why wish ye the Stuarts ba
again, Norman? Were they wise rulers? Oh, t
early Jameses were worthy kings, I grant ye; b
what of Charles II. and his dissolute court, and Jam
VII. wi' his Popery and his persecutions, and tl
weak Chevalier St. George, whom ye persist in calli
James the Eighth? And wha kens aught o' Prin
Charlie,—just a handsome, reckless lad, afire v
youth's madness! Is it for these ye'd pour out p
cious blood, an' waste the lives o' men? Rules n
George II. wisely enough, though he be foreign-bre
Does he no' uphold the established faith? Norma
man, as ye're a Scotsman and a friend, tak' warnin
Dinna gi'e yoursel' and yours to sheer destructi

for the sake o' a lad's folly! Remember how much
brave blood ye ha'e shed already in this vain cause!"

But Sir Duncan's words produced a far different
effect than he had intended. Leslie's eyes had kindled with the old ardent fire of his youth at mere
mention of the Stuarts; it was with difficulty that he
controlled the passionate quiver of his voice.

"Dinna talk to me, Duncan, o' the House o' Hanover, an' ye value my friendship! Dinna seek to
dissuade me frae what's dearer than life! Ye speak
o' the blood shed a'ready,—d'ye think I'll be forgetting it?—I, who lost six brothers in my country's
cause! Three died upon the battlefield, and one in
chains, and one upon the scaffold,—and one of a
broken heart, and d'ye think I'll disgrace their name
wi' a coward's caution?

"Because I died not upon Sheriffmuir, because I
lived through weary years o' exile to return to Scotland at the last, think ye I'm free to dwell here in
ignoble quiet, serving a German alien in the stead o'
my rightfu' King? I'd rather ha'e back the Church
o' Rome than buy my freedom thus! Think ye I'll
sit inactive when the Stuarts call? Nay, by a's that's
just and true, I ask no greater favour o' God than to
live and die,—fighting as they fought,—dying as
they died,—for the son o' my country's kings, for a
Prince o' the Stuart line!"

And his voice, which had risen high in ardour,
sunk to a tremulous undertone, and made the last
words a prayer.

Sir Duncan rode homeward to Inverness, musing
sadly upon the failure of his mission; but the memory

of that song at twilight was to haunt him often in the after-years.

* * * * *

Norman Leslie had meditated sending Agnes to France to be educated, "like our little Scottish Queen," he had said to Locheil,—" But it cannot be. She is too fair a maid to return unwed, and I would not see her married to a Frenchman. A Scotswoman should wed none but a Scotsman." And he had dismissed the idea with a light heart, rejoicing that duty did not compel him to send her away from him.

Now, although he felt a keen pang at the thought of separation, he was too unselfish to consider his own feelings, for he regarded the girl's happiness alone. When he entered Agnes's room, he found her sitting by the window, gazing out into the twilight. The wind from Ben Nevis, sweet with heather, blew in at the lattice. At first she would not even consider the contents of the letter, but gradually she grew more reasonable, and they sat pondering the matter till the moon flooded in through the casement.

"Ye'll have a chance, lassie, to improve the French and Italian I've taught ye, and to study the harp ye lo'e sae weel, and to learn the city-ways."

"'Tis for the Highlands alone I care!" she cried passionately.

"But it's right ye should go," he insisted; "ye must learn to trip the stately minuet, and to bear your train like a court-lady, for when our King comes hame, an' ye are Lady o' Rothes, ye may be maid-of honour to the Queen," he said, with pride in her loveliness.

"O Saw Ye Bonnie Lesley"

The prospect failed to allure her. "I winna go to court, if I maun wear a train!" she cried. "I winna wear one; I should trip, I know. D'ye really want me from ye, laddie?"

"Lassie!" he cried, "that ye should say it! But 'tis but for a little space; an' ye owe it to William Leslie to make the most o' your bonnie life!"

"Then I will go!" she said.

. . . . .

Two weeks later Norman Leslie kissed her farewell, and entrusted her to the care of Donald Cameron for the ride to Edinburgh. Locheil was to accompany them as far as Blair-Athole.

On a bright summer morning the little party, winding round the Salisbury Crags, beheld their journey's end. The beautiful grey city of the north, queenly Edinburgh, lay before them. Ancient Holyrood, wrapped in piercing, piteous memories, the Castle, frowning proudly from its grim crag, the long windings of the Canongate between tall palaces of blackened stone, the lion-form of Arthur's Seat, and the infolding hills that rim this Scottish Athens,—all burst upon Agnes's eyes for the first time. Not long hence was it to be called "mine own romantic town" by the Wizard Scott. Not less romantic was it half-a-century earlier when the tales of fair Mary and John Knox had been handed down but three generations on the lips of men, and when the days of Montrose and Dundee had barely ceased to be memories of the living.

Agnes entered Edinburgh in state befitting a princess, for beside her rode Donald, and Dr. Archibald,

Locheil's brother, and behind, four Highlanders, Angus among them,—all gorgeous in gay tartan and Glengarry bonnets. On the steps of the old grey house at the foot of Canongate stood Kenneth and Mistress Campbell to greet their guest, and the fair maid in blue-and-silver flashed like a vision upon Kenneth's delighted eyes. The girl of seventeen had become the young lady of twenty, and the three years had deepened her great beauty and added stateliness to her manner. Kenneth bowed low, and held open the door for her to enter. But she paused, and gave her hand to the young clansman.

Donald, with courtly grace, pressed her fingers to his lips. His handsome young face was quite pale, to hers the colour rushed.

"When I am Lady of Rothes I will return," she said.

CHAPTER V

"AWA, WHIGS, AWA!"

"Awa, Whigs, awa!
 Ye're but a pack o' traitor loons,
 Ye dae nae gude ava!"

THE year that followed the eventful day when Agnes came to Edinburgh was fraught with [m]any and strange experiences in her existence. She [ha]d adapted herself with marvellous readiness to the [li]fe of the household, although her freedom-loving [sp]irit often rebelled against the restraints and con[ve]ntionalities of Lowland society, and the yearning [fo]r the Highlands was an almost constant reality. [B]ut she had little time for actual grieving, for every [m]oment was crowded full with new interests. There [we]re French and Italian lessons; hours for practice [on] the harpsichord, and above all, the beloved harp [fo]r which she had developed remarkable skill. The [sw]eet lilt of her voice, mingling with the rich chords, [m]ade exquisite harmony through the old house. Her [so]ngs were all the lays of the Cavaliers, and the pi[br]ochs of the clans as they marched to battle,—gay, [de]fiant, thrilling with unutterable pathos,—that pas[si]on that flowed in her very life-blood. And Sir Hugh [wo]uld listen angrily, and leave the room, or he would [bi]d her cease her rebellious ballads and sing some [fi]tting song, or not at all. Endless were the pas[sa]ges of arms that took place between them, when

Sir Hugh, brutally regardless of her feelings, attacked her dearest sentiments, while she, quivering with indignation, returned him thrust for thrust. When he upheld the execution of Charles the First she flung scorn at Oliver Cromwell; when he arraigned Mary, Queen of Scots, she heaped accusations on John Knox; and it was only respect for his age that restrained her rebellious tongue.

Indeed it was Sir Hugh's fondness for Kenneth, to whom he clung as the last of his family, that induced him even to tolerate Agnes's presence. He had a sour dislike of women, and had often been heard to say "that of a' created beings a maid could do the maist mischief in the least time." Indeed, his nature was strangely lacking in the softer virtues, of which his love for Kenneth seemed the sole representative, a love largely compounded of pride. But whatever its composition, it stood Sir Hugh in the place of a warmer affection, and he was prepared to forego some prejudice on its account. If Kenneth really loved Agnes, if she were indeed to be his wife, she must not be deprived of all advantages of culture and education. Sir Hugh had great faith in the power of a dominant will, and did not entertain the slightest doubt that Agnes, although the sauciest of Jacobites, might yet be transformed into a sober Whig. He had used his tyrannical power with great success upon shrinking Mistress Campbell, and other yielding spirits, and he did not realise that this girl was moulded of vastly different stuff, and was no more to be moved by threats and storming than the Castle wall by rain-drops.

Poor Mistress Catherine, whose delight in Agnes was unbounded, was a terrified spectator of these encounters, and when they were over, she would endeavour to soothe the girl's passionate resentment.

"Lassie, I'd no' sing that song which ca's George Second 'an auld carlie'; it makes your uncle sair angry."

"Then Sir Hugh needna speak o' King James as the 'Old Pretender'!" cried Agnes, with brown eyes flashing.

"Wae's me, lassie, there'll ne'er be an end on't! An' a house at strife is aye a misfortunate thing. Why need folk to be fashin' themsel's ower politics? If ye're happy at hame, it doesna matter greatly whether Geordie or Jamie be King!"

And when the talk reached this point Agnes ceased to insist, divided between indignation at such apathy and perplexity as to how there could be a heart which beat neither for Stuart nor for Hanover.

Angus MacDonald at frequent intervals bore various missives to and from the Highlands. A strange history had Angus MacDonald: his grandfather, Lachlan, had dwelt with his clan in the lonely valley of Glencoe; whither, upon a certain wild mid-winter evening had come, with murderous intent, a number of King William's troops led by a Campbell of Glenlyon. Lachlan MacDonald and his little household, escaping from the foul carnage, that left so dark a blot upon King William's reign, fled through the snowy mountains to Lochaber. Half-dead with cold and hunger, they were succoured by Sir Ewen Cameron, grandsire of the "gentle Locheil," who adopted

Lachlan into his clan, and gave him lands among the Camerons.

As gratitude stood foremost among Highland virtues, Lachlan, in return, became one of Locheil's body-guard, and occupied the enviable position of foster-father to the chieftain's children. This honour he had bequeathed to his descendants, and in consequence each Master of Locheil had a son of the MacDonalds for his foster-brother and devoted follower. Angus, accordingly, was possessed by a vehement hate for all Campbells, and a fervid devotion for all Camerons,—the son of his chief in particular.

Apparently Agnes's zeal for the Stuarts had banished all thoughts of love, and although Kenneth seized every opportunity to offer passionate petition to the Court of Venus, he seemed to win no nearer place in that goddess's affections. Moreover, he soon discovered that he was not to be left in unrivalled possession of her sweet companionship. For Agnes had taken Edinburgh by storm; her name was upon all lips; tales of her beauty and wit and daring were nightly subjects of discussion among the youths of both parties. "The Lady of Locheil," "The Lass of Lochaber," and "Agnes of Auchnacarry," were some of the names by which the lovely Jacobite was toasted by her numberless admirers.

And in truth hers was a matchless charm, an irresistible witchery. There were many beautiful girls in Edinburgh, but this maid of the Highlands outshone them all, as the lustrous cairngorms of her native hills outshone a common pebble. Hers was the beauty of the blossom,—a springtime gaiety and grace; hers was the light heart of William Leslie in the days before the shadow of death had fallen across his youth; a heart that laughs and hopes, nor dreams of evil days to come. She had the fascinating Stuart beauty, the beauty with which Mary, Queen of Scots, had bewitched the world,—so said the Jacobitish gossips; but the Whigs asserted that with the splendid brown eyes and proud bearing of "that deil o' Dundee," she had inherited something of his disposition; his fiery devotion and utter recklessness. Sir Hugh strongly upheld the latter opinion. To have a beauty and a Jacobite under the same roof, and combined in the same person, was a tempting of Providence, he considered. "The deil's a hand in the matter," was his terse observation.

About a month before the arrival of that mysterious slip of white bark which wrought so strange an effect on Agnes, Kenneth was obliged to visit London. He was absent from Edinburgh no longer than could be borne by a lover, yet he returned to discover that even a short space may suffice for mischief, and that his fair lady had wasted no time in idleness.

Kenneth had formed an acquaintance with a handsome young Englishman of fine family, who was a student at the University of Edinburgh, and almost the only one of Agnes's admirers that he had brought himself to regard with friendship. But Edward Farrington possessed a frank and genial disposition, tempered by much sound judgment, and thus became an excellent balance to the fiery young Scot, restraining as best he might Kenneth's wild flights of rage and jealousy.

The day after his arrival in Edinburgh Kenneth met Edward Farrington near the Netherbow Port; the young Englishman called a merry greeting and caught him by the arm.

"And what, think you, is your fair Jacobite's latest achievement? Why, nothing less than drinking King James's health in the presence of his enemies. And this is how it came about: there was a gathering the other evening at Mistress Forbes's, and our fair lady attended, wearing her Leslie tartan as proudly as 'twere ermine. And of course the King's health is proposed, and we all rise to drink it,—Brunswickers every one, save my Lady Mischief! Then up springs Mistress Leslie, glowing like a rose, her eyes, two diamonds, dangerously bright, and faith, thinks I, she'll pull the Castle down about our ears!

"Well, there she stands, a white rose at her bosom, the wine-glass lifted in one hand, and her glance flashing round the hall as if in search of something. Then suddenly the pretty rogue runs across the room to a globe of gold-fish,—the only water she could find, —and *passes her glass across it*, crying as merry as a peal of bells, 'I'll gi'e ye a tex' o' scripture,—the tongue no man can tame; *James Third and Eighth!*' And there we all stood, dumfounded, without a thought in our heads, just turned daft by her wit and her daring. And before we can catch our breaths, she cries in her pretty Scotch, 'Aweel, frien's, an ye dinna mak' a change o' heart I'll deave your ears wi' an auld sang o' Bonnie Dundee's!'

"But at that your uncle comes forward, greatly

angered, as all may see, and snatches her by the sleeve, and trouble there would have been had not Mistress Forbes turned the talk upon the East Indies, where 'twas safe for a time.

"But upon my soul, I envy you, Kenneth, the task of making my Lady Whig, as you must if you marry her. She's been bred up in Lochaber in the midst of a very nest of Jacobites, and she's the incarnate spirit of Montrose and Dundee, and being woman, can do a thousand times more havoc than they ever did. Faith, she's worth more to King James than all his Highland claymores, for she's as fair as his own white roses, as ardent as a summer sunbeam, and enough to bewitch every man in his senses into turning Jacobite on the spot!" He grew grave as he ended, and added in a mournful tone, "On my honour, if I thought she'd have me, I would join the white cockade this very instant!"

Having utterly failed to convert Agnes, Sir Hugh consoled himself by selecting a suitable bride for Kenneth, and after some search secured his object in the person of Mistress Janet Munro, who not only came of a staunch Whig family, but also possessed no small fortune, two requisites Sir Hugh thought quite sufficient to outweigh the "bonny looks" of which he stood in scorn. Unfortunately, Kenneth did not share his uncle's opinions, and could not be brought so much as to glance at Miss Munro, much less to admire her charms; which course of action caused Sir Hugh further to rage against fate, and especially to invoke maledictions on the witchery of woman and the obduracy of man. He never ceased to curse the unlucky mission which sent Kenneth to Lochaber, and brought him under the spell of that saucy enchantress, Agnes Leslie, for he knew too well that Kenneth, although bred a Whig, had never exhibited any particular zeal for that party, and if temptation appeared in the shape of a Jacobite beauty, who could foretell the outcome!

The cause of Sir Hugh's misgivings was indeed near at hand. Late summer of that year of tempest, 1745, found strange rumours afloat in Edinburgh; rumours, which, although persistently denied, as persistently clamoured for a hearing; rumours of a French ship, the *Doutelle*, which had sailed from France with a royal youth who claimed the title of three kingdoms; of his landing on the west coast of Scotland among the MacDonalds of Moidart, and of his resolute determination to gather an army and win a crown. Then, in the slow-footed fashion of those days, came the news of the rising of the clans; of how the gallant Lochiel had espoused the Prince's cause, and had led his Camerons to the place of gathering in Glenfinnan; and of the Stuart banner unfurled on Scottish air. Close on the heels of all this trod the tidings of the march southward; of the swelling ranks of the impetuous Highlanders; and, above all, of the strange charm of the young Prince who made friends of foes, and of sober friends passionate followers. But Edinburgh,—or rather Whig Edinburgh,—viewed the entire enterprise with superb scorn, and after General Cope, commander of the King's forces, had marched northward to quell the audacious rebels, remarked

"Awa, Whigs, Awa!"

confidently in every close and market that "Cope would soon cock up the Pretender's beaver." Nevertheless, despite this assurance, guns were mounted along the old Flodden wall that still girdled the city, guards were set at the West Port, the Netherbow, and other points of entrance, and volunteers, hastily collected, paraded daily along the streets with an air of mingled dash and trepidation.

From that August morning of the missive Agnes showed a delight she hardly troubled to conceal. When the word came that Cope, not daring to meet the Highlanders in their mountains, had left the road to the Lowlands open, her joy took tantalising form.

> "He's comin' frae the north that's to fancy me,
> A feather in his bonnet, and a ribbon at his knee"

she chanted in a provokingly careless tone, very irritating to Kenneth, to whom Highlanders were especial objects of jealousy, and who felt uncertain, in the present case, whether reference was intended to blue-eyed Donald Cameron, or to the Bonnie Prince himself.

CHAPTER VI

"SAE NOBLE A LOOK, SAE PRINCELY AN AIR!"

"Sae noble a look, sae princely an air!
Sae gallant and bold, sae young and sae fair!
Oh! could ye but see him, ye'd do as we've done,—
Hear him but ance, to his standard you'll run!"

EACH day increased the stir and apprehension that shook those gloomy mansions of High Street and Canongate, so proudly lifted toward the stars. There, in the crooked wynds and closes, where richest and poorest elbowed each other at every turn, where wealthy banker and belted earl climbed the steep, dark stairs to their lofty eyries above the town, while labourer and apprentice hived in rooms below, the noblest lady, lifting her satin gown out of the filth of the street, shared the thrill of fear with the meanest beggar. For Edinburgh had dreamt so long in peace that the ways of war were all forgot, and rudely awakened now, she trembled before the foe. Jacobite and Whig, both equally excited, pulled opposite ways: to "defend" or "not defend" the city was wildly advocated at every corner. Whatever preparations were made to oppose the advancing army were of a curiously inadequate nature;— some of them suspiciously so;—and when at the order of Archibald Stewart, the Lord Provost, a ditch, dug beneath the castle wall, showed the earth thrown outward instead of inward, the indignant Whigs declared it to be intentional, that their foes might ascend thereby.

So the days surged on with stormy argument and growing rumours of the young Chevalier's swift approach. Meanwhile, Cope's belated transports, hurrying from Aberdeen, were daily expected off Dunbar, and loyal Whigs gazed anxiously for northward-pointing weathercocks, while the Jacobites rejoiced at every south wind.

On Sunday morning, September 15, Agnes and Mistress Campbell set out for service at St. Giles's, for although zealously High Church, Agnes was liberal-minded enough to join her aunt's devotions; and indeed the stern, grey beauty of St. Giles's, the pillared stateliness of nave and transept, the warm glow of coloured windows, glorified by sunshine, and the solemn stillness pervading all the sanctuary, could not but touch her soul. While Mistress Campbell sat with bowed head the girl would kneel on the footstool, with opened prayer-book, inaudibly repeating the morning prayers. On the present occasion, however, Agnes fiercely resented the Presbyterian zeal of the minister, who, with a sword girt above his Geneva gown, prayed for the reigning monarch and the deliverance of Edinburgh with unnecessary fervour. She had risen angrily with the intention of leaving the church, when the heavy clang of fire-bells brought the rest of the congregation to their feet with looks of consternation. "The Highlanders! The Highlanders!" was the cry upon all lips.

Agnes and Mistress Campbell joined the throng,

who were hastening from the church to the Lawn
market. There the volunteers were collected, preparatory to marching on the enemy, who were now
reported to be only eight miles distant. The dragoons, with clanking swords and valiant bearing,
came galloping along, and their courage spread to
the volunteers, who thereupon cheered lustily, while
the people swung their hats with a vast show of
loyalty. But a few moments wrought a mighty
change, and the troopers had hardly disappeared before weeping kinsfolk and anxious friends besought
the brave volunteers not to risk their noble lives in
the open, but to remain behind the walls, and protect
their native city. And so successfully did they plead
that when Captain Drummond, fearing lest their advice be taken, rode off down the West Bow, he found
himself in undisputed solitude, his devoted company
having seen fit to vanish into neighbouring closes,
and the city's fame finally rested on less than two
hundred dejected men.

Edinburgh knew little sleep that night. Every
slight disturbance in the streets was taken for the
enemy, and anxious heads appeared at every window,
and frightened voices cried for help. Morning was
productive of still more extraordinary antics on the
part of Edinburgh's defenders, for the timorous dragoons, encamped two miles westward at Coltbridge,
had sent forward a small reconnoitering party, who
at first sight of the Highlanders, and first sound of
their pistols, turned tail to, and with guns unfired
scampered back to their comrades; whereupon the
entire troop, wholly panic-stricken, galloped helter-

"Sae Noble a Look!"

skelter toward the city, not with the intention of seeking refuge behind the walls, but of gaining the open country beyond. The people of Edinburgh, amazed and incredulous, beheld this disgraceful flight, the Jacobites with scornful pleasure, the Whigs with fear and humiliation. Agnes gave a ripple of sweet, contemptuous mirth: "They looked, they saw, they scampered," she said in saucy imitation of the great Roman, and was rewarded by an angry glare from Sir Hugh.

The streets were now filled with terrified townsfolk, who, bereft of one more defence, assembled in frantic council to decide on their course of action. In the midst of their wild discussion, a messenger entered with a letter for the Lord Provost, which bore the signature of Charles, Prince Regent. It commanded them peaceably to surrender the city, promising that in this case no violence should befall them; but, should they longer resist, his Royal Highness would be obliged to use force, and would not hold himself responsible for the consequences. This ended all dispute, and it was straightway agreed that a number of citizens should visit the Prince's camp to settle the terms of surrender.

Meanwhile, outside, a fresh alarm was spreading. A clatter of hoofs smote the street, and up the steep West Bow dashed a gentleman on a grey horse, hot with spurring, crying to the assembled volunteers, "I have seen the Highlanders; they are sixteen thousand strong!" and was off again, ere one could scan his face. But the cry bore instant fruit, for the volunteers lost no time in reaching the Castle and flinging down their arms before General Guest, from whom they had received them. Thus proud Edinburgh hauled down her flag without a shot, and stood, defenceless, at her young foe's mercy.

At ten o'clock that night the deputies returned from their errand with a second letter from the Prince to the same purport. Meantime, the city had caught a false rumour of Cope's landing at Dunbar, and with the prospect of deliverance, despatched a second embassy to prolong the treaty. It was now two o'clock in the morning, and Prince Charlie, weary of subterfuge, dismissed them imperatively, with the same reply. Then, determined to delay no longer, he gave orders for the immediate capture of the city.

Moonlight was fading into dawn when Agnes was awakened from a light slumber by hurrying feet which her quick ears recognised as shod in Highland brogues. Springing from bed, she wrapped a plaid about her and ran out on the narrow balcony that overlooked the Canongate. Just then a familiar voice hummed a bar of "Sir Ewen's Salute," and instantly she leaned over, whispering, "Donald, what do you here?"

"We go to seize the Netherbow," the low voice replied. "Pray for us, Agnes, that we gain the town!"

"Oh, Donald, that will I do, and God befriend you!" she cried in an anxious whisper, and crept back, trembling with excitement, to fulfil her promise.

Up to the Netherbow, intent upon its capture, stole the brave Locheil and his followers. After vainly attempting to gain entrance by artifice, the

"Sae Noble a Look!"

were warned by the growing dawn that they must either retreat or use more violent measures. At that moment a coach came rumbling down the High Street with the returning deputies, and upon its approach the sentry unlocked the port. Like bees out of a hive rushed the Highlanders from their lurking-places; they surged in at the gate, they swiftly disarmed the guard. The High Street was filled with plaided figures, advancing sword in hand, who rent the air with battle-cries, while through the grey dawn pealed the exultant pibroch, "We'll awa to Sheriffmuir to haud the Whigs in order." Gate after gate was surrendered so peacefully that half the inhabitants knew nothing of the momentous happening. One gentleman in particular, taking his usual morning walk along the ramparts, was astonished to see a Highlander sedately seated on a gun, and upon asking if he belonged to the guard of the day before, received the calm reply, "Och, no, she pe relieved." So when the sun rose over Arthur's Seat, Locheil held Edinburgh for Prince Charlie.

There were many pale faces among the Whigs that morning, but Agnes rose with sparkling eyes and glowing cheeks. She and Donald had a rapturous meeting, but they had barely time to inquire for each other's welfare before Donald was summoned thence by manifold duties. Agnes tripped away to the garden to water her Stuart roses, herself a fairer flower than any there. They grew upon a magnificent tall rose-tree that had flourished, tradition said, in the days when Dundee rode forth to Killiecrankie, and an ardent Jacobite had plucked a snowy rose-bud for the Chevalier St. George, the uncrowned monarch of the "'15." Now, thirty years later, they still throve luxuriantly. They had bloomed in white glory all the summer, but in August their beauty had taken on new lustre, due, Agnes believed, to the mysterious influence of Prince Charlie's landing at Moidart. Agnes surveyed them now with blithe satisfaction, her head tilted as gaily as a flower on its stem. "A fine bouquet I shall have for. King James!" she observed. Then, with a sudden widening of her bright brown eyes, she leaned over and plucked the loveliest blossom of them all, a snowy bud just opening to full flower. "And if by any chance Prince Charlie comes to-day, I'll e'en wear this rose in his honour!"

Early that same Tuesday morning the Prince and his little army began their march to Edinburgh winding southward of the city to avoid the castle guns, for General Guest still held the fortress for King George. Upon reaching the Queen's Park, the royal estate adjoining Holyrood, the Prince left his army and rode forward alone, accompanied only by two of his nobles. He drew rein beneath the hill crowned by ruined St. Anthony's Chapel, for here he first caught sight of the home of his forefathers —sad, grey Holyrood,—lying at his feet. He stood dismounted, gazing down upon the ancient palace and with the glorious tragic memories of this old mansion of the Stuarts a strange thrill of melancholy mingled with the triumph of this young descendant of that royal line. But a rousing cheer, rising from the throng below, dispelled his reverie, as the most ardent of the Jacobites pressed forward to fling themselves at his feet and kiss his hand. Charle gracefully acknowledged their homage, then mounting his handsome bay horse, proceeded slowly toward the palace.

Agnes and Kenneth Campbell had made their way to a little knoll whence they could obtain a view of the Prince's approach. At sight of the young hero Agnes drew a quick breath of ecstasy, and clasped her hands to her bosom as if to restrain her wildly beating heart. Like a leaf in the whirl of the stream, she was seized and shaken by the rush of that moment's rapture, for she looked on the realisation of the dearest dream of her life,—a dream to be lightly purchased with precious blood and tears.

No wonder an enthusiastic murmur escaped the lips of the excited throng, no wonder men pressed forward to render him allegiance, for a bearing more princely, a mien more noble and winning, had never graced an heir of the Stuart line, since the days of Bruce, and the delighted Jacobites marked with joy the resemblance between the youthful hero of their hopes and the renowned victor of Bannockburn. Well did gallant Charles Edward deserve the adoring title of the "Bonnie Prince." His slender but rounded figure was moulded upon almost perfect lines of suppleness and grace, and set off to the utmost advantage by his short tartan coat, red velvet breeches, and military boots; and so spirited and winsome was his face that his every glance compelled admiration, while its almost feminine beauty of feature,— the bright hazel eyes, fair skin, and red, curving lips, —was illumined by a man's determination and a youth's courage. A blue velvet bonnet, enriched with gold lace and a white satin cockade, sat upon his flowing yellow curls, a blue sash, embroidered with gold, crossed his shoulder, a silver-hilted broadsword hung at his side, and on his breast shone the star of Scotland's Order of St. Andrew.

Upon reaching the group on the little knoll, the Prince paused for a moment, held by the beautiful face so steadfastly regarding him, by the brilliant hazel eyes, so like his own in shape and colour, that flashed on him that rapt, adoring gaze. But Agnes suddenly became aware that while others showered roses and white ribbons down, she had naught with which to show her homage. Then she bethought herself of the bud she had plucked that morning. Blushing, half-hesitating, with trembling fingers, she loosed the rose from her bodice, and it fluttered downward to the Prince's saddle-bow. He caught it ere it fell, bowed low and pressed it to his lips with a bright smile,—that smile of rare sweetness which had won him so many hearts. He gazed an instant upward with wondering admiration, and then rode on,—amid the plaudits of the loyal throng who dimmed his very boots with their adoring kisses,—to Holyrood and triumph!

The rose was but one of a myriad roses that had been flung in heart's devotion at his feet; the face was but one of a thousand fair faces that had gazed at him in ardent admiration; but that one rose, alone, found a resting-place within his tartan coat, very close to the royal young heart, now beating high with triumph; and that one fair face alone,—so winsome and brave and tender,—was mirrored in that heart itself.

CHAPTER VII

"WHA'LL BE KING BUT CHARLIE?"

"Come thro' the heather, around him gather,
Come Ronald, come Donald; come a' thegither,
And crown your rightfu', lawfu' king,
For wha'll be king but Charlie?"

THE day of Prince Charlie's entrance into Edinburgh lived for Agnes in a golden mist of memory through which certain wonderful moments shone like stars: that interchange of words in the moonlit dawn by the Netherbow; Prince Charlie pressing her rose to his lips; and her meeting with Norman Leslie in the dark apartment at Holyrood that had been Darnley's audience-chamber.

Enough of the September sunshine entered to light up the ancient tapestries and faded furniture, and rob the chamber of its wonted gloom; or perhaps the radiance of glad hearts lent the place a momentary brightness. They sat hand in hand, the grave face and the gay alike illumined by a joy too great to find immediate expression.

"So it has come true at last," Norman Leslie murmured, "that we ha'e hoped and prayed for sae mony weary years! Oh, that your father had lived to see it, lassie! Then I had been content."

She lifted her glowing face to his: "Perhaps he, too, sees it, and is happy; happier than we! God must let a' who died for the Stuarts behold their triumph, will ye no' be believing it, laddie?" Then, after a pause, "To think ye were the first man to welcome the Prince to Holyrood! Kenneth told me how, when the Prince entered the courtyard, you came forward and knelt to receive him, then drew your sword and led the way up the staircase like some grand marshal. And 'twas your right, laddie, as Duke o' Rothes!"

"So said our Prince," he answered, smiling at her eagerness; "''tis for a Leslie to bear the sword *before* his monarch, as well as *for* him. An earlier Leslie bore the Sword of State for the Second Charles, and if ever I am crowned Charles the Third, you shall do me the same service.' And it was the Prince himself arranged our meeting here, for he is kind and thoughtful as he is brave and princely. When he heard of Sir Hugh's hatred he turned to me, saying: 'So long as I have a roof above me, it shall shelter my friends; you and Mistress Leslie shall meet to-day at Holyrood.'"

Fully an hour had passed before Agnes finished telling all that had happened in the year since she left Auchnacarry, and the time seemed all too short before Norman Leslie was compelled to return to his insistent duties.

"We'll no' forgither aften, lassie," he said as he kissed her good-bye. "It'll be far frae me to stir up auld hates wi' Sir Hugh, so we maun be content wi' seeing little o' ane anither for a time."

"He's a hard man, laddie," Agnes said, her pretty mouth set bitterly. "Has he ony softer side, I wonder? I ha'e ne'er seen it. An' 'twas no' for

Aunt Catherine and Kenneth I wouldna bide beneath his roof a moment!"

Norman Leslie scanned her face intently. "Ye speak o' young Campbell, lassie! It's he that'll be wanting ye for his wife. Does your hairt incline to him?"

"Laddie, I canna lo'e a Whig!" she cried impatiently. "I'll no' be denying he's a leal friend, but he's nae mair."

That same afternoon beheld a brilliant spectacle enacted in the old High Street. The ancient Market-Cross, its steps richly spread with carpet for the ceremony, was surrounded by a large company of Highlanders, Locheil, on his black charger "Bruce," foremost among them, while his son, Donald, appeared on foot with the Cameron men. The King's heralds came forward, arrayed in their gorgeous robes, and their trumpets echoed far over the assembled throng. Amid the silence which followed, Norman Leslie ascended the steps of the Cross, and in a clear, ringing voice, proclaimed James VIII. King of Great Britain, and then proceeded to read the proclamation, written in Rome two years earlier, conferring the regency upon Prince Charlie.

This was hailed by tumultuous cheers from the vast assembly, and a fluttering of kerchiefs and white ribbons from the ladies whose windows overlooked the scene, while the Highlanders, wildly exultant, discharged their muskets into the air till the old grey mansions rang with the echo, and the bagpipes sounded "The Stuarts' White Banner," a stirring pibroch to King James, following with "The Prince's Salute" in honour of Bonnie Charlie.

Throughout this victorious pageant, Agnes, at Locheil's behest, sat beside the Market-Cross on her white horse, named for the Prince, while the impetuous colour flooded her face with shy elation. In one hand she held the ancient broadsword with its knot of King James's ribbon, and in the other a bunch of gay rosettes, and so entrancing was the picture she made in her silver-laced riding-dress, that many a lad pressed through the throng to receive the white cockade and fasten it in his bonnet, for the sake of her lovely face and winning smile.

But there was one who felt little pleasure in the scene, or rather in his own part therein, and this was Kenneth Campbell. Disdaining to join the timorous volunteers, he had taken, at Sir Hugh's bidding, the position of captain under General Guest at the Castle; and accordingly had been obliged to endure Agnes's scornful displeasure, manifested in all the sweet, tantalising ways of which she, alone, was mistress. To-day, having extracted a brief leave of absence from the General, Kenneth had mingled with the crowd about the Cross, and was still further tormented by Agnes's triumphant joy in the part she was playing.

That evening, as he sat musing despondently in the dim parlour, Agnes fluttered merrily in, and thinking herself alone, began to sing with gay abandon:

> "There ne'er a lass in a' the land
>   But vows baith late and early,
> To man she'll ne'er gi'e heart or hand,
>   Wha wadna fecht for Charlie!"

To her great amazement Kenneth came forward, and caught her hands in his, exclaiming earnestly:

"Do you really mean it, Agnes? Would you give me your heart and hand if I——"

"I will be making no promises," she returned archly, "but I winna deny I'd like ye better as a Jacobite than as a Whig." And her bright glance inspired him to hope.

He released her hands, went over to the table, and took up his cocked hat.

"Do you think I don't value you more than the Hanover succession, more than all the kings and crowns on earth? I will offer myself to the Prince this very hour!"

Agnes drew a quick breath of utter astonishment, finding it rather disconcerting to be thus taken at her word. Keen as was her delight at Kenneth's change of allegiance, she was yet pricked by certain qualms of conscience as to his motive. Clearly knowing that it was no devotion to Prince Charlie which prompted him, but devotion to a more exacting monarch, she wondered if it would be honourable in her to encourage his decision.

"Are you sure, Kenneth——" she began, then paused as suddenly. Her wild enthusiasm for the cause she loved overbalanced every other thought, and swept her momentary scruples into the nether scale. She ran to him, laying eager hands upon his arm.

"Kenneth, will ye in truth draw sword for Prince Charlie?"

Her fair face was aglow with that strange fervour. His was as radiant with another fervour.

"Aye, Agnes, upon my honour, that I will!—for the Prince,—but—more—for you!"

And when she had watched him disappear beneath the carven Scottish lions on the palace gate, she turned from the window with a half-troubled, half-triumphant face.

CHAPTER VIII

"ALL PLAIDED AND PLUMED IN THEIR TARTAN ARRAY"

"When her bonneted chieftains to victory crowd,
  Clanranald the dauntless, and Moray the proud,
  All plaided and plumed in their tartan array"—

KENNETH'S decision had,—to put it mildly,— an astounding effect upon the Campbell household. All Sir Hugh's acquaintance declared that Kenneth would pay for his apostasy by disinheritance, but they reckoned without due knowledge of the inconsistency of human nature in general, and of Sir Hugh in particular. There did follow a stormy interview, but without the expected termination, for at its close Sir Hugh laid a hand on Kenneth's shoulder, and observed in a conciliatory tone that although it was to be greatly regretted that the lad had taken so rash a step, still, youth would be ever impetuous, and there was no need to quarrel over a matter that would right itself ere long. "Ye'll come to a sound mind soon enow, lad!" he concluded, while Kenneth, who had nerved himself to meet the full force of his uncle's wrath, could only stare at him in amazement at such magnanimity.

No one rejoiced more at the outcome than Mistress Campbell, to whom contention was a sore grief, and who had dreaded Kenneth's banishment with all her fearsome, affectionate soul. She was still further gladdened by the increasing warmth of the friendship between Agnes and Kenneth. So fond was she of her nephew, and so great was her love for Agnes, that her one wish was to see them happily married to each other, that through them she might find recompense for the lovelessness of her own life. Agnes, for once, was in a quandary, for since Kenneth had joined the Prince for her sake alone, she was obliged to grant him every favour possible, although at the same time she blamed herself for the emotion which every bright smile and friendly word spoken in comradeship only served to deepen. She never dreamed of using coquetry, though her mischievous gaiety too often unconsciously resembled it.

In truth, a wide rift lay between them, for Agnes had not a particle of the Puritan in her, save perhaps in her utter devotion to duty. Hers was the Gaelic temperament in all its intensity,—with all the fiery hates and warm affections born of centuries of feud and friendship. Kenneth could only mutely wonder when she kindled in passionate memory of Montrose or Dundee. To him the deeds of the past were but ashes,—to her they were living flame.

The Prince was naturally much gratified by the accession of this influential young Whig, and the more so as he had been well informed of Sir Hugh's proclivities, and had little looked for aid in that hostile quarter. He received Kenneth graciously, welcomed him warmly to the cause, and offered him the position of major in one of the Lowland regiments. But in spite of this good fortune and of the followers hourly flocking to his standard, the young Prince knew well that this victorious entrance into the home of his fathers was only a loosening of the sword in the scabbard,—the first step toward the battles he must win ere he achieved the throne. On the very day of his triumph, while he was gazing with all youth's rapture upon Holyrood, Cope's evasive forces were landing at Dunbar with the purpose of disputing his possession of the Lowlands. But the Prince was only too eager to meet the enemy, and so after less than three days' bivouac at Edinburgh, he marched his little army to Duddingston, called a council of the Highland chiefs, and decided to offer battle next day, assured by Keppoch, the gallant head of the MacDonalds, that the courage of the chieftains was indisputable, and that the clansmen, loyal to the death, would follow where they led. Accordingly, on the following morning the dauntless Highlanders advanced under the leadership of their belovéd Prince to engage in their first conflict with the King's troops.

Throughout that day and night Edinburgh again endured a state of anxious suspense, which was startlingly broken in the early morning of Saturday, September 21, by the sight of some terrified dragoons, who tore frantically up the High Street on horses exhausted with spurring, closely pursued by a solitary rider, before whom they fled with the precipitancy of frightened sheep. Agnes, recognising the intrepid pursuer as Grant of Glenmorriston, ran out on the doorstep crying breathlessly, "What tidings?"

Without checking his headlong course, he swung

his bonnet high, and shouted, "The day is ours, Mistress! Victory! Victory for Prince Charlie and the White Rose!"

Never once stopping to face their single foe, the dragoons fled on, and slacked not rein till they were safe within the Castle; while their bold pursuer rode scornfully up to the gate, stuck his blood-stained dirk into the gate-post, and turned leisurely back to rejoin his clan.

Partly because the Lowland regiment in which he was to serve as major was not fully organised, and partly owing to the Prince's tactfulness, Kenneth had not joined the Highland army in their march against Cope, but had remained in charge of affairs at Edinburgh, and thus was spared a direct part in the humiliation of the Whigs.

Agnes, aflutter with excitement, danced gaily on up the Canongate to buy a white breast-knot. She was engaged in fastening it at her bodice when she caught sight, from the shop-windows, of people running wildly toward Holyrood, and she hastened eagerly after them. She had not reached Sir Hugh's house when the skirling of bagpipes smote her ears. Dizzy with delight, Agnes flung open the door, and darted up the steep stairs as fast as flying feet could take her. She gained the attic, sprang to the window, and poised herself, half-kneeling, on the broad sill, her heart pulsing faster and faster to the weirdly thrilling strains of the exultant bagpipes. It was the clan-music of the Camerons that she heard,—the wild notes rushing in a tempest of stormy triumph,— and it stirred her with an unutterable thrill to hear

"All Plaided and Plumed"

the belovéd pipes sound the old familiar music of her childhood,—" The Head of the High Bridge," and ' The Pibroch of Donald Dubh."

Now they swept into sight, these gallant Camerons, seven hundred strong, to whose impetuous courage the victory was largely due. On they came in firm, unbroken ranks, their brilliant tartans waving in the wind, their blue, plumed bonnets stirred like wind-swept bluebells by their swinging tread, the sun glowing down on the rich hues of kilts and belted plaids, and flashing lustre back from every sporran and cairngorm brooch, from every dirk and claymore. Afar, they were a mass of living, fluttering colour, hemmed by high grey walls;—near, when the thunder of their feet shook the stones below, they were the flower of the Northland, like the archers of fatal Flodden, chosen like them for vigour and manly grace, supple-limbed as panthers in the barbaric beauty of their dress, white-skinned, fair-haired, with eyes the blue of a sunlit sea. Above their heads the white and crimson banners tossed fitfully like roses and red poppies intermingled.

Upon his proud black horse rode the "gentle Lochiel"; his noble features, lit by triumph, were yet none the less courtly and chivalrous. His son, Donald, marched on foot by his side, and near him Angus MacDonald, bearing aloft one of Cope's captured standards, whose folds clung in humiliation to the staff.

As the procession came abreast of Holyrood the pipes changed to a tune which shook the watching thousands with thunderous applause. They were playing that old Cavalier air known to the days of Cromwell and the Restoration,—"The King Shall Enjoy His Own Again." Agnes, who had sung it from childhood, found herself unconsciously repeating the words to the weird melody of the pipes:

> "Though for a time we see Whitehall
> With cobwebs hung about the wall,
> Yet Heaven shall make amends for all,
> When the King shall enjoy his own again."

As they passed beneath the window from which the "Lady of Locheil,"—the fair adopted daughter of the clan,—was looking down upon them with bright, exultant eyes, whose pride was for their triumph, every Cameron, from Locheil to the lowest, raised his broadsword in salute. And Donald doffed his blue bonnet, decked with the oak-leaves of his clan, and bowed his yellow head as to a princess.

That day, and the next, and the week that followed, shone out in memory like jewels strung upon the golden chain of triumph. Tales of the battle crowded thick and fast;—of the Highland army sweeping swift and noiseless through the mist upon Cope's astounded ranks; the headlong impact of the clans, the panic-stricken flight of the English,—Cope himself escaping to Berwick with the news of his own defeat; the mercy displayed by Prince Charlie who had spent hours upon the field caring for the wounded, and how as he rode over the battleground strewn with the English dead, and an officer had observed to him, "Sir, there are your enemies at your feet," he had answered solemnly, "They are my father's subjects."

"All Plaided and Plumed"

Donald, with whom Agnes enjoyed a canter through the Park, told her all this, and many a tale besides, some of them so mirth-provoking that she could not but laugh merrily. The rank and file of the Highlanders had eagerly seized upon the spoils of the battlefield, although with scarcely an idea of their value; and one of them, Donald declared, to whom a gold watch had fallen, sold the article immediately, saying he was glad to be rid of it, for " it had died the night before," quite ignorant of the fact that it had simply stopped for want of winding.

The day after the battle of " Gladsmuir," as the Jacobites best liked to call their victory, the rest of the army, which had been encamped near the battlefield, marched triumphantly into the city, playing the same jubilant air to which the Camerons' pipes had sounded, and bearing with them their prisoners and captured flags. The young Prince took no part in this display, but that evening he rode quietly to Holyrood, with Lord Murray and Locheil. He found the palace thronged with elated Jacobites who greeted him with wild applause, and strewed the ancient courtyard with tartans, roses, and white breast-knots.

Edinburgh rang with toasts to " Bonnie Charlie," who, they declared, " could eat a dry crust, sleep on pease-straw, take his dinner in four minutes, and win a battle in five," and the fair Jacobites treasured ribbons adorned with pictures of " The Highland Laddie." And before the month was out the town was echoing to a mocking ballad of Sir John's defeat, alleged to have been written by a collier of Preston, who, on going forth to his work in the morning, had stopped to watch the battle, and whose scornful amusement at the cowardice of Cope's army had found satirical expression in a song which would have aroused indignation in a snail. Endless were the feuds it created, numberless the duels it inspired. To the day of his death Kenneth recalled the taunting, challenging words, set to the sauciest melody ever sung. But perhaps it clung to his mind less because he heard it everywhere, than because he heard it afterward at a memorable crisis in his life.

CHAPTER IX

"DUSKY SHADOWS OF THE CAIRNGORMS"

"Dusky shadows of the cairngorms
All among her golden hair."

ON the evening of the 24th of September, Charles Edward gave a magnificent ball at Holyrood to celebrate his victory. Kenneth had come from the palace that afternoon with a stately message from the Prince, who earnestly besought the honour of Mistress Leslie's attendance upon that occasion. Kenneth's presence was a matter of course, for it was the duty as well as pleasure of every officer connected with the cause to appear at such an assembly. Having delivered the Prince's request, Kenneth chanced to mention that the young Master of Locheil would be absent from the gathering, as he had departed on an important mission to the Isle of Skye. A shade of disappointment clouded Agnes's face, followed by a deeper blush than the occasion seemed to require. Kenneth did not notice this, however, so absorbed was he in the anticipated delight of Agnes's company for the evening; a joy which enabled him to bear Sir Hugh's displeasure with a light heart.

Candles were beginning to shine through the autumn dusk when Agnes fluttered blithely upstairs to don her festive attire. So brightly did the early moonbeams illumine the chamber that her first prep-

arations were made by that light alone. Having
removed her kerchief and unlaced her gown, she drew
forth from the shadows into the moonshine a small
leather-covered trunk, studded with brass, and worn
with the marks of age and travel. She unlocked it
carefully propped open the lid, and began her search
in its fragrant interior, lifting one article after an
other from the linen folds that showered rose-leaves
down upon the floor. The moonlight streamed the
while with mellow radiance over her white neck and
fair, flushed cheeks, and sparkled in the hazel depths
of her eyes, and upon the warm gold of her hair
Presently she paused, having found what she sought
and shook out into lustrous folds a splendid court-
dress of shimmering yellow satin, whose rich lengths
fell about her like spun gold as she held it up against
her bosom. But strangely enough it was not upon
the beauty of the gown she turned such shining
eyes, but for the wonder that Fate had allowed her to
wear it.

For it was sixty years and more since that rich
gown had known a wearer, though twice had it been
drawn from its rose-scented nest by lovely fingers
trembling with their hopes; and twice had it been
folded away again, unworn, when those bright hopes
had perished, by fingers whose lingering touch
thrilled with a passionate sadness.

Fair Lydia Leslie, Countess of Lindores, a beauty
at the court of James the Seventh, had walked
through stately measures in this golden gown with
no less a personage for her partner than the handsome and fated Duke of Monmouth, concerning whom

Agnes's sentiments were strangely mingled, since she must needs revere him as a Stuart, while at the same time she condemned him for his rebellion against his lawful sovereign. Then had come the Revolution, the fatal Battle of the Boyne, and the flight of broken-hearted James to his place of exile and of death at St. Germain; and the lovely Lydia herself had died afar in France, bequeathing her splendid dress to succeeding generations with the imperative command, tradition said, that never again should it be worn till a descendant of the Stuarts trod the halls of Holyrood. Thus was it linked like its wearer with the love and anguish of two generations; with that pathetic passion of loyalty which the royal race of the Stuarts, above all other kings, inspired in their subjects.

It seemed to Agnes, kneeling in the moonshine,—itself a light of memory,—clasping this precious heirloom of the Leslies to her heart, that she clasped to her heart as well, in fashion subtle as exhaling perfume, the very spirit of that Past. A shiver of rapture thrilled her from head to foot; her bosom was heaving wildly with a joy that was almost pain. She returned with a start to a sense of the present, shook off with a dreamy effort the Past's enchantment, and swept aside the web of dreams by lighting all the candles, before whose yellow radiance the moonlight faded to a ghostly memory.

Agnes busied herself in spreading out her finery on the great canopied bed, fingering delightedly the white satin lacings of the bodice and the fairy falls of Brussels lace at neck and sleeves; but she could

not help wondering, as she studied the gown, why so
much material had been wasted on the train, while so
little had been bestowed on the bodice. She next produced the yellow satin slippers, set with amber clasps,
and their accompanying silken stockings clocked
with silver thistles. When Mistress Campbell tapped
gently at the door, Agnes was in the midst of all the
delights of experiment and adjustment. The dress
fitted remarkably well, but the bodice was cut much
lower than accorded with the ideas of Highland modesty. But the girl was ingenious, and she speedily
devised a way to alter this defect. She caught up a
silken scarf of the Leslie tartan, crossed it over one
shoulder, and knotted it at the waist, letting the
fringed ends fall down over the glimmering skirt.

From time to time her dressing was interrupted
by the merry voices of those passing without, and
she would flit to the window toward Holyrood, whose
dark walls now shone with firefly brilliancy. But at
last the final touch was given to her hair and gown,
and she tossed her plaid over one arm, caught up the
despised train, and swept majestically down the winding staircase. Kenneth was awaiting her in the hall
below, and he caught his breath with wonder at the
sight of her.

For this mischievous little maid of the Highlands
had bloomed a court beauty. Clad in the shimmering folds of her yellow satin, she moved in stately
mien, with lifted head and calmly smiling lips and
haughty grace befitting any queen. Her golden hair,
parted above her brow, was secured by a white velvet
ribbon, leaving free a few fair curls to fall against

the flower-like whiteness of her neck like gold on marble, or, Kenneth fancied, like sunshine upon snow. Her only ornament was a necklace of cairngorms, brilliant as topazes, the gift of Locheil. A single snow-white rose gleamed among her curls, and with the white snood and breast-knot, and the dark silken folds of the Leslie tartan, shone in vivid contrast to the golden lustre of her hair and gown. Even Sir Hugh stood entranced by her loveliness, as, gathering up her satin train, she swept past him with all the stately grace of an empress.

But Agnes was not equally pleased with Kenneth's costume of dark wine-colour.

"The crimson becomes you nobly, Kenneth," she said, surveying him, "but why wear you not the King's colours, instead of those of Hanover? You have not so much as a white rose among your ruffles!"

"Why, you sweet tormentor, the Prince's very standard is crimson. And as for posies!—beshrew me, you have plucked the rose-bush bare; and besides, they are more beseeming a flower like yourself. So away with your displeasure, haughty dame!"

And he playfully brushed her cheek with his ruffles. She returned the caress by tapping his fingers with her fan in mock punishment. Her spirits soared so high that, despite her fleeting disapproval of his choice of colour, she was pleased with all the world. There was so much sweet comradeship in her that evening that Kenneth's goblet of joy was full to brimming, and he quaffed it jealously, fearing to lose a single drop. With her splendid robes and stately manners she had donned a graciousness which might befit some titled lady of the court, and he scarcely recognised in her the saucy and capricious beauty for whose favour he had sued so long.

It being time for them to set forth, Kenneth, wrapping Agnes in her plaid, offered his arm to the proud demoiselle, and they picked their way across the street to where the lamps burned brightly above the palace gates. Torches flickered redly in the wide court within, and merry groups of people ascended the great staircase on the left,—of massive iron, wrought with thistles,—which led to that portion of the palace built by James the Fifth, hallowed by Mary, Queen of Scots, and now honoured by Prince Charlie as his place of residence. It was brilliantly illumined, and snatches of gay music floated fitfully to those below. Agnes's hand tightened upon Kenneth's arm, and he felt her tremble, as she leaned against him, with the pang of a joy too mighty.

And looking down he caught a glimpse of her enraptured face,—of eyes lit like stars in the half-shadow, and he heard her tremulous whisper, "The day has come for which *they* suffered! O father, do you know? And the King—the King enjoys his own again!"

CHAPTER X

"GLORY OF LIFE, GLORY OF SOUL"

"Glory of life, glory of soul,
Where is that glory now?"

AGNES entered a small ante-room at the head of the staircase to lay aside her plaid, and adjust the rose in her hair, and joined Kenneth at the entrance to the long portrait-gallery which served the Prince for a ballroom, producing no small sensation among the throng of fair Jacobites who were lingering there, aflutter with expectation. Agnes met their gaze with the utmost composure, scattered a gracious smile or two, as a queen scatters gold, and entered the hall on Kenneth's arm with becoming stateliness. Resisting an impulse to bestow a gentle kick upon her train, she allowed that superfluous portion of dress to trail gracefully behind her as she swept across the floor.

Brilliant indeed was the scene before them, with every sombre shadow expelled by golden luminance of candlelight. The long bare hall of the palace blazed with colour;—the shimmer of satin, the sheen of velvet and the lustre of gems; and the ancient portraits of the Scottish kings looked down upon as blithe a company as ever shone on dark old Holyrood.

All Jacobite Edinburgh was in attendance, almost

beside themselves at a triumph beyond their wildest dreams. They had drunk deep of that most intoxicating of all wines,—the wine of joy. Thistles and white roses bloomed everywhere, clustered in the tall marble vases, or sewn in rich resemblance on the hangings of faded purple which recalled the mournful splendour of Queen Mary's day. Musicians in Highland costume occupied a dais at the further end of the hall, and dispensed a strange variety of music, the violins now emitting some classic melody, and now yielding their softer strains to the wild, heart-stirring monotone of bagpipes, adored by every Highland heart.

Prince Charlie, the soul of all this passion of rejoicing, stood slightly apart, conversing with his officers, yet ever alert to welcome each advancing guest with the kingly graciousness of which he was the born possessor. This he gave to each, known or unknown to him; but when Agnes entered, he broke off the conversation, and watched her approach, with a strange agitation.

As Kenneth presented her, Agnes swept so low a courtesy that she appeared to kneel, and she would have kissed the hand in which the Prince had taken hers if Charles had not gently prevented her, while he whispered a chivalrous protest which deepened her blush of pride. Very splendid he was,—this bonnie young Stuart,—in his satin court-dress of stainless white, vividly contrasted with the rich scarlet hues of the royal tartan that glowed against it, and adorned by the embroidered garter at his knee, and the order sparkling on his breast. His long curls, thickly powdered, set off the fairness of his skin, and the darkness of his laughing, brown eyes. To Agnes, he was a god from Olympus, in his white jewelled splendour, and mysterious charm; her radiant eyes grew dreamy and wide with wonder; and as for Charles, he thought her fairer by far than any carved or painted Venus, or Dian of the chase.

But the presentation was brief enough, for even the Prince could not neglect the stream of guests impatiently waiting to pay him homage. He was forced to murmur his greeting and farewell in almost the same breath, and see Agnes pass on, promising himself, however, that they should meet again during the evening.

Agnes was soon surrounded by a bevy of admirers, each clamouring for the honour of a dance, and she was kept busy parrying honeyed compliments with the merry sword-play of her wit. In spite of numberless petitions, she had succeeded in eluding a promise for the opening dance, and had just yielded to Edward Farrington's entreaties for the second, when her attention was suddenly called to her partner for the evening, who had been engaged by the Prince in earnest conversation.

Whether he felt himself ill at ease in the unwonted company of these joy-mad Jacobites, or for some other and more subtle reason, Kenneth had remained aloof, more haughty and reserved than usual. Now he approached Agnes and informed her in a low voice that he had been despatched by the Prince on an errand to the West Bow, excused himself for leaving her, and assured her that he would return long before the opening of the ball. Agnes accompanied him to the staircase, laughingly charged him to return in season, and when he had gone, seated herself by a window in the little ante-chamber.

It was late September, yet a summer breeze stirred the heavy window-curtains. Agnes sat in their shadow, oblivious of the world about her, her hands clasped idly in her lap, her eyes fixed dreamily on the grim mass of the Castle, looming mistily above the Canongate. Moment after moment glided by, and still she sat there heedless of their flight. The musicians ceased to play, and there fell a lull, broken only by fragments of happy laughter that floated out into the evening air. To her they were dream-sounds, and less; they did not break the spell. She was equally regardless of Kenneth's failure to reappear; indeed, she had forgotten his existence. She was holding communion with the Past in this old palace of the Past.

But something,—a voice in the street, perhaps,—smote her frail fabric of dreams, shattering it ruthlessly, like spider-woven gossamer, and left her alone again, bereft of her spirit-comrades, and petulant at the rude awakening. She could not build again—that was out of the question, for the mood was gone. Moreover, the dance-music had begun—a lively Scotch strathspey, to which Agnes's satin-shod foot kept restless time. She could not bear to sit inactive, and wished impatiently that Kenneth would return;—wished still more that Donald Cameron, the best dancer in the Highlands, were there to trip a measure with her. They had so often sped through reels together, when the great hall at Auchnacarry had glowed with a myriad candles, and all the gentry of Lochaber had assembled there to pass a merry evening, and to drink grave toasts to the King above a bowl of water. With a little sigh she turned again to the window.

Just then the curtains at the door stirred softly as some one lifted them and entered. Half-startled, Agnes rose; but the exclamation on her lips was one of awe and wonder, for there beside her, all radiant in his rich attire, stood the Prince. He shone like a star in the grey dusk of the room; for the jewels on his breast caught lustre even in that deep shadow, and his eyes sparkled with triumph as he took her timidly yielded hand.

"Fair Mistress Leslie," he said, bowing grave and low, "will you grant me the priceless honour of your hand for this dance?"

She caught her breath audibly; her eyes sought his in wistful unbelief.

"Oh, your Royal Highness, you cannot mean this! You cannot mean that you have chosen me,—of all the noble dames of Scotland here to-night,—for this undreamed-of honour?"

She spoke in tones half-shy, yet quivering with rapture.

"A Prince's word is not to be doubted," he answered, smiling. "Can you be cruel enough to question mine? I could command your fealty, I suppose," he continued laughingly, "but I will not use authority in this case; I will plead instead: 'His Royal Highness' entreats you for the honour. Come, fair lady, away with all objections; they are waiting for us to open the ball."

She hardly knew how she murmured her assent, for she was mute with the strangeness and marvel of it all; but she took the arm he offered her, and let him lead her toward the door. She was vaguely conscious of the rustling of the curtains as they passed through; of the swift dividing of the throng to give them entrance; of the blaze of light and colour doubly dazzling after the semi-darkness; dimly aware, too, of the whisper that stirred the brilliant company like wind-tossed poppies, as they moved, the centre of all eyes, to their place at the upper end of the long hall.

Yet, however conspicuous the position, Agnes was not one to yield to her sense of shyness. She straightened her slender figure proudly, and poised her lovely head a trifle higher than its wont, looking neither to the right nor left, with wide, wistful eyes and lips just parted.

As the Prince and Agnes turned to face the vast assembly, the musicians sounded a flourish, and the notes of "Welcome, Royal Charlie!" pealed out and mingled with the thunder of acclaim. Why should not Agnes thrill with triumph, with the proud blood of Leslie and "Bonnie Dundee" pulsing hotly in every vein, her very heart afire with love and loyalty, as every knee was bent, and every head bowed low, before Charles Edward Stuart! As the girl sank softly to one knee, pressing her lips to the hand in hers, the Prince made a gesture of remonstrance, and quickly raised her to her feet, acknowledging with a

"She was concious of nothing save the wild sweet witchery of the moment"

"Glory of Life, Glory of Soul"

graceful bow the homage of the loyal throng. Among them knelt the brave Locheil, his eyes alight with pride at the vivid beauty of his foster-daughter, and the royal honour conferred upon her.

How the dance fared Agnes hardly knew, for she gave no heed to her footsteps, and could not have told with whom she touched hands as they glided through the gay, familiar measures;—she was conscious of nothing save the wild, sweet witchery of the moment; that "glory of life" which transfigures youth with its mysterious splendour.

This beauty of Scotland was all gold and snow; the gold of gleaming hair and shimmering gown and lustrous yellow cairngorms; the snow of throat and brow and breast-knot white as Stuart roses. Her lips and cheeks alone were traitors to Prince Charlie, for, despite her, they bloomed crimson roses that the House of Hanover might have proudly claimed.

She moved in a splendid dream, a trance of rapture from which she could not bear to waken;—she wished the pipes would never cease to play their saucy, haunting melodies. Glorious visions swept before her eyes: visions of Scotland's triumph, of the Bonnie Prince king of actual empires as of Highland hearts, of Norman Leslie Duke of Rothes, and of the closed gate at Auchnacarry unbarred at last to the loved Stuarts. She moved in a mist of radiant joys, dreamily conscious of the dazzling figure in white-and-tartan by her side, of the warm pressure of his hand upon hers, and of the delicious fragrance of Stuart roses.

Meantime Kenneth, returning from his belated

errand, sought vainly for Agnes where he had left her, and through several rooms besides, till at last he turned toward the portrait gallery. But on the very threshold his steps were stayed by an astonishing sight. For Agnes, after winding her graceful way among the dancers, was in the very act of extending her hand to the Prince, as they rejoined each other at the head of the line. Kenneth gazed one moment, incredulous, then his face darkened ominously, like a sky beneath a thunder-cloud, while his eyes supplied the simile of lightning, as he made his way to a vacant seat by the wall near a dark dame in crimson, whose eyes, like his, were fastened savagely upon the central figure of the scene.

The bewitching beauty of the Highlands had snatched the Prince from the very midst of a galaxy of city beauties, all vieing with each other for the inestimable honour of opening the ball with the Prince.

And yet the jealousy was less because the victor wore her triumph lightly, and had not, so far, shot a single glance of exultation at the vanquished from beneath her brown lashes. But one vivid exception to this moderation of ill-will presented itself in the form of the Countess of Menteith, who, besides her high rank, had ample pretensions to beauty,—in her own opinion at least,—to prove an attractive claimant for the Prince's hand,—for the length of a dance if not more. The Countess was indeed sufficiently handsome, but her manner bordered upon boldness, and was certainly far removed from maidenly reserve.

Now, although foiled in her chief desire, she welcomed Kenneth warmly, with faith in the ancient principle of half-a-loaf. But Kenneth sat there, grim and glowering, a statue of sullen rage, while the Countess toyed with her jewelled fan, and followed the Prince and Agnes with burning eyes. At length, however, she turned to him again, and having once engaged him in reluctant conversation, proceeded to ply him with questions, to which he made strange and abstracted answers, unpleasantly aware that he denied when he should have assented, and said "*yes*" when the occasion demanded "*no*." The Countess, with the keen insight of her sex, had speedily guessed at his source of displeasure, and since he would pay no attention to her, took a malicious delight in fanning the flame of his fury.

"The Prince seems quite enamoured of your fair lady, Major Campbell," she observed with a scornful smile; "but beauty ever adores a royal lover!"

At this Kenneth turned on her a face of intense indignation.

"Oh, my dear Major, never look so shocked!" the Countess murmured, with veiled malice; "'tis but the fashion of the sex, as all history will inform you."

And without waiting for Kenneth to absorb this poisoned morsel, she caught his arm in mock solicitation, exclaiming:

"Never mind, Major, let her think herself secure in the royal graces. *We* know what kings' favour is! But see, the dance is over! How proudly your pretty lady trips it among the throng!"

Kenneth saw Agnes coming toward them on the

Prince's arm, her eyes, jewel-bright, searching the company in anxious quest, but resting not on him.

His gaze followed her feverishly till she disappeared through the low doorway beside the radiant white figure of the Prince.

CHAPTER XI

"TO SEE HER IS TO LOVE HER"

"To see her is to love her,
　And love but her forever,
For nature made her what she is,
　And ne'er made sic anither!"

AGNES and the Prince strayed slowly from one room to another, directing their footsteps toward the small, dark chambers, so piteously hallowed by the most tragic memories of Queen Mary. As they went, Charles repeated the mournful legends that clustered, grey as lichens on a rock, about this ghost-thronged palace of his race; and Agnes listened, stirred like vibrant harp-strings by the minor cadence of his voice and theme. At length they crossed the worn and narrow threshold admitting to the tiny, shadow-haunted chamber that had been the bedroom of the fated Queen. It was lighted dimly by tall candles burning in quaintly wrought candlesticks of tarnished gold, and this faint light diffused a mystic glamour. If the Scotland of the sixteenth century had decked the chamber with any richness of royal state, small trace remained of it now. The time-worn tapestries with which the walls were hung retained so little of their ancient colouring that only a vivid fancy could repaint the gay profusion of figures they had once portrayed.

Agnes gazed with a shudder at the faded curtains concealing the secret stairway,—the self-same stairway up which the assassins stole to the murder of Rizzio; and her eyes grew dark with dread as they entered the shadowy supper-room where the deed was done.

"Oh!" she cried, with a quick breath of pitying horror, "what a terrible thing! And it happened here in this very room, not two hundred years ago! Ah, the unhappy Queen! My heart bleeds for her when I recall that night! And the coward Darnley —how I hate him!—I do not wonder that she wished his death! Oh, I know that it was wrong to kill him, —wrong for her to let them kill him if she had known. But I will never believe she knew! I will never believe wrong of Queen Mary!—No true Scotswoman will! She was so beautiful and so unhappy! And it was Fate that was cruel,—not she who sinned!"

Her hazel eyes, not unlike Mary's in brilliancy and beauty, shone with defiant lustre, as she upheld the memory of the hapless Queen.

Charles listened eagerly to her warm defence.

"I, the Queen's descendant, thank you in her name, Mistress Leslie. Yet I am tempted to add, in my own behalf, that you extend that ardent loyalty to me."

The words were spoken laughingly, but with none the less serious meaning.

"Your Royal Highness asks for what is yours already," she answered just as seriously. "Are you not a Stuart?"

Perhaps the Prince was not entirely satisfied with

the answer, but he made no demur; only proposed after a moment that they return to the Queen's bedchamber. Yet Memory still held them in its thrall, for here the "Rose of Stuart's line" had left the haunting perfume of her presence, sweet as roseleaves; and in the place where she had knelt to offer pleading prayer, or had sobbed herself to sleep with an aching, embittered heart, they must needs remember her, even amid youth's triumph.

So they talked together in that old haunted chamber,—the royal descendant of Queen Mary and this lovely daughter of the Cavaliers. And Agnes gazed into the dim little glass that had so often reflected the beautiful features of Mary, and now mirrored those so strangely like them.

Charles touched with reverent fingers the faded hangings of the bed; and again Agnes shuddered.

"It chills my very blood to think of the scenes that have been enacted in this place! Brave indeed must one be to sleep in that bed, for surely spirits walk here. We are superstitious, we Highlanders; and more afraid of ghosts than of living men. I should think they would haunt your dreams."

He smiled faintly. "They would, were I not so weary that sleep is sound. But you speak the truth," he continued, a slight shade of melancholy clouding his handsome features. "Holyrood is thronged with shadows. Here the ghosts of memory rise, and the past lies heavy on the soul! *Shadows! Shadows!*"

But Charles was too young and buoyant to remain long under the influence of hereditary gloom; and Agnes, though equally sensitive to sad impressions, as quickly recovered her natural gaiety. The Prince would have her sit in a tall, time-blackened chair, heavy with rich carvings, and brought another for himself.

Joy dispelled the gloom with a stronger radiance than that of candles, and they were soon engaged in a lively discussion of all that had happened in the age-long week just ended. Agnes, too, related the story of the dress she wore, and the Prince listened with absorbing interest.

Charles had never been susceptible to feminine influence; the Stuart failing in that respect was not his; he had endured with indifference the tender looks and ardent adoration of half the beauties of Europe. But since the day of his entrance into Edinburgh, the image of a girl had flitted constantly across his vision. Now that image was a warm reality, he found himself moved by the strongest passion that had yet laid its grasp upon him.

And indeed, in all France and Italy and Scotland he had seen no face so fair. Her hair, the golden lustre of cairngorms; her cheeks, the pink glow of the Highland heather; her eyes, the clear brilliance of a mountain stream reflecting the hazel light of the pebbles in its bed; and above all,—her heart,—pure tender, loyal,—that held the Stuart cause above all else in life.

The Prince, secure in so devoted a confidant, had begun to unfold some of his plans for the future, and was rather ruefully emphasising his need of money to equip his army, when he met with a startling response from his fair listener.

Agnes unclasped the golden necklace from about her white throat, and held it out to him.

"Will you not take it, your Royal Highness?" she pleaded earnestly. "'Tis of some little value, and perhaps may be some slight aid——"

"Do you think I will allow you to sacrifice your jewels for my sake?" Charles cried vehemently.

"I beg your Royal Highness to accept of it," she insisted sweetly. "It is no sacrifice on my part, for to aid you, however slightly, were a joy beyond all jewels, and never would I wear it were you not King of Scotland!"

"Ah, can you mean this, Mistress Leslie?" he cried, with an ardent tenderness in his tones perilously near betrayal. "Is it for me you feel such great devotion?"

He broke off, struggling with the flood of feeling that was threatening to overwhelm every barrier of restraint and surge into passionate expression.

"Tell me!" he repeated fervently, "tell me, is all this splendid loyalty for me alone?"

"It shall never be given to another!" she answered very low.

She did not look at him, but gazed straight into the dim shadows of Queen Mary's chamber. Her cheeks flushed a soft crimson, her eyes grew dreamily bright, and her hands instinctively clasped themselves against the white breast-knot. As for the Prince,—he was but four-and-twenty after all, and the throne seemed suddenly an empty honour, and the crown a weary weight, and a girl's beauty and a girl's loyalty were vastly more precious treasures.

While this scene was passing in the Queen's bed room, Kenneth had wandered restlessly about the palace like an avenging ghost, avoiding the light-hearted throng about him, and brooding grimly over the affront he had received. He reflected bitterly, seeing now through jealous eyes which changed the world from rose-colour to grey. So this little beauty of the Highlands, whose moods had appeared to be merely those of a capricious child, was not so artless after all! She was playing for high stakes,—a duchy, it would seem. And every bewitching smile she gave the Prince was as much a coin of favour as if it had been a golden guinea. All her sweet, mischievous ways, as natural to her as its song to a bird, he laid to the studied wiles of a cruel coquetry which plays with hearts as with dice, risking all for the highest throw.

At this point in his wretched musing he observed the Countess standing in one of the deep recesses of the windows. At sight of him she came forward with an amused smile.

"Are you still pursuing, Major Campbell?" she exclaimed playfully. "I think I can guide your footsteps, for not five minutes since I beheld the Prince and Mistress Leslie admiring the prospect from the north window. The view is remarkably fine at this hour of the night!"

And with this biting sarcasm she left him. Kenneth, grinding his teeth with rage, muttered, "Confound the lovely witch! She would as soon coquet with a prince as with any other mortal!" and followed the direction the Countess had given him.

In the meantime, Charles and Agnes, little dreaming of the feelings they had aroused, continued their delightful conversation. Agnes was leaning back in the great chair, the sheen of her dress and the exquisite curves of her arms showing vividly against the dark background like a white-and-golden lily against a sombre wall. The Prince could not withdraw his eyes from her, and as he gazed he was seized by a singular impulse. Agnes's white arms rested on the carved supports of the chair, and the pretty fingers, which needed no rings to adorn them, proclaimed their proud blood in every curve of their tapering slenderness.

Charles was strongly impelled to seize those delicate fingers, and not release them till they had been warmly kissed.

But the wild impetuousness of youth had been tempered in the Prince by the royal necessity of prudence, and now, although much annoyed by being compelled to weigh his actions, Charles was too clear-eyed not to consider what their effect might be. He could not begin his conquest of Britain by making ardent love to this adorable little Jacobite, however strong his personal desires.

As a means of controlling his rebellious impulse, he withdrew his eyes from the cause of it, and allowed the conversation to cease, at a loss, for the first time in his life, where to turn it with safety.

Agnes, quite innocent of the peril of her presence, resumed the dangerous subject.

"If prayers would win a kingdom, then would your royal Highness be secure already. My one prayer is——" she paused, thrilling with emotion, unable to proceed.

"For what do you pray?" he whispered, leaning toward her.

"*For the kingdom of God, and the reign of the Stuarts,*" she murmured softly.

His mighty resolution dissolved like fragile mist. One moment more and he would have caught her in his arms, clasping her to him as the embodiment of all his joy and triumph, forgetting everything in the wide world besides.

Instead, a footstep sounded in the adjoining chamber, another force than the breeze parted the curtains, and the romance was rudely dispelled by the abrupt entrance of Kenneth Campbell. Both had risen and stood facing him, Charles in evident annoyance at the interruption; Agnes in deep amazement at his aggressive bearing.

The Prince, concealing with difficulty his vexation, said inquiringly:

"To what do we owe your presence, Major Campbell?"

Kenneth bowed slightly. His face was very cold and stern.

"I have come to seek Mistress Leslie, who appears to be unaware of her promise."

The angry blood coloured Agnes's face at the rebuke; and she met Kenneth's gaze with one of proud defiance. But, strangely enough, she controlled her temper, and turned to the Prince, saying calmly:

"I must beg your Royal Highness's pardon for

"To See Her is to Love Her"

having so long detained you from your guests. The honour conferred on me this evening I shall remember always. And now I ask your Highness to permit me to withdraw."

She made a profound courtesy, and gave the Prince her hand in farewell, quite unconscious of the feeling she had invoked. He touched her fingers with his lips in a grave salute, very different from the passionate caress he longed to bestow; bowed very low, and held the curtains back for her to pass. And walking straight and proud, by Kenneth's side, she left the presence of the Prince.

Once they were alone, however, she twitched her hand from Kenneth's arm, and flashed him a challenging look. It was the inevitable clash of parties; the century-old hostility of Puritan and Cavalier. All her gay and brilliant blood, bequeathed from generations past, took fire from the flint of his iron dominance.

"You are a fine model of constancy!" raged Kenneth.

"Constancy? To what?" queried Agnes, maliciously.

"You may well ask, indeed," he exclaimed bitterly. "Constant to nothing, Mistress April!"

"Aweel, frien', April is a guid month," quoth that saucy spirit, lapsing into provoking Scotch. "I weel ken ane while she laughs, ane while she greets, but ye'll have the gran' variety!"

This was unbearable. Kenneth was distracted between admiration of her beauty, and rage at her behaviour.

"Might I inquire what has become of your necklace?" he said, observing that her snowy throat was bare.

Agnes's fingers flew to her neck in a gesture of dismay. "Why, I must have lost it!" she exclaimed in a tone of consternation, but he noticed that she did not suggest a search for the missing ornament.

"I trust you did not lose your heart as well," he added meaningly.

"I wear my heart neither upon my sleeve nor on my necklace, sir!" she retorted instantly.

"I think I have had enough dancing for one night," he observed with grim significance.

"And I have received all the glory that one night can give," she replied serenely. "Kindly tell Captain Farrington that I am too exhausted to dance with him." She shut her eyes with an air of weariness, and began to fan languidly. "Since the Prince of Scotland has paid me the honour of dancing with me, I desire nothing more!"

. . . . .

That night Agnes could hardly sleep for happiness, and through her dreams glided the white jewelled figure of the Bonnie Prince; but amid all the splendour, there brooded, like a dark avenging wraith, the tragic memories of Holyrood.

CHAPTER XII

"O'ER HIGHLAND HEARTS SECURE HE REIGNS"

"His right these hills, his right these plains,
O'er Highland hearts secure he reigns;
What lads e'er did, our lads will do;
Were I a lad, I'd follow him too!"

MORNING brought no abatement of Kenneth's resentment. Directly he and Agnes were left alone together he alluded angrily to the troublesome topic.

"You are so unreasonable, Kenneth," Agnes insisted calmly; "you left me with a promise to return, and then the Prince sought me out to dance with him, and you are angry that I did not refuse so great an honour." Her colour mounted, and her calmness disappeared. "I did not break my word with you; no honourable maid would do that, even in small matters. You did not come, and I was free to dance with whom I would. And 'tis not every day a maid is asked to dance by a prince,—*our* Prince of Scotland!"

Her eyes had begun to sparkle. "Kenneth, bethink you of the honour his Royal Highness did my uncle, in asking me to lead the ball with him! There was many a titled lady, and many a fair city-maid he might have chosen, yet he bestowed this great distinction upon me, because of all the Leslies did and suffered; and was it not right I should receive this wondrous honour for the sake of my uncle's house?"

She flung the last words at him with an air of final vindication. But Kenneth would not leave the subject.

"I think 'twas not 'the honour of your house' alone that won you favour," he observed grimly. "The fact that you were by far the most beautiful maid in the hall may have had a share in his decision. Even princes are not always impartial."

"Indeed, Major Campbell, I think you have e'en lost your mind!" was the indignant retort. "His Royal Highness is concerned with other things, and has something better to do than pick out pretty faces like ponies at a fair. Pray have the courtesy to drop the conversation, Major Campbell!"

And with a haughty straightening of her slender figure she swept past him into the garden.

Agnes would have thought more seriously of Kenneth's displeasure had she not deemed it quite as possible for him to feel jealous of the sun, as of the Prince. Each seemed equally absurd, and therefore each seemed equally imaginable. Mortals and stars are not comparable. Moreover, despite her lack of worldly knowledge, she was quite sensible enough to be free from all romantic follies in regard to the Prince; while, on the other hand, she was entirely blinded to any passion from a source as remote as royalty. And, furthermore, all her wild dreams of Stuart glory were for her uncle, her coun-cry, and her king; her own share in them had always seemed a very insignificant part, scarcely worth thinking of. She therefore laid Kenneth's ill-temper to one of his sullen moods, and paid small heed to it; though it cooled her friendship considerably, and widened the rift already forming between them.

She was also obliged to encounter Kenneth's partner in displeasure,—the resentful Countess of Menteith. The meeting took place on horseback in the very courtyard of St. Giles's, and it was the Countess who began the battle.

"Stop a moment, Mistress Leslie," exclaimed that lady, reining her horse at Agnes's side; "do you know you were quite the most envied person at the ball last evening? By what secret did you win the royal favour? Was it by your beauty alone? You must not be too rash, you know," she concluded maliciously.

"You might advise me, perhaps," said Agnes, whose eyes were beginning to glisten dangerously.

"My dear, I trust you did not follow this course:

"'She bade good angels and saints defend her,
 And sank in the arms of the young Pretender!'"

the Countess quoted bitingly, in the words of a popular ballad. But she failed to disconcert her rival.

"Aweel, aweel!" the girl flashed saucily, "it isna every one has the chance!"

But the next instant she coloured to her temples and bit her lip in fierce vexation at herself for having made so indiscreet an answer, and one which the Countess could interpret in so different a spirit from that of mischievous daring in which it was uttered. She felt that she had overshot the mark, and in spite of victory had given her enemy the advantage.

As for the Countess, although a year passed by before she again ventured to encounter her brilliant rival, she treasured wrath against the day of wrath and never rested till she had turned the sharp edge of that reckless speech against the fair inventor.

. . . . .

On a Thursday evening, nine days after the ball, Agnes found herself alone in the house, and free to do what she chose. Sir Hugh had gone to console with a fellow-Whig over the madness of the world in general, and Mistress Campbell had betaken herself to service at St. Giles's with Kenneth for her companion. But although Agnes had been usually anxious to attend her aunt, she had remained at home on this occasion on the plea of practising the harp which had been sadly neglected of late. As the maid, Betty Macrae, had hied herself to a neighbouring close for an evening's gossip, the girl found ample opportunity to indulge her heart's desire in the songs which she adored.

Agnes, exulting in her freedom, betook herself to the great parlour; lighted a couple of candles on the mantel, and then drew her harp into the shadow, as she needed no music for the songs she knew by heart. At first she let her fingers wander idly, and sat with drooped head, like some inspired minstrel waiting for the flood of impulse to rush from soul to harp-strings. Instinctive as a breath the impulse came; and the passion-stirring song echoed wide:

"O'er Highland Hearts He Reigns"

"Charlie is my darling, my darling, my darling,
Oh! Charlie is my darling, the young Chevalier!
Oh! there were mony beating hearts,
And mony a hope and fear;
And mony were the pray'rs put up
For the young Chevalier!"

The royal visitor on the door-step delayed to lift the brazen lion's head that served as knocker. The ringing words floated out to him, borne on the sweet, passionate voice, a strange pathos quivering through its gaiety. Many fair lips had sung his triumph, but these alone thrilled his heart. He waited till the song was ended, and then knocked, half-reluctant to disturb the singer.

Agnes obeyed the summons with a curious premonition of wonder, instantly fulfilled when, upon opening the door, she beheld the Bonnie Prince himself, and, starting back, almost dropped the candle in her amazement.

He laughingly put his hands behind him, thinking to dispense with the usual homage; but she foiled his purpose by kissing the fringed ends of his plaid. He was plainly dressed in dark-blue velvet, without a sign of his royal rank.

"I encountered one of my own sentries yonder," he said, laughing. "I coaxed him to let me through; it was too dark to see the colours of my plaid," glancing as he spoke at the glowing folds of the royal Stuart tartan which fell across his shoulder.

She had recovered presence of mind enough to murmur some words of greeting, and lead her guest into the parlour, explaining rather confusedly that she was the only one left to act the part of host. The Prince seemed rather pleased than otherwise, and seated himself in a large arm-chair, with a smile of boyish delight.

"Then I suppose you and I will be allowed to enjoy ourselves. And you must play to me, Mistress Leslie, for music is my great delight, and few chances have I of indulging in it. Lord George Murray never lets me so much as glance at my dear violin, my 'fiddle,' as he disrespectfully calls it, without reminding me of the tyrant who fiddled when Rome burned. I trust the parallel is not a strong one!"

Agnes was lighting the candles along the wall in honour of her royal guest, and she faced him, taper in hand, its lustre glimmering over the gold of her hair. She wore a simple blue dress, whose straight-laced bodice and full skirt did not conceal the grace of the lithe figure; and over it, shawl-fashion, as the night was cool, a plaid of the Leslie tartan, clasped in front with a cairngorm brooch.

The Prince glanced at the sombre furniture of the room, and especially at the hangings of gloomy crimson from which even the candle-light drew no warmth of colour.

"Sir Hugh has a liking for crimson," he remarked, "he seems a lover of red roses."

Agnes laughed archly. "There are those who love white roses better," she replied, looking down at the snowy blossom at her breast.

"Let's dispense with formal names and titles. Take warning, fair lady! At first mention of 'Royal Highness' or 'Your Majesty' I fly away like a indignant fay, or goblin—as you will," he said, smiling.

"I may call you 'Mistress Agnes' for this evening? As for me, why call me——"

"I would not think of calling you aught unbecoming your rank," Agnes interposed gravely.

"Well, if a title there must be, take 'Prince Charlie' then. The name sounds sweeter as we of Scotland speak it, than it ever did before."

"'Prince Charlie' it shall be, as you desire it. Though perhaps you would prefer ' 'Phrionnsa Teàrlach,'—as we say the name in Gaelic."

"That is how my brave Locheil addresses me," said the Prince. "Oh, you must teach me Gaelic, Mistress Agnes; it will never do for me to remain ignorant of the language of my most loyal subjects."

At the Prince's entreaty Agnes returned to her harp. Her delicate fingers swept the strings, and she began to sing to the accompaniment of rippling chords. And such a bewitching variety of songs the Prince had never heard before; saucy Jacobite ballads, mournful love-lays, fragments of border-minstrelsy, and laments over Scotland's slain. And into each she put the strange, compelling glamour of her personality, making each incident glow with life. She drew smiles from him at the gay defiance of

"THE SONG OF THE CHEVALIER."

"To daunton me, and me sae young,
　And guid King James's auldest son;
　O that's the thing that ne'er can be,
　For the man is unborn that shall daunton me!

> O set me ance on Scottish land,
> My guid braidsword into my hand,
> My guid blue bonnet 'bune my bree,
> And shaw me the man that will daunton me!"

She made him laugh merrily at the bold sarcastic wit of "This Is No' My Ain House"; and thrill with pity at the tragic fate of fair "Helen of Kirkconnel." And when she sang "The Flowers o' the Forest," that touching dirge over the slain of Flodden, she brought before him with a magic power that blood-stained field where gallant James the Fourth and the flower of Scottish chivalry lay cold in death.

Brought up in a Highland castle among those of the opposite sex, Agnes had none of that mock modesty that girls so often acquire. Her feeling of shyness toward the Prince was not due to the fact that he was a man, but because he was of royal blood. She would have had the same feeling,—perhaps in a greater degree—before a princess,—for it did not occur to her to make any change in her demeanour. She talked to him very much as if he had been a girl of her own age,—as freely and upon the same subjects,—those she had been always used to discussing, —music, war, politics, or whatever new and wonderful had happened throughout the world.

The Prince picked up one of his long fair curls, and playfully compared it with a tress of Agnes's, declaring "they were somewhat like, but that hers was by far the finer and more golden," an advantage she blushingly disclaimed.

To-night they were not sovereign and subject, but boy and girl,—they were scarcely more in years,—

frankly and innocently happy in each other's company.

The Prince proposed that Agnes should teach him the Highland Fling, and forthwith she sprang up, with a child's delight, and pirouetted through the lively steps. Next they attempted it together, Agnes applauding the Prince's efforts, while he laughed at his mistakes.

When they were weary of dancing they resumed the conversation which the lively exercise had somewhat interrupted. Charles told Agnes of his determination to invade England, and encouraged by her enthusiasm, spread out some maps on the table between them, and pointed out to her the especial points of vantage. He also related several entertaining stories concerning his little army; among them how Lady Macintosh, wife of the chieftain of that clan, upon her husband's declaring for King George, had proclaimed her allegiance to the Stuarts by raising her clan for the Prince, and thereby gaining the title of "Colonel Anne."

"I believe Alexander MacGillivray has been chosen to lead them," Charles concluded.

"Alexander MacGillivray,—he is a fine, brave man," cried Agnes, kindling at the familiar name. "The Lady Anne did well in choosing him for the leader. I mind me clearly how he came to Auchacarry and lifted me in his arms when I was a little child.

"But, oh, your Royal—Prince Charlie, do not leave Scotland! Believe me, Scottish hearts love you more dearly than any others!"

She had risen, and was bending toward him in entreaty; and she spoke with a sweet solemnity, her beauty glowing in the candle-light.

"Will not Scotland suffice you, Prince Charlie?" (pronounced *Chairlie*). She spoke with the Scottish softening of the *a* which made the name a caress.

She leaned so close to him that one of her bright curls brushed his sleeve. And at that involuntary touch,—that sweet nearness,—a quick thrill ran through him; he wished that fleeting moment would never end.

But there is always the serpent in paradise, and on this occasion the serpent presented itself in human form;—to drop the simile and the unpleasant inference,—Kenneth Campbell appeared. Perhaps the scene was sufficient to warrant the whirlwind of jealousy that swept his spirit.

Agnes and the Prince were very near each other, she with downcast eyes and deepened colour, one slender hand resting on the table close to that of Charles, while the expression on the Prince's face was unmistakable.

Kenneth, with the preternatural insight of the jealous, stood smitten by the Medusa; but when Charles inquired carelessly, "Well, what is the evening?" he managed to answer drily, "I *had* thought it frosty, your Highness, but I have changed my mind."

CHAPTER XIII

"GALLANT YOUNG DONALD"

"I ha'e but ae son, my gallant young Donald;
  But if I had ten they should follow Glengarry;
Health to MacDonald and gallant Clanronald,
  For these are the men that will die for their Charlie!"

CHARLES EDWARD had the royal faculty of disregarding dangerous speeches when occasion required, and he replied to Kenneth's irony only by remarking that the temperature seemed to him very seasonable. But when he bade Agnes farewell he had the very natural satisfaction,—not confined to majesty,—of observing his own supremacy over his sullen rival; and his brown eyes flashed with irrepressible triumph as he glanced at Kenneth. Agnes, who never lacked an appropriate ditty, left the room demurely the instant the Prince had departed, singing with quite uncalled-for emphasis, "Charlie, Ye Are Welcome to Scotland and to Me." And though Kenneth longed to take her to task for such audacity, he hardly desired another clash of arms with this quick-witted and ready-tongued little Highlander.

He could not realise what warmth and steadfastness and lofty courage lay beneath her saucy speeches and mischievous ways. He knew very little of women; how, then, was he to judge aright this most perplexing of her sex,—a creature half shy, half saucy, half serious, half gay,—and wholly irresistible;—a flower dancing in the wind, yet ever faithful to the sun;— a being steadfast to the right as is the guiding-needle to the pole, yet as changeful in her moods as the pole-star in its orbit. He was no more capable of estimating her character than he was of measuring the moon, though he had often wrathfully compared her to that mutable planet in beauty and caprice. He judged her very falsely; her moods were mere eddies on the river's brim;—the stream was very clear and deep. She was as pure of heart as her own mountain-mists, but, like them, often vexing and delusive.

Nothing happened, however, during the next two weeks, to rouse his smouldering suspicion; and his attention was so much absorbed by his duties that little time was left for musing. The Prince had ordered a strict blockade of the Castle, and General Guest retaliated by opening fire upon the town. Sir Hugh's loyal sentiments amply protected his own house in spite of Kenneth's deflection; Agnes, seated at a western window, could safely watch the shot raining down upon the High Street, and hear the cries of the terrified people, seeking comparative security in the Canongate. Excitement became frenzy when some of the houses near the Castle caught fire, and those attempting to extinguish it were slain by the cannonaders. Many of the citizens fled to Leith, the seaport of Edinburgh, only to discover that a British warship in the Forth was bombarding the town, and that refuge there was none. Even Holyrood was in

danger, for the Castle commanded the entire city, and
Agnes trembled for the Prince's safety, remembering
that on the very moment of his first arrival at the
palace a shot had struck the tower of James Fifth.
But Charles, though fearless for himself, was too
merciful to cause needless suffering, and he restored
quiet by raising the blockade on the day following
that of its commencement.

The Jacobite Journal of Edinburgh, which bore
the name of the *Mercury,* gave minute accounts
of the Prince's movements, describing the morning
councils, daily reviews of troops, and state levees,
which made up the life of this young leader. Agnes
devoured these accounts with unfailing delight; Kenneth read them as carefully, with different motives
and a less degree of zeal.

Charles had reached the noonday of his triumph,
and hours were reckoned years; it was the crowding
of a lifetime into six short weeks. The Prince
sought to bury his troublesome passion under numberless urgent cares, and allowed himself no chance
of temptation beyond catching a few distracting
glimpses of Agnes from his windows. He longed to
remind her of the promised lessons in Gaelic, but he
knew this would be unwise, and resolutely suppressed
the desire. But however successfully he banished the
thought of her by day, she completely dominated his
sleeping hours. Whether he sought repose in his
stately palace, or lay wrapped in his Highland plaid
among his clansmen, the vision of her did not cease
to haunt him.

On a sunny morning in mid-October the Prince met

the lady of his dreams in the shaded windings of the
Duke's Walk, a path through the wooded park behind Holyrood, named for the Prince's grandfather,
the exiled James VII. Mounted on her white horse,
she looked as radiant as the sunlight in her gay riding-dress with its snowy breast-ribbon. She drew
rein at sight of the Prince, and bent her saucy head
in grave obeisance.

"I beg your Royal Highness to pardon my steed
and me for not kneeling," she cried archly, "but he,
too, is a Prince, and so can make no reverence, and
'twould sadly disarrange my riding-dress, besides giving your Royal Highness the trouble of assisting me
to mount."

The young monarch's eyes were sparkling, and as
he doffed his blue bonnet, the wind spread his yellow
curls over his shoulders, and fluttered the silken folds
of the Charles Edward tartan which was looped over
his velvet coat. Never had the "Bonnie Prince"
appeared handsomer or more kingly than at this
moment, with his winsome face illumed by unuttered
love. No wonder Agnes's eyes shone with fervent
pride, a passionate loyalty which deepened the
traitor-roses in lips and cheeks.

Side by side they rode through the wooded beauty
of the park till they reached the ruined chapel of
Holyrood, and there drew rein to separate. But
again Fate showed a frowning face, for from the foot
of the Canongate Kenneth Campbell rode to meet
them. He gave one look at Agnes's dancing eyes,
and his face grew dark and almost savage. Agnes,
though fearless of all things, cast several restless

"Gallant Young Donald" 113

glances in his direction, as she parted from the Prince. And for the little way that she and Kenneth had together she showed a remarkable interest in a knot of her bridle rein. For the time, however, their mutual distrust revealed itself by a sarcastic word or two from Kenneth, and a biting rejoinder from Agnes. The height of the climax was yet to come.

The 25th of October was a brilliant autumn day, unusually warm for the time of year. Directly dinner had ended, and the family had dispersed, Agnes sauntered out into the garden. The season was very late, and here and there along the leaf-strewn paths flowers still bloomed in summer beauty. The old garden itself was an enchanting spot with its wild luxuriance of shrub and thicket, its low-leaning fruit-trees, and shady seats, embroidered thick with moss. The view it gave was of the massive gates of Holyrood, flaunting their rampant lions, and the ancient fountain in front, with its procession of carven figures.

Agnes, seated upon one of the mossy steps, her chin sunk in her hand, was watching the group of moving figures about the palace-gates; and as she looked, a form in Highland dress came toward her across the wide street. She sprang up, glowing with delight, recognising her belovéd playmate and foster-brother, Donald Cameron.

She ran merrily to meet him, unlatched the vine-wreathed gate, and then, grown shy in the midst of her eagerness, made no more attempt at greeting than the yielding of both her hands to his warm pressure.

"Oh, Donald!" she cried, blushing, yet half-reproachful, "to think ye've been in Edinbro' so long, an' I've seen scarce a glimpse o' you. Had you really forgot your old playmate, since ye had climbed so high in honour?"

"Forget you, Agnes?" he exclaimed; "forget our happy childhood, and all our sweet companionship? 'Tis a part of my very life, and will never be forgotten so long as that life lasts!"

"Ah, it is so with me," she answered; "every hour my heart longs for the Highlands, and the sweet days in the old Castle. Shall we never return to it, Donald?"

"It is God alone will decide," he responded gravely. "We have drawn the sword from the scabbard; it will be long unsheathed. Duty forbade our meeting before, Agnes, and now we shall meet no more for many weeks, for to-morrow we set out for England, and for that purpose I came hither,—to bid you farewell!"

She sat with averted face, looking out into the sunny garden. She had turned quite pale; and her mouth was quivering. Neither found it easy to continue.

They had seated themselves beneath a wide-spreading tree, and Agnes had taken up a bit of Donald's plaid and was winding it mechanically about her fingers, as if the trivial action relieved her restless anxiety.

She rose abruptly, exclaiming with forced gaiety, "Let us not sit here and fashion ill of the future. We have an hour to ourselves in this lovely garden

Let us be children again, and talk of hopes, not fears!"

So they strayed along the garden-paths; but they did not go hand in hand in the old familiar comradeship; curiously reserved they were for those who had been children together. Donald's thoughts flew back into the years, questioning whether the little maid with whom he had lived in brotherly intimacy could really be the queenly beauty who walked beside him.

He could not have told when the boy-and-girl friendship ended for him; or rather when it had changed to that deeper feeling which possessed his soul, and seemed to dominate his every thought. But there had come a day when he could not touch her hand in daily greeting, or come into her presence, even with others by, without a thrill of consciousness that was almost rapture. Yet there was awe as well in his thought of her, for she seemed suddenly removed from the region of familiar friendship to some mysterious realm of dreamland where every act and word and look of hers was coloured by that golden atmosphere. Of her own feelings he could not judge, save by delusive tokens, and if she blushed when he appeared, or grew strangely shy when they were left alone, or looked away whenever he looked at her, he was by far too modest to imagine that these signs were in his favour.

He had the simple, tender, trustful loyalty of the Highlander; love and confidence were one with him. That the Prince had honoured Agnes at the ball was to him a cause for pride, not jealousy. If he had been told that Agnes had coquetted with every man in Edinburgh it would not have shaken his faith in her. He would have indignantly denied the charge, and have felt no other emotion than unquenchable wrath against the tale-bearer. He had known that the life would make no change in her; that she would still be the sweet, true Agnes of the Highlands though she had become the belle of Edinburgh, the nightly toast of admiring Whigs and adoring Jacobites.

They now paused by a magnificent cluster of tall purple thistles, fitting symbols of that beautiful warlike country. Beside them grew Agnes's treasured roses, of which one flower alone remained, coquetting with the autumn breeze. Nestling in the shadow of the rose-bush, and the arméd thistles, some delicate spires of white heather swung their fragile bells. Agnes stooped and plucked a slender spray, adding to it a thistle bloom, and the solitary rose.

"See, Donald!" she cried, "this little Jacobite was left to nod in your bonnet. But, oh, I wish 'twas not plucked on a Friday, for I have strange forebodings." And she ceased suddenly, gazing at him in fear.

Donald made a brilliant picture in the rich hues of his tartan, his fair head uncovered to the sunlight, and his blue eyes glowing with youth's unbounded hope. His lithe figure, hardy and healthful grace in every line, was especially adapted to the most picturesque of costumes, the Highland dress.

Agnes took the blue bonnet from his hand, and fastened beside the eagle's plume, the rose, the thistle, and the heather.

"Look, Donald, are not these precious tokens? They bear a three-fold charm! The rose is for the cause we love,—the white rose for Prince Charlie; the thistle goes ready-armed against your foemen,— the thistle is belovéd Scotland; and the heather "— here she coloured deeply, and her eyes drooped— " the heather is for the Highlands and all our joys together. May it prove mighty to protect you! Wear it in token of your little playmate. Agnes Leslie!"

CHAPTER XIV

"THOU ART A QUEEN, FAIR LESLEY"

> "Thou art a queen, fair Lesley,
> Thy subjects we before thee;
> Thou art divine, fair Lesley,
> The hearts o' men adore thee."

AFTER her meeting with Donald in the garden Agnes's longing for the Highlands grew to a heart-hunger deeper than anything she had known before. She yearned unceasingly to be back in Lochaber, galloping over the moors on her pony, drifting on the loch in her boat, roaming brae and mountain for wild flowers and bracken. She knew where the golden broom grew fairest; where the rosy heather nodded its fairy bells, and its fragile white sister, shy and inaccessible, hid, elf-like, in the clefts of the rock. She could feel the breeze from Ben Nevis blowing in at the window, as she had felt it on that night of Duncan Forbes's visit. They cried to her heart, and her heart cried out to them.

Upon one only her thoughts dwelt with shy tenderness after the manner of maidens, and the feeling was so instinctive that she was yet hardly conscious of it. It was twined as closely in her heart with love of country and of king as the rose and the thistle had been twined with the heather on Donald's bonnet; and it throve with the delicate sweetness of heather-bells.

For the past week Kenneth had noted Agnes's every act with the vigilance of a spy; but he had discovered nothing by this surveillance, and his suspicions were lulled considerably. That same Friday evening he was to attend a banquet with the Prince's officers at Holyrood, and he set off in a better humour than he had felt since the fateful ball. Agnes he left gazing thoughtfully into the fire, wherein she was building Highland castles, with walls wrought out of fancy and battlements of hope.

Unfortunately, the banquet-tables were spread in the long portrait-gallery, forcibly reminding Kenneth of his recent discomfiture. There were present a large number of Jacobite officers, both Highland and Lowland, most of them mad with eagerness for the proposed invasion, though here and there might be seen the graver face of one who realised the odds against them. The Prince, gayer and winsomer than ever, was like a mischievous boy engaged in some desperate enterprise. He was dressed in complete Highland costume, further enhancing the fine proportions of his figure, and the extreme fairness of his complexion.

But the Prince's choice of attire seemed to jar on Kenneth's humour in some way,—perhaps because he remembered Agnes's partiality for the tartan; and he sat staring moodily at the portrait of Fergus the First, which happened to hang opposite him, without beholding the painted features of that legendary monarch, and made only brief replies to Edward Carrington, who occupied the seat beside him.

But when the Prince rose to address the gathering

his gaiety had disappeared, and his face was grave
and steadfast, and alight with unfaltering purpose

"Comrades!" he cried, "comrades and fellow
Scotsmen, are we agreed? Shall we challenge the
usurper's power? Is it 'on to England'?"

And into every face, alike, whether grave or confi
dent, there flashed the fire of devotion! Every man
drew his sword and kissed the shining blade. From
end to end of the long hall the answer rang: "T
England or perish!"

When the excitement had lulled a little they bega
to discuss the plans of the campaign; then, having
transacted the main business of the evening, they fe
to drinking healths to various fair ones. But th
Prince remained silent, apparently absorbed in med
tation, not responding to their demands for a toast
and when at last he rose, he wore a look of sti
deeper determination than that which usually dom
nated his winsome features.

"Gentlemen, I have but one toast: 'Agnes
Auchnacarry': the Fairest Face, the Purest Sou
the Bravest Heart, in all brave Scotland!"

Deep feeling breathed through the tone; it cou
scarcely have been more reverent had he invoked
prayer. He stood motionless, the goblet lifted
his outstretched hand, and the red wine sparklin
in the glass like rubies.

As Agnes's name fell from the Prince's lips, Ken
neth's hand sought his sword, his face grew whi
with fury, and he started to rise, but was forcib
restrained by Edward Farrington, who seized h
arm, whispering wildly, "In Heaven's name, Cam

bell, have you gone stark mad, that you seek to fight a duel here and now? Patience, man, the Prince couldn't have named a saint with more respect!"

Kenneth submitted angrily, and resumed his seat; but throughout the scene which followed, his fingers remained clenched on the sword-hilt, and his eyes, brooding and ominous, never left the Prince's face. Charles apparently did not observe the hostility he had roused; he was too much absorbed by the intensity of the passion which swayed him to notice trivialities. He lingered for a moment with his glass uplifted, then bowed, as if to her he honoured, and touched the goblet with his lips. And each man rose in solemn silence, and drank as to a queen.

But Prince Charlie's toast, despite its grave deference, did not appease the embittered Kenneth. He left the banquet raging, he spent the night brooding fiercely over the incident, and morning found him still heaping fuel upon his hotly flaming wrath.

Immediately on rising he hurried out into the open air, and wandered feverishly to and fro, struggling with his fury, and all the maddened impulses it created. In the midst of his wild roamings about the city, he caught sight of Edward Farrington emerging from the White Horse Close, an ancient courtyard off the Canongate, named, said tradition, from a snowy steed belonging to the fated Queen of Scots.

Upon beholding Kenneth, Edward halted suddenly, and then approached him, exclaiming, "Heavens, man, why wear you so grave a face to mock this merry morning? You are pale enough to be en route to the gallows, and I would swear you have not been to bed the whole night through. Never tell me 'tis for what passed ' yestre'en,' as you Scots say. What! so 'tis true? But we must not discuss this on the street; come where we may talk apart."

So saying, he drew Kenneth's arm through his, and led him toward the courtyard. Once they were seated on the stone steps within the Close, Kenneth began to speak fiercely of the Prince and his behaviour toward Agnes. His words came in a torrent, wild and reckless, without reason or restraint. The passion of jealousy drew him on like a twig in the clutch of the whirlpool, while Edward, like some peaceful counter-current, sought to draw him into safer channels.

"For Heaven's sake, man, summon a ghost of sense! Because your loved one wears white tokens, sings Charles Edward's praises, and glows at mention of his name, is that proof positive she has done a thing so mad as to lose her heart to him altogether? Why, you must needs accuse every maid in Edinburgh on the same grounds! And because the Prince is moulded like Apollo, with the winsomest way,— save one,—that e'er was seen, should her loyalty gain not in warmth thereby? Ye fates, man, you would have our lovely goddess a very iceberg, lest she melt at the sight of royal grace. Fate defend us from more brown-eyed, fair-haired beauties of either sex! First comes this lovely maid of Lochaber and sets all Edinbro' a-tremble with one glance of her hazel eyes, and then follows this golden-haired Prince

Charlie to win us with his Stuart wiles. And which of them works more ruin the sphinx may decide!"

But Kenneth was only further irritated by this half-whimsical yet serious reasoning.

"As well ask counsel of a comet!" he exclaimed resentfully. "You go whisking headlong without the least perception of the truth. The Prince loves Agnes Leslie and does not trouble to conceal it, as a mole might see; and what is worse, she has given her heart to him and none other!"

"You and I may not blame him for his passion, Kenneth," replied Edward reflectively. "Do you love the maid the less for bright eyes and golden hair? As well love not the sunshine and the flowers as bonnie Agnes Leslie! But indeed you do her wrong, Kenneth, in this suspicion," he continued rather sternly. "With some maids one might doubt, but not with her. Love and jealousy are often bedfellows, they say; but mistrust never won a woman's heart. Kenneth, it takes a lover's mind to build black dungeons out of air, and mould darkest midnight from a morning cloud."

But Kenneth was not seeking for reassurance; rather he desired the company of one who would support his own miserable belief, and foster his bitter hatred to the Prince. Since Edward would not agree with him, he had no desire to prolong the interview, and announced quite coldly his intention of returning home.

But he had barely reached the entrance to the courtyard, when Edward, who had been studying the ground perplexedly, hurriedly detained him.

"Kenneth," he exclaimed, with the air of one suddenly enlightened, "you are right in one thing. The Prince adores Mistress Leslie if ever knight loved lady! I venture to prophesy that if Charles Edward ever comes to the throne, Agnes——" here he was forcibly interrupted by the rough pressure of a hand over his mouth.

"How dare you breathe her name with the name of that curséd Stuart!" hissed Kenneth, beside himself.

But he was cut short in turn. Edward snatched the restraining hand from his lips, crying indignantly:

"For insane jealousy, commend me to you, Kenneth Campbell! How dare you think I would speak of any woman in aught but honour, above all, the woman I love and reverence?"

His brave young face had grown very noble "You might at least hear me through before judging. My name does not begin with Charles that you should vent your rage upon me. Therefore listen, O mad Othello! If Charles Edward ever comes to the throne, Agnes Leslie"— he uncovered his head at the name,—"Agnes Leslie, if she wills it, will be *Queen of the Three Kingdoms!*"

CHAPTER XV

"THE BRIGHTEST JEWEL IN MY CROWN."

"Or were I monarch of the globe,
  With thee to reign, with thee to reign,
The brightest jewel in my crown
  Would be my queen, would be my queen!"

MEANTIME, the future "Queen of Three Kingdoms" sat in her room, knitting her pretty brows in perplexity over a letter bearing the royal seal, which lay open before her. Angus MacDonald had brought it an hour earlier, looking unusually important, and when she had sought to question him, had closed his lips more tightly with an expression of mysterious secrecy. Agnes had immediately recognised the clear, bold hand of the "Bonnie Prince," for she had seen his writing frequently in documents of Locheil's and Norman Leslie's, and it was with fingers trembling with eager expectation that she broke the seal. As she read, her wonder increased to absolute amazement, till, from sitting in dignity beside the table, she sprang up, and began to pace excitedly through the room, her eyes shining, her cheeks glowing, as she pondered the contents of the Prince's missive.

She was thinking how she could best fulfil his request, when the voice of Mistress Catherine from the stair-foot interrupted her musing, and hastily concealing the letter beneath her plaid, she ran to obey the call. Having discharged the various household tasks for which she had been summoned, Agnes did not return to her chamber, but rather rashly retired to the parlour, which, however, seemed secluded enough at that morning hour.

A fire of coals burned brightly on the hearth, diffusing a welcome warmth, for the white haar or sea-fog was creeping up from the Forth and wrapping Edinbro' in a mantle of gloom. Agnes, intent upon her letter, had no thoughts for the weather, nor indeed for anything save the wonderful honour which the Prince was about to bestow upon the House of Leslie.

Curiously lacking in self-conceit, she no more dreamed that his interest in her was warmly personal than a peasant girl might deem that the sun shone for her alone, dispensing all his rays to give her warmth and light. The Prince showed kindly care for her, she thought, such as he might show toward the humblest of his subjects; she could only feel intensely grateful that so large a portion of it fell to her share.

Her splendidly loyal nature never dreamt of fault in her object of worship; for her, the Prince was surrounded by a halo that hid all defects and blemishes. "The divine right of kings" found in her its most absolute advocate; whatever their manifold failings, the Stuarts reigned by the will of God, and although it perplexed her to reconcile with this belief the weaknesses of James the Seventh and his predecessors, her loyalty was never diminished

"The Brightest Jewel in My Crown" 127

thereby. "The king can do no wrong" was to her a law of the universe, unswerving and eternal as all other laws.

She gave Charles Edward the love her ancestors had given to every being of his hapless race, laying all life held, and the breath of life itself, at his feet, with an unfaltering devotion that asked nothing, gained nothing, in return, save a passion of love that burned the fiercer for its hopelessness;—all this she gave the Prince,—the worship and devotion of generations past,—generations whose hearts' blood had fed the flame, only with her it burned upon the purer altar of a woman's heart.

Again Agnes started impulsively to her feet, clasping the letter to her bosom, and exclaiming with passionate feeling: "I would never refuse should it cost my life! Whatever the Prince asks me, I will do!"

At this point in her soliloquy, she became unpleasantly aware of the fact that she was speaking aloud, and that some one had entered the room, and was watching her. This instinct was promptly fulfilled, when, upon turning abruptly, she beheld Kenneth's eyes fixed upon her in savage questioning.

Her first impulse was to hide the letter, her second to pretend it was of no importance; and acting upon the latter prompting, she made no attempt at concealment, but glanced carelessly at Kenneth, and snatching at the first thought which presented itself, said indifferently: "Oh, so 'tis you! And did you enjoy the banquet last evening?"

It was a chance shot, and as luck would have it,

the worst she could have made, for to Kenneth, who was not calm enough to remember that she could not know what had occurred, the words seemed pointed with malicious meaning; and he answered with bitter irony:

"Most enjoyable, I assure you, Mistress Leslie."

Perhaps it was his formal manner of address that increased her nervousness, or with the consciousness of something to conceal she lost for once her self-possession, for she stood gazing down distractedly, the very picture of guilt.

With all his splendid qualities, Kenneth had a touch of that sternness which had reached such harsh predominance in Sir Hugh, and the present crisis forced it into sharp relief.

"This deception shall go no further!" he cried accusingly. "I insist that you tell me——" with the words he took a step toward her.

Agnes, startled by his manner, made a quick movement. The luckless letter fluttered from her fingers, and with a cry of consternation she flew to recover it, while at the same instant, Kenneth, catching sight of the crimson seal, and instantly suspicious, sprang forward to possess it. But Agnes proved the quicker, and snatching it from under his very fingers, she drew back,—flushed, angry and reckless of the consequences, exclaiming, "'Tis a pretty pass things have come to, sir, when you seek to read my letters! Pray, who appointed *you* as my guardian?"

"Necessity," he replied grimly, "and if ever maid needs master it is you! Yet for all your cruelty and waywardness I cannot let you suffer the consequences of your folly——"

"Stop where you are, sir, and explain your meaning!" The words came fiercely as a trumpet-blast. Never had she been addressed thus in all her young life; neither Norman Leslie, nor Donald, nor the gentle Locheil, had ever spoken one word to her in anger or suspicion. Kenneth's stinging speech acted upon her hot, impetuous nature like blows upon a spirited thoroughbred who had never known the lash; they roused her to tenfold recklessness.

Kenneth did not immediately reply to her indignant question. He had caught only glimpses of the letter as it fluttered past him, but those fragments played wild havoc in his brain, and he felt like a man stunned by a heavy and unexpected blow. Two sentences wrote themselves indelibly upon his very heart:—"*the turn is to the left, and the door is unbarred,*" and "*the King can never repay for all.*" They maddened him as he watched her; they spoke with sinister meaning through his words.

"Agnes," he said sternly, "show me that letter! I demand to see it!"

"Sir, the letter happens to be addressed to me," she replied defiantly, "and I reserve the right of reading it for myself!"

Her one thought being to keep the hapless missive from Kenneth's hands, Agnes ignored the meshes of suspicion in which she was entangling herself.

"A curse upon this dastard Prince!" he cried, losing his last vestige of control. "He dared not play the man; he has stolen your heart like a skulking robber! But he shall not go unpunished, if I have to offer my sword to Cumberland for the purpose!"

"What right have you to insult the Prince?" blazed the girl. And then in her fiery Scotch: "It's weel I ken ye're no' leal, Kenneth Campbell! Are ye na blate to speir at me sic a way! Aweel, ilka man for his ain! 'Up an' rin awa, Geordie!' Gang awa to Weellie, Whiggie!" drawling out the Duke of Cumberland's Christian name in a taunting tone that would have kindled ice.

"I pray Heaven I may live to see Charles Edward on the scaffold!" he hurled at her from between locked teeth.

She sprang toward him like a burst of passionate flame, her brown eyes blazing, her hands clenched at her sides, her slender figure drawn to its fullest height.

"You never will!" she cried in a fierce whisper that breathed defiance;—yes, even triumph, "You never will! You will see *me* there first!" And her last words, despite their fury, bore a strange thrill of self-devotion.

With that challenge ringing in his ears, she left him to his tempest-torn solitude.

While this stormy scene was passing, Prince Charlie sat alone in his morning-room at Holyrood absorbed in deep reflection. He was musing, especially, upon his letter to Agnes, which he had succeeded in writing only after a long and obstinate struggle with himself; a conflict between duty and desire, from which he had finally emerged victorious. As four-and-twenty is an age at no time remarkable

"The Brightest Jewel in My Crown" 131

for deliberation, and the Stuarts had never been noted for self-control in matters of heart and will, it was greatly to the credit of the young Prince that he had at last written so sober and dignified an epistle, which suppressed so resolutely the fire of passion burning dangerously near the surface. For whatever stain darkened his after-life,—a life poisoned by bitterness and despair,—not the slightest blot disfigured the bright escutcheon of his reign at Holyrood,—of his youth in Scotland.

As he mused, he raised his eyes to the dark-framed mirror hanging opposite, and the reflection therein recalled still more vividly that lovely face so strangely similar and yet unlike. The Countess of Menteith had once said petulantly that "the Prince could save further trouble by making love to himself in the looking-glass if bright eyes and red lips and fair hair were all he wanted." Charles leaned forward and studied the image intently.

"They say we resemble each other," he murmured, "but I cannot see it beyond the passing likeness of our features. Her face has a wondrous something that mine never had."

He paused an instant, and sighed deeply.

"What slaves we are, we of royal blood! We have not even the common rights of men; we are mere puppets in the hands of nations. We have not even the liberty of loving; we may not wed as we choose. O Heaven, what a mockery of power! I think I guess the reason why young Campbell glared at me so last evening. He looked upon me as a rival, and an unlawful one! This lovely Agnes!—there is not a gentleman in Scotland but has the right to woo her, and to me it is denied!"

He rose and paced feverishly up and down.

"Were it not for my unhappy father's sake I would fling every consideration to the winds, and offer myself to her before this hour was ended! But no! I must not bind myself thus on the eve of this desperate expedition; to my father belongs the prior claim! Restraint, restraint is my only course! But should God prosper us, should I win the crown, ah, then, Agnes, it is you alone who shall share my triumph, *you* that shall be my Queen!—*Queen Agnes,*—ah, how fair a name!"

He sank into a seat beside the table, and rested his chin between his hands, saying dreamily:

"I can conjure up fair visions as well as any wizard's glass. I can see this dark old palace illumed with love's glory; and beauteous children playing here, in whom their father's failings shall be counterbalanced, and their father's follies rectified. And Scotland shall be a free and prosperous people, restored to all her ancient splendour; her King the happiest ruler in the universe, and her Queen—ah, God fulfil my vision—her Queen shall be bonnie Agnes Leslie!"

CHAPTER XVI

"THE ROSE SAE LIKE THE SNAW"

"A bonnie laddie tended the rose baith aire and late,
He watered it, and fanned it, and wove it wi' his fate;
But the thistle-tap it withered, winds bore it far awa,
And Scotland's heart was broken for the rose sae like the snaw!"

THE Prince continued his pleasing reverie by unfastening his velvet coat, and drawing from under his richly embroidered vest a lace handkerchief with the initials C. E. worked in the corner. Standing in the light of one of the windows, he unfolded it carefully, and shook down upon the table a shower of white rose-petals, scarcely faded, that still retained their delicate spicy perfume. He stood motionless for some moments, touching them with his finger-tips as if they were things possessed of life.

"'Tis the rose she tossed me the day we entered Edinburgh; the rose she wore at her breast. Sweeter it is to me than all my triumph, for it recalls her whose presence is fragrant as white roses:—you, Agnes, the only rose I would wear against my heart!"

And with impetuous tenderness he kissed the crumpled petals.

How long he would have yielded to the influence of this sweet day-dream must remain a quandary; a cautious knock upon the door aroused him. He started slightly, and summoning his vagrant thoughts, restored the rose-leaves to their hiding-place, and seated himself at the table, before he answered "Enter!"

The door slowly opened, and Angus MacDonald, who served in the Prince's body-guard, approached reverently, and informed his Royal Highness that Major Campbell of the Lowland Light Infantry desired an immediate interview on a matter of urgency. Charles raised his eyebrows at this intelligence, but gave orders that the Major be admitted; and Angus withdrew, muttering something in Gaelic about "a snake among the bracken."

As Kenneth entered, the Prince rose, remarking pleasantly, "Why, my dear Major, you are omnipresent——" and stopped short, for Kenneth's look of uncontrolled hatred was not to be mistaken. The Prince's hesitation was only momentary, however; he came forward and held out his hand, but Kenneth made no pretence of grasping it.

For all his gracious ways Charles could be stern upon occasion.

"Sir," he exclaimed with biting coldness, "to what do I owe this discourtesy?"

"To behaviour, sir, befitting neither a Prince nor a gentleman!"

Charles's eyes flashed ominously.

"Have the kindness, sir, to explain your insinuation as quickly as possible!"

"With the greatest pleasure! I allude to the base manner in which you have gained an influence over

Mistress Leslie's affections, to the mysterious letter,—doubtless *letters*,—you have written her, proposing a secret meeting—probably not the *first* which has taken place between you. Did you think your royal blood entitled you to pluck by stealth this 'White Rose of the Leslies' and yet go unscathed? Such a flower blooms not for a *Pretender's* pastime! If this is not enough to warrant my interference——"

"Silence, sir! How dare you pollute your lips with such damnable lies? How dare you seek to sully the fame of one who is whiter than the whitest roses? You have conjured up evil, where not even the shadow of evil fell. God knows, if ever love was pure!—but what avails it to waste words? The fact that your charge is vilest falsehood does not lessen your guilt in having uttered it! Had you insulted me alone, it had been a small matter, but to have cast such insinuations upon Mistress Leslie,—upon Agnes, whose very name means purity—this, sir, passes endurance."

The gentle young Prince was quite transformed by the mingled magic of love and indignation. His fiercely blazing eyes, angrily mounting colour, and sternly compressed lips made him a being to command both fear and admiration had his rival been in a state to be moved by either; but above all, his voice and appearance gave so strong an impression of sincerity that for an instant Kenneth hesitated, uncertain of his ground, like one, who, astray in the marshes, beholds a sudden light.

But the blinding mist of doubt shut down again,

more impenetrable than before; he felt doubly assured that the Prince played the part of deception; and with augmented rage he heard Charles repeat: "This base calumny shall not go unpunished!"

Kenneth had come with the express purpose of challenging the Prince to combat, but strangely enough, the challenge passed out of his hands, and it was Charles who took the initiative.

"Sir," he said furiously. "name the place of meeting and the hour!"

"I suggest the 'Duke's Walk' at sunrise——" began Kenneth.

"No! I tell you no!" Charles cried emphatically, "no distant place, and no future hour! I will not sleep upon this insult! With your assent, it shall be decided *here* and *now!*"

Kenneth did not conceal his astonishment at such precipitancy, but he answered "that the present could not be too soon, provided there was no danger of interruption."

The Prince smiled composedly. "Oh, no fear of that! The arrangement is quite providential, for young Locheil and I have had the habit of sword practice at this hour, a fact which will amply account for any peculiar sounds."

Kenneth having bowed a cold compliance to this explanation, the Prince locked the door, remarking as he did so, "We may fight to the death and none shall separate us!"

So saying he began by unbuckling his sword-belt, removing his coat and waist-coat, and rolling up his lace ruffles.

Kenneth quickly followed his example, and in barely two minutes' time the two stood in fighting attire. The Prince deftly drew the heavy table to one side, and pushed the chairs back against the wall, leaving a cleared space of sufficient size for free movement.

The chamber, with its dark furniture and ancient tapestries, afforded a sombre background for the impending crisis. It had three doors, the one opening on the hall which the Prince had just locked, another, seldom used, leading into Queen Mary's apartments, and a third apparently giving access to some secret passage. Opposite the last hung the tall mirror into which the Prince had lately gazed. The antagonists took their places, Kenneth with his back to the mirror, and the Prince facing it. Sword in hand they stood, each watching the other intently; a breathless pause ended by the Prince's uttering the fateful words "On guard!"

The next instant heralded the low clash of swiftly crossing rapiers, the bright gleam of blade intercepting blade, and the dexterous, wary movements of the opponents at their deadly task. Each read the other's purpose in his eyes, and drew from thence the knowledge for parry or for thrust, and both were desperate, relentless, determined never to lower sword till that insult should be retracted which both sought to avenge.

. . . .

Directly Kenneth had left her, Agnes hurriedly summoned Angus MacDonald, and despatched by him a sealed note with many instructions for secrecy.

The interview with Kenneth had taken place before nine o'clock of that eventful morning, and it was still early when Agnes, it being Saturday, took her basket on her arm, and set out for market, a task she regularly fulfilled for Mistress Campbell.

Opposite the gate of Holyrood she lingered for a moment, recognising the Cameron tartan of the Highland sentries, and hoping to see Locheil. But the gallant chieftain did not appear, and she resumed her way at a brisk pace. She had just turned the corner of the street, when she encountered an old woman she had often met during her rambles about Edinburgh. This acquaintance appeared to be in some anxiety, for she caught Agnes's sleeve, as the girl was passing, and besought her to stop. The old woman, it seemed, had a grandson, a likely lad of twenty, whom she was exceedingly eager to enlist in the Prince's service, could she but find some friend at court to further her petition.

"Oh, lassie, ye ken the Prince weel, will ye no' ask him to help the puir lad, an' do an auld wife an unco favour!"

"I might speak to Locheil, I suppose," pondered Agnes, "but it may be he's away."

"Na, na, it'll be your ain sel' that can best do't. Your ain fair face will do mair than Locheil. Come awa, bonnie lassie, will ye no' gang wi' me to the Prince?"

And with this, the persistent old woman, who had never loosed her clutch upon Agnes's arm, began gently to pull the girl in the direction of the palace.

Agnes, who always acted upon impulse, and never

paused to consider the consequences, instantly conceived an idea, which she proceeded to put into immediate execution.

"I'll tell you what we will do," she explained to her protégée as they turned toward Holyrood, "we'll just win in some quiet way, an' we can, for if we gang by the gates, what with Lord Murray and the rest 'twill be an hour or more ere ever we gain an audience, and the Prince meets with the council at ten, and that will be too late, for the army marches this very day. So we'll try what luck may do," she concluded gleefully.

The morning was misty, which favoured their design. The white haar swept blindingly down, obliterating every object more than a few yards distant, and again it lifted as suddenly, admitting eerie glimpses. Protected by the fog, Agnes guided the old woman around to the north side of Holyrood, and into the ruined Chapel Royal where the fatal marriage of Darnley and fair Mary had taken place two hundred years before.

Leaving the old dame seated on the fragment of an ancient tomb, Agnes stole forward to investigate. She remembered that Norman Leslie had once told her of a secret passage connecting the Chapel with Darnley's audience-chamber, which at present served as the council-room. By treading over Rizzio's tragic grave she reached the angle of the wall whence a steep and winding staircase of broken stone led upward to the Queen's bed-room, down whose worn steps Mary had often stolen to prayer in the royal chapel.

Following the wall to the left, Agnes at length discovered a small door, which she tried, half expecting to find fastened, but to her surprise it opened easily, admitting her to a long and narrow passage-way.

At this point it occurred to Agnes that she had better assure herself of the location before she returned for her protégée. Accordingly, she closed the door, and began to make her way softly but swiftly along the dim corridor. Norman Leslie knew every turn of the old palace by heart, but Agnes, save for that day in Darnley's audience-chamber, and the night she had danced with the Prince, had never even crossed the royal threshold, and she had not gone far before she felt doubtful of her way; began indeed to regret the impulse which had led her thither. She paused, considering whether she should not retrace her steps; then, impelled by some strong inclination, continued onward, though slowly and with increasing hesitation.

The passage now turned sharply to the left, and ended in a narrow door, whither leading, Agnes could not surmise. Lost in perplexity, she leaned against the wall, and pondered her next course. Could she have seen what was happening beyond that narrow door she would have sprung forward with the speed of an arrow from the bow.

CHAPTER XVII

"I'LL TO LOCHEIL AND APPIN, AND KNEEL TO THEM"

"I'll to Locheil and Appin, and kneel to them;
   Down by Lord Murray and Roy of Kildarlie;
Brave Macintosh, he shall fly to the field wi' them,
   These are the lads I can trust wi' my Charlie."

THE Prince and Kenneth had continued their combat for several minutes without much gain on either side. Both were skilful swordsmen, versed in the Continental mode of duelling, though Charles excelled in natural aptitude for the art, and in constant practice from boyhood up. The Prince was pressing his rival hard, forcing him backward step by step, when his quick ear caught the sound of footsteps in the passage behind him, and pausing instantly, his eyes upon the mirror opposite, he lowered his sword in mid-stroke, while Kenneth, unprepared for the act, thrust fiercely, wounding Charles in the sword-arm.

It was at this moment that Agnes's alert ears detected voices beyond the mysterious door and a sound that resembled crossing steel. Tense with excitement, she listened breathlessly, heard the Prince say, "Bravo, that was struck to kill!" and waited to hear no more. One thought alone possessed her: *the Prince was fighting for his life!*

True to her impetuous nature, she did not dream of summoning aid; her one impulse was to reach the scene of danger, and save the Prince from whatever threatened.

She flung herself wildly against the door, desperate with the fear lest it be locked, but it yielded instantly to the strong pressure, and she fairly burst into the room, comprehended with one lightning glance the scene enacting, and sprang with incredible swiftness between the Prince and his rival, seizing Kenneth's blade with both hands, and crying in fierce amazement, "What do you mean, sir? Are you mad that you seek to kill the King?"

"My God! Agnes!" cried the Prince, alarmed, "supposing you had been injured!" So great was the tension of the moment that Agnes did not notice his use of her name; Charles himself was unconscious of it. Kenneth it naturally did not escape.

Swift as her act had been, she had not failed to notice that although Charles stood calmly beside the table upon which he had laid his sword, there were flecks of crimson on the lace at his wrist, and a slender trickle of blood was staining his velvet sleeve.

With a quick gasp of horror she released Kenneth's blade, and ran to the Prince, exclaiming, brokenly, "Oh, your Majesty!—your Majesty!—he has wounded you!"

Then turning on Kenneth like a lioness at bay, she cried fiercely: "Explain your reason for this assault, sir! Know you not that the King's person is sacred, and that it is not only murder but sacrilege you have attempted?"

"Are you mad that you seek to kill the King?"

Curiously enough the one thought of both men was to conceal from Agnes the reason for their duel. Deadliest rivals in all else, in this they were allied.

"Oh, my dear lady," the Prince protested, "if this gentleman came hither with the intention of murdering me, I assure you he proceeded about it in a most refined and civilised manner. We disagreed upon a very important matter. There were blows delivered on both sides."

Agnes responded only by bestowing on Kenneth another indignant glance; and again addressed herself to the Prince.

"If your Royal Highness will permit me, and will pardon the liberty I take——"

As she spoke she gently lifted the wounded arm, and with the Prince's dirk deftly cut away the blood-stained sleeve, disregarding his protests that the hurt was trivial. She quickly removed her plaid, tore from it a large piece, and, having wrapped a handkerchief about the wound, proceeded to bind it dexterously with the strip of plaid.

All the while Charles stood silent and motionless, pale with emotion, not pain. She had finished her task before he recovered his self-possession.

"How came you hither, my loyal little champion?" he inquired in a voice that was low and agitated.

Agnes hurriedly explained her mission in the old woman's behalf, while Kenneth, standing coldly by, looked his unbelief at the glib tale which seemed to him coined for the occasion.

"And I thank God who led me hither, for the purpose of saving your Majesty from one who would have slain you!"

Here she faced Kenneth, and cried with passionate hatred: "Traitor! How dared you lift your sword against your lawful King? A pity 'tis the Regicides are not alive to bear you company!"

She flashed on him the angry lustre of her hazel eyes, two bright and very hostile stars.

Stung beyond endurance, Kenneth drew the weapon he had sheathed, and extended the hilt to the Prince with a look of proud defiance, saying to Agnes: "*Your* King he may be; but he is *my* King no longer!" Addressing Charles, he continued: "Here is the sword I drew in your service; with it I offer my resignation from your army, and request an immediate release from my position!"

Charles bowed with cold courtesy.

"It is granted, Mr. Campbell, and here is the proof in writing."

And the Prince caught up pen and paper, and using his left hand, wrote out a discharge, signed "Charles, Prince Regent," which he handed to Kenneth, remarking, "This will carry you safely to my cousin Cumberland, or to any other friend of Hanover, as you shall choose!"

Kenneth received it coldly, his eyes flashing at Charles's allusion, and with a stern glance at Agnes standing straight and haughty beside the Prince, unlocked the door, and bowed himself out of the room.

Left alone with the Prince, Agnes suddenly recollected the remarkable manner in which she had enered his presence, and with the remembrance began to colour confusedly.

"Oh, your Highness," she exclaimed in distress, "I have left good Dame Christie sitting all this time on a stone in the chapel, and 'twas in her behalf that I came hither so rudely."

Charles quickly put her at her ease by saying laughingly, "Oh, never mind; 'tis not likely she'll get lost, and 'tis not cold enough for her to freeze. See, her wish is granted; I have made the boy a sergeant."

Agnes raised her eyes almost timidly to the Prince, as she murmured broken thanks for the letter he had written. She was still further embarrassed when Charles took her hand in his, saying gravely:

"The gratitude belongs with me; it is not for you to thank me. The courage and devotion you have shown is a debt I cannot repay; though, believe me, it shall never be forgotten!"

Footsteps sounded in the hall without, and the Prince moved toward the door, exclaiming:

"Lord Murray, I presume, come to command my attendance."

There was nothing left for Agnes but to remain where she was, for the next moment Lord Murray entered.

"I would inform your Royal Highness that the council is waiting," he commenced, and paused in surprise on beholding the girl.

"So you summon your fair counsellors to aid in your decisions," he concluded, with another keen glance at Agnes.

"If I did I should need no other advice, my lord," said Charles carelessly, but with a warning look that Murray understood. "Mistress Leslie has kindly interested herself in young Christie's behalf,—see to it that the lad gets his promotion."

Agnes, only too eager to escape, murmured something in acknowledgment, swept an elaborate courtesy, and disappeared through the door by which she had entered.

Murray, however puzzled he might be by Agnes's presence at Holyrood, was by far too discreet even to mention the episode; besides, he had no time to devote to the Prince's love affairs, and he at once dismissed the matter without another thought. Long afterward a fateful circumstance recalled it to his mind.

So it came about that the Prince attended the council that morning with his arm wrapped in a fold of the Leslie tartan, a fact which did not escape the keen eyes of the "gentle Lochiel," and which caused him much inward wonder.

Charles, noting his glances, saw fit to observe lightly:

"Just a mere scratch I came by, which your fair foster-daughter, whom I met with, kindly bound up thus in a strip of her own tartan, which I am honoured by wearing. 'Tis not the first time it has protected the King."

"By my faith, if this comes from a sword-thrust of Donald's"—began Lochiel, aroused—"I never before knew him to mistake friend for foe!"

"Nay," replied Charles meaningly. "*His* sword

"I'll to Locheil and Appin"

was never drawn against me. This blow was not of Donald's dealing."

. . . . .

Agnes's neglected marketing wrought sad havoc in Mistress Campbell's dinner, but there were two who did not notice it, and who made but a pretence of eating. Kenneth, indeed, was hardly able to conceal his agitation, and though Agnes, woman-like, succeeded better, she was self-absorbed, and paler than usual, and as soon as the meal was ended, she withdrew to her room, and remained there for the rest of the afternoon.

It was that same evening during supper that Kenneth announced his change of allegiance, with the same startling effect he had produced a few weeks earlier.

"Uncle," he said to Sir Hugh, and despite himself his voice betrayed him, "I have returned to my rightful sovereign, and to-morrow morning I propose to set off for London to join the Duke of Cumberland."

Sir Hugh was fairly overcome with joy. He uttered a resounding shout, and struck the table a heavy blow with his fist.

"My soul, lad, ye've gladdened my auld heart at last! Did I no' tell ye ye'd find your senses before mony days? Ye havena been dazzled lang by a blink o' the Pretender's ee. I'll live to see ye and braw Duke William sweep the Stuarts out o' Scotland! And here's to your success, lad, in guid Brunswick port."

Port was always considered a Whig beverage, while claret was claimed by the Jacobites. Sir Hugh was on his feet waving the decanter wildly in lieu of a wine-glass. Indeed, the excitement moved the entire family, although with varying effect. Mistress Campbell had left her chair, and Betty Macrae lingered, dish in hand, with eyes and mouth wide open, to hear the astonishing news.

Agnes had risen with the rest, and stood quite motionless, her eyes lifted steadfastly to Kenneth's face. There was no answer, save a calm defiance, to the mute entreaty with which his gaze questioned hers. Yet she was decidedly pale, even in the candle-glow, and the hand she rested on the chair-back trembled slightly. Kenneth could not trust himself to speak another word, but turned suddenly, and hurried from the room to conceal his emotion.

Sir Hugh, who was not troubled by delicacy, followed him upstairs.

"Whisht, lad!" he cried, "why will ye be lookin sae glum ower a sly coquette of a lass? Dinna tel me ye're greetin' for that?"

"Uncle, do not question me,—I cannot speak o it," stammered Kenneth.

"D'ye mean she's daring to refuse ye?" flame Sir Hugh. "Never ye mind, lad, there's a thou sand mair as bonnie as she would be ower proud t have ye! 'Fair and fause' are the Highlanders,— ye can never trust them. Ane minute a kiss fra them, and the next a dirk at your breast! 'Fai and fause,' ilka ane o' them."

But his nephew only sighed and did not answer.

. . . . .

Kenneth sat for hours that night staring griml

out at the haunted mass of Holyrood, as if it were
the dark embodiment of all his fears. But Agnes,
before she slept, turned her head upon the pillow to
gaze with wistful eyes at those moon-silvered towers,
and pray for him they sheltered. And she fell asleep,
content, a smile upon her lips, for Fate was kind at
last, and a Stuart reigned over Scotland!

CHAPTER XVIII

"HEY! JOHNNIE COPE, ARE YE WAUKIN' YET?"

> "Hey! Johnnie Cope, are ye waukin' yet?
> Or are ye'r drums a-beating yet?
> If ye were waukin' I wad wait,
>   To gang to the coals i' the morning!"

KENNETH looked back upon that 26th of October as a man looks back upon the terrible hour that shattered his last hope. He was absolutely assured now not only of the Prince's passion for Agnes, but of Agnes's wild infatuation for the Prince, and with this pitiless conviction every slightest shadow of doubt took substance, every word and act of hers, however trivial, reflected light upon the bitter truth. If she gave her love in the same lavish measure in which she gave her loyalty, he trembled for the consequence. She was but little more than an impulsive child, for all her twenty years, yielding herself heart and soul to one who had gained her love. If he had passed the night after the banquet in a tempest of rage and jealousy, he passed the night after the duel in far greater agony of mind. For now to jealous anger was added the cruel knowledge that Agnes had given her love to one who would never requite it, even if he could, and who doubtless thought of her with no deeper feeling than a man might give to some lovely rose-bud of his plucking once he had wearied of its fragrance.

So his decision to join Cumberland flowed from mingled sources. Revenge upon the Prince was undoubtedly the strongest, but beneath it lay the feeling that he could not linger here to face the tragedy that must follow when the girl awoke from her dream of rapture.

Heavy-hearted, he rose at dawn, and began some hurried preparations for his journey. The Duke of Cumberland, second son of King George, who had been summoned from the war in Flanders to conduct the campaign against the gallant young Stuart, had arrived in London a few days before; and it was Kenneth's intention to travel thither as rapidly as the slow and irksome methods of those days permitted. It did, indeed, occur to him that so precipitate a journey might seem like flight in the Prince's eyes, and he even pulled out the passport Charles had given him, with the rash intention of throwing it into the fire. He was saved from this, however, by the fact that no fire had been lighted in his room, and before he could find the means to kindle one, cooler reflection prompted a more prudent course, and he reluctantly returned the paper to its former place of security.

After what seemed an age of waiting, he was roused by a low tap at his door, and going to answer it, discovered Mistress Campbell, anxious-eyed and pale. He faced her in dull despair, for he did not dare to breathe a single word of his suspicions, through terror lest it reach Sir Hugh, a possibility at which he might well shudder.

"Laddie, laddie!" she cried, "tell me what it is

that ails ye, and why ye're bent on leaving us sae strangely. Tell me, is it Agnes?"

"Do not ask me!" cried Kenneth, bitterly. "Can you not see that all is broken between us? And my heart is broken, too! But never speak one word of this to Agnes! And do not blame her for my going, nor let my uncle blame her. And promise me you will not allow her to leave you, whatever happens!"

He suddenly turned away, and buried his face in his hands.

"Oh, Agnes, Agnes!" he moaned. "God in Heaven, how I love you!"

Poor Mistress Campbell wept piteously at this cruel shattering of her fondest dream.

"Eh, laddie, my puir laddie," she sobbed, "i maun be a fearfu' thing that'll be makin' ye gree sae sair! Oh, I had hoped to see ye and Agnes wedded, and happy thegither, for she is dear to me a an ain daughter, an' now it's a' ower wi', there's na mair joy in my hairt!"

And choking back her sobs, she left the room.

When the family gathered at the breakfast-table Agnes did not appear, and her absence was almos a relief to Kenneth. No one spoke a word, till Si Hugh remarked that the London coach set off "a nine preceesely, and were the lad's belongings a'read to carry doon?"

"Preserve us, laddie, have ye forgot the day!" cried Mistress Campbell, in genuine horror at a fac she had hitherto overlooked. "Ye'll no' be gangin on the blesséd Sabbath!"

Kenneth groaned. "Good heavens! I nev

thought of it's being Sunday! But I *must* go! I cannot endure it until to-morrow!"

Here Sir Hugh interposed in his nephew's behalf.

"Hoot, wife!" he cried, "dinna name your scruples! The lad's awa to save his country; could he gang on a better errand? Cumberland travels o' Sunday, why shouldna he? If 'twas to aid the Pretender 'twould be anither tale, eh, lad?" jocosely slapping Kenneth's shoulder, and accompanying this endearment with a sly wink, the humour of which was lost upon the recipient.

Half-an-hour later Kenneth came disconsolately downstairs, and stood waiting in the lower hall till the last of his luggage should be bestowed in the heavy coach at the Netherbow. He was wondering wretchedly whether he had better make an attempt to see Agnes, or leave a message of farewell for her, when his uncertainty was solved in a most astonishing manner.

Kenneth had thought himself prepared for anything that Agnes might say or do,—for an outburst of contrition, or renewed defiance, or even an explanation of her presence at Holyrood on that fateful morning. But her mine of amazing behaviour was unlimited, as he was soon to learn.

He was restlessly pacing the hallway when a slight sound from above diverted his wretched thoughts. At the turn of the stairs stood Agnes, one white arm resting on the balustrade as she leaned over and looked down at him. Never was there a picture of more exultant triumph! Her brown eyes shone with passionate disdain, her proud, fair head was held in queenly poise, and her crimson lips curled contemptuously.

The evening pallor had completely vanished, and the wayward rose-bloom rioted in her cheeks. There was scorn in every line of her lightly balanced figure, scorn even in the white and exquisite curve of the arm she leaned upon.

Held by the very steadfastness of her imperious gaze, Kenneth could not withdraw his eyes from her. Suddenly she descended a step, leaned still further over the railing, and began to sing,—that saucy, unbearable ditty of Cope's defeat:

> "Sir John Cope trode the North right far,
>   Yet ne'er a rebel he cam' naur,
>   Until he landed at Dunbar,
>   Right early in the morning!"

The mocking emphasis she flung into the words was indescribable. But she had no intention of letting him escape so easily, and with added fervour of bitterness she leaped into the next verse:

> "He wrote a challenge frae Dunbar,
>   'Come fight me, Charlie, an' ye daur!
>   And I'll teach you the art o' war,
>   If you'll meet me in the morning.'
>
> "When Charlie look'd the letter upon
>   He drew his soord the scabbard from;
>   'So Heaven restore me to my ain,
>   I'll meet ye, Cope, in the morning.'"

Pausing only to gather breath, Agnes continued mercilessly:

"Fye, now, Johnnie, get up and rin,
 The Highland bagpipes mak' a din;
 It's best to sleep in a hale skin,
 For 'twill be a bluidy morning.

"When Johnnie Cope to Berwick came,
 They spier'd at him, 'Where's a' your men?'
 'In faict,' says he, 'I dinna ken,
 For I left them a' i' the morning.'

"Now, Johnnie, troth, ye were na blate,
 To come wi' the news o' your ain defeat,
 And leave your men in sic a strait,
 Sae early i' the morning."

Kenneth stood with bowed head, unable to endure longer the exultant scorn of her gaze. The words: "Agnes, Agnes, how can you?" leaped to his lips, but they died unspoken. He was powerless under the spell of his sweet persecutor, for he observed to his anguish that she looked lovelier than ever.

All the venom of her animosity was poured into the last stinging lines:

"Hey! Johnnie Cope, are ye waukin' yet?
 Or are ye'r drums a-beating yet?
 If ye were waukin' I wad wait,
 To gang to the coals i' the morning!"

The soul of rebellious daring that breathed through the taunting words stung him as nothing else could have done. That the woman he loved so hopelessly should mock him thus was a heart-stab sharper than he could bear. Like a man passive under repeated blows, he turned without a word, cast a single upward glance at his beautiful tormentor,

and went despairingly out of the door, still pursued
by the sweet, taunting voice, with its derisive burden.

But when he had disappeared, Agnes leaned
against the balustrade with a face well-nigh as woeful
as that which Kenneth had turned to her a moment
before. And when she had reached her room, she
flung herself upon the bed, and burst into passionate
tears. But her tears were not of pity for Kenneth
hurrying southward, broken-hearted; they were shed
in bitter chagrin at having estranged so strong an
ally at a time when the Prince most needed his allegiance. It is doubtful whether Kenneth would have
derived much comfort from knowing that she had
shed them.

. . . . .

Agnes's pride impelled her to go to Mistress
Campbell that very day, and explain the precarious
footing on which she and Kenneth stood.

"It is only fair, Aunt Catherine, for you to know
that Kenneth went away because of me," she said
with admirable candour. "We were very angry
with each other, and we quarrelled bitterly, but the
reason I may not tell you." At the mere remembrance of the scene her colour rose; yet she continued steadily:

"Perhaps I had better go away; you asked me
only for Kenneth's sake. I do not wish to take advantage of your generosity, when he and I are friends
no longer. Sir Hugh has endured me only on Kenneth's account. Should I not return to Lochaber?"
she questioned gravely.

She was really thinking of the desolation that would await her at Auchnacarry while every soul that made the place so dear was far away in England, fighting for the King. But she resolutely repressed her dread; it was pride alone that spoke.

Agnes's words gave Mistress Campbell the second pang she had felt that day. The thought of parting with the girl was unbearable. She answered only by folding Agnes in her arms, and exclaiming piteously: "Oh, lassie, why will ye be ganging awa? Would ye be breaking the hairt o' me wi' greetin'? An' mayhap 'tis but a wee misunderstanding atween ye, an' the lad will be comin' back ere lang."

But Agnes shook her head with grave conviction.

"He will never come back to marry *me*, Aunt Catherine. I am sorry it happened,—for *your* sake."

And Mistress Campbell, strong in the hope that all would yet be righted, did not notice the emphasis that Agnes had laid upon the last words.

With woman's tact, Mistress Catherine soothed Sir Hugh's rancour by observing that although the quarrel between Agnes and "the lad" had resulted in Kenneth's departure, it was probably no more than a slight disagreement between lovers, which would soon end in complete renewal of the sundered friendship.

"Ye'll no' be sending the lass awa for a thing sae wee?" she pleaded artfully; while Sir Hugh, whose grudge against Agnes for having discarded Kenneth was somewhat counterbalanced by that young gentleman's restoration to the Whig party, replied with unexpected blandness:

"Aweel, there'll be nae harm in letting matters bide as they are, till we hear frae the lad."

"I misdoubt 'twas the Prince himsel' they were fashed aboot," observed his wife, relieved by his answer. "Agnes will aye be believing in the divine right o' kings."

Sir Hugh snorted scornfully: "A great pity 'tis she couldna ha'e been a man; she could ha'e got hersel' hanged for the Pretender wi'oot ony trouble. But being a lass, and a beauty at that, she maun draw to destruction ilka puir lad that sets eyes on her. Aye, she bewitches them a', even the Prince himsel'!"

"Now, Hugh, what nonsense 'tis ye talk!" retorted Mistress Campbell. "'Tis true the lass hath a bewitching way, that's a' her ain, but as for the Prince, he doesna lack to bow to ilka lady, auld or young. And where's the harm indeed!"

CHAPTER XIX

"WI' A HUNDRED PIPERS, AN' A,' AN' A'!"

"Wi' a hundred pipers, an' a', an' a',
Wi' a hundred pipers, an' a', an' a',
We'll on an' we'll march to Carlisle ha',
Wi' its yetts, an' castles, an' a', an' a'."

AGNES'S mind was occupied during the next five days by events of far greater moment than Kenneth's apostasy. On the very day of the duel the main body of the Scottish army had begun their march toward England, and on Thursday, October 31, Prince Charlie himself proposed to leave his ancient capital, in order to lead the bold invasion.

Agnes thrilled to alternating fears and expectations, each for the moment dominant, as she watched, from her eastern window, the final preparations for the march. About noon Edward Farrington came to bid her farewell, brave in his handsome laced uniform, and imparting his cheery confidence to every one he met.

"Adieu, fair Mistress Leslie," he said gaily. "I shall think of you when I raise the Prince's banner above Carlisle. And when I arrive at London, I will send you a wreath of white roses to twine in your hair. Will you wear it for my sake?" he pleaded.

She promised him, smiling, and was watching him ride away, when she beheld Norman Leslie approaching from the palace. He was dressed, as Donald had been, in the garb of a Highland chief, his broadsword by his side, his silver-mounted dirk and pistols secured within his belt, and on his left arm a target of thick leather, studded with brass, which glinted brightly in the sunshine.

They two were the last of the "loyal Leslies"—not the last of that brave old fighting clan which had given so many leaders to the armies of Britain and of Europe, but of that devoted family which for centuries had yielded unswerving allegiance to the Stuarts, they were the sole survivors.

Agnes's heart leaped with pride at his noble bearing, then, smitten by quick foreboding, sank with leaden weight, as she was clasped in his arms.

"Oh, will ye no' be takin' me wi' ye, laddie?" she entreated. "Sir Hugh is cold and hard, and for a' Aunt Catherine's kindness, this place will ne'er be hame. Oh, laddie, laddie, when ye will ha'e captured London, an' our Prince rules at St. James's, will ye no' come back to Auchnacarry, an' keep me wi' ye, laddie?"

And she clung to him, trembling, pressing her fair young cheek against the folds of his plaid, and holding him in a piteous clasp that would not let him go.

There was a solemn, a prophetic sadness in his face as he kissed her tenderly and answered, "Aye lassie, ye shall have your wish. When we ha'e conquered England, I'll come back to ye, and where'er I am on earth, ye shall be with me! We will never part again!"

The autumn sun was sinking, throwing purple shadows over Arthur's Seat, and the stern crest of the Salisbury Crags, and touching with mellow glow the grim old palace at their feet. Through the lofty gateway, surrounded by his life-guards in their brilliant uniforms of blue, faced with scarlet, his winsome, debonair young face alight with steadfast purpose, rode the Bonnie Prince. His dress was a belted plaid of his own royal tartan, bound by a wide blue sash, and upon his curling golden hair a blue velvet bonnet, decked with a rose of white ribbons.

Again Agnes knelt within the dark old casement, her heart throbbing with suppressed emotion, and gazed mutely down at the daring little band, marching southward on their desperate mission. As Charles passed beneath the window, Agnes caught a glimpse of his grave eyes, and pale resolute face, upon which a shade of melancholy was already falling. And seeing his look, her eyes grew wide, and darkened, and a sudden fear swept her soul like a ruthless hand on harp-strings. It was but momentary; the flood of buoyant hope surged back, burying that dim fear as a mountain-stream engulfs some ugly pebble that has dared to darken its brightness.

. . . . .

Autumn waned, and glided into winter, threading the leaden days on a chain of life once jewelled. Northward-wafted tidings of the gallant little army were scanty and imperfect. Time crept wearily by till mid-December, when a Highland messenger brought two letters, stamped with the royal seal, for Mistress Leslie. They were not from the Prince, however; he had sealed them simply to insure their safe arrival. And at this thought of her she blushed with gratitude. One missive was from Norman Leslie, the other from Donald Cameron.

Owing to some contradictory impulse Agnes opened Donald's first. It was a lively, vivid account of their progress southward, written somewhat in the form of a diary, and characteristically gay and hopeful.

"Friday, November 8," so it began. "At last, dear Agnes, we are over the border, and James the Eighth has been proclaimed King of England. What a shout rose from our ranks as we forded the swollen Esk and felt hostile ground beneath our feet. We were drenched to the skin, but we cared not, for with flags flying to the English wind we danced ourselves dry to the music of a pibroch, one hundred pipers playing manfully.

"Sunday, November 10. We have surrounded Carlisle, and the Prince has demanded the surrender of the city, which must inevitably yield, in spite of determined resistance. As I write, I can hear the report of the cannon from the walls. The mayor has taken pains to announce that he is not *Paterson*, Scot, but *Pattison*, an Englishman. Whatever he be, he will soon be our prisoner.

"Friday, November 15. Carlisle has fallen! This morning at ten we entered the city, under the command of the Duke of Perth, and now our flags are flying from the walls like white and scarlet birds. By this capture we have supplied ourselves with arms and provisions, besides gaining great prestige from so brilliant an achievement. We all believe mo fervently that God Himself is guiding us to victory, and in this confidence our Prince relies most strongly. This evening I opened the Testament by chance to these words:

"'And shall not God avenge His own elect, which cry day and night unto Him, though He bear long with them?'

"O Agnes, shall not prayers prevail with God? They have risen to Heaven on the lips of three generations, like the purple rays of vapour from Loch Arkaig when the mountains burn with sunset. Believe you not as I do, Agnes? My heart is with yours in the Highlands, little playmate!

"Wednesday, November 20. At the council of war this morning it was decided to march directly upon London, in spite of the fact that Cumberland's army, 10,000 strong, is between us and the capital. The Prince, like his gallant ancestor the Bruce, takes for his motto, 'Never retreat!' 'Rather than go back,' he said, 'I could wish to be twenty feet underground.' Last evening he came to my lodgings, and talked long with me; and at parting he quoted the words of your ancestor, the great Marquis Montrose:

> "'He either fears his fate too much,
>   Or his deserts are small,
> Who dares not put it to the touch,
>   To gain or lose it all.'

"Wednesday, November 27. For the week past I have had no chance to write, so rapid has been our march. Every morning we have risen before dawn and pressed forward by the waning moonlight. Our food consists of the oat-meal we carry in our sporrans, which we eat mixed with cold water. We astonish the English folk by marching thirty miles a day upon nothing else. The Prince walks in Highland dress at the head of his men. As we crossed the mountains at Penrith, he was so exhausted that he grasped my shoulder-belt for support, and walked several miles half-asleep, but he absolutely refused to mount a horse. What Scotsman would not toss his bonnet for such a King?

"I can hardly write for laughter when I think of an episode which happened but two days past. was entering my room for the night when the old woman who was my hostess suddenly flung herself at my feet, almost crazed with terror. Upon my inquiring the cause of her fear, she clasped my hands entreatingly, and prayed me to slay her if I must, but not to destroy her children. Convinced of her madness, I yet strove to pacify her, when she still further amazed me by saying she had been told that *the Highlanders devoured children.* You can judge from this, dear Agnes, what an impression the English have of us and our manners, that they imagine us cannibals. It was not till I had repeatedly assured her of my total innocence of such behaviour, that she dragged the children out of a clothes-press, announcing joyfully, 'Come out! come out! the gentleman will not eat you.'

"Late this afternoon we entered Preston amid the ringing of bells, and the shouts of the populace who are strongly Jacobite. But some of the clansmen remembering the tragedy that here befell our cause in 'the '15,' were troubled by the superstition that they could never proceed further, and in order to prove this false, our clan forded the Ribble, and encamped on the farther side.

"Friday, November 29. Good fortune still attends us! At 2 o'clock this afternoon our Prince marched into Manchester at the head of the Highlanders. This evening bonfires are blazing,—as we used to light them, Agnes, on the shore of Loch Eil:—and every house is glittering with candles in the Prince's honour.

"'Grandmother' Wade, as we call him, could not *wade* through the snow to encounter us, and is still at Newcastle. The Prince has kindly given orders to repair the bridges for his benefit.

"Sunday, December 1. *On the road to London!* Yesterday at Manchester the Prince reviewed the English regiment, newly organised under Colonel Francis Townley, and we Highlanders thought it an evil omen that the church-yard should be chosen for the reviewing-ground.

"You must know of a beautiful incident which occurred as we crossed the Mersey. A number of loyal gentlemen awaited the Prince on the southern shore, and with them Mistress Skyring, a lady of ninety years, who had been lifted as an infant in her mother's arms to behold the landing of Charles II. at Dover. From that day she had lived in the most ardent devotion to the Stuart cause, yearly sending the half of her means to our exiled King, though never mentioning the sender's name. Having sold her jewels and her silver, she laid the money at the

Prince's feet, and passionately pressed his hand to her aged lips, murmuring with devoted rapture the words of the 'Nunc Dimittis,'—'Lord, now lettest Thou Thy servant depart in peace!' Is not this a sublime example of the spirit of the Cavaliers?" . .

Here the letter ended so abruptly as to indicate that the writer had been unexpectedly interrupted. Agnes, with tears awakened by the pathos of the closing lines, turned self-reproachfully to her uncle's letter. Donald's missive had fairly pulsated with the buoyant spirit of youth, but that of Norman Leslie breathed an undertone of deep foreboding, of half-revealed despair;—it was so vividly the conviction of a man who has ceased to hope. Long before she had finished, Agnes's eyes were wet with sadder tears than those she had just shed in passing sentiment.

She read with growing apprehension: "Ere we return, your birthday will have passed, little maid, but wherever I am on the Old Year's Night, serving my King, whose birthday is your own, my heart will be with you when the bells are ringing for the birth of the New Year. And I choose never to see that year rather than behold his fair young head bowed in defeat, rather than know that the bonnie brow which was fashioned to wear a crown, must go forever undiademed. God protect him! God keep from him the demon of despair!—for sooner than ill should touch one lock of his golden hair I would die and death to save him, and in any grave, neglected and unhonoured, I would sleep content. And so would you do, Agnes, *so would you do!*"

CHAPTER XX

' THE BROKEN HEART, IT KENS NAE SECOND SPRING
AGAIN "

" The wee birdies sing, and the wild flowers spring,
 An' in sunshine the waters are sleeping;
But the broken heart, it kens nae second spring again,
 Tho' the waefu' may cease frae their greeting."

THE profound melancholy of Norman Leslie's
words haunted Agnes continually. Perhaps if
he had read them first the effect might have been quite
different, but set against the background of Donald's
gay assurance, they loomed in black relief—like
clouds on the horizon, remote yet darkly ominous,
whose shadow dims the brilliant summer blue.

But Agnes hid her disquietude, and made no outward sign when she heard the alarming news of the retreat from Derby, the advance of Cumberland, and the thickly clustering perils encompassing the dauntless Scots. She came of a race that had always endured in proud silence the utmost Fate could inflict.

Agnes spent Christmas-day in her room, reading the appropriate selections in the prayer-book, for she had refused to attend service since that day,—the Sunday following Prince Charlie's departure,—when the minister of St. Giles's, relieved from all restraint, had exultantly chosen for his text the nineteenth chapter of St. Luke, and the fourteenth verse:

"We will not have this man to reign over us."

Sir Hugh regarded the prayer-book with Presbyterian abhorrence. "As well Papist as Prelatist," he was wont to observe. "She had better get her a rosary, and tell her beads." But he had long since learned that Agnes would alter neither politics nor religion at his behest.

At intervals, Sir Hugh received a letter from Kenneth, now a Colonel under Cumberland. On such occasions, the girl would withdraw without a word, leaving Sir Hugh to unrestrained enjoyment of the contents. Not even to Mistress Catherine did she mention Kenneth's name.

Agnes, brushing the bitter rime from her chamber window, felt the chill clutch of a terror deadlier far than cold. The Edinburgh of sleet and snow and pale enfolding mist was vastly different from the Edinburgh whose grey walls had lain golden under summer sunshine, or purple in autumn haze. And the silent, wistful Agnes was strangely unlike the gay and mischievous creature who had gathered roses in the garden, or darted like a fleck of sunshine through the winding wood-paths of the Queen's Park.

The brilliant victory of the Prince at Falkirk, on the very plain where Bruce had triumphed at glorious Bannockburn, awakened in her a gleam of hope, and for a few days she was her own radiant self. But on the 30th of January the Duke of Cumberland reached Edinburgh, intent on annihilating his daring young cousin, and Agnes, inherently superstitious, opened the prayer-book to the death of King Charles the Martyr, and shuddered at the suggestion it con veyed. When, on the following morning, the Duke clattered up the High Street in a coach drawn by twelve horses, while the chimes of St. Giles's performed the obnoxious Whig tune of "Up an' waus them a,' Willie," Agnes, with flashing eyes, drew the window-curtain close, and refused so much as to glance at the hated Hanoverian.

.   .   .   .   .

April had come to Edinburgh with gleams of fitful sunshine and shimmer of opal rain, with snow-storms sweeping down from the Pentlands like flocks of white-winged birds, and mantles of pearly mist trailing softly over the stern shoulders of Arthur's Seat. No flowers bloomed as yet, but here and there the fields were flecked with green, and at night under the faint white lustre of the moon, and the fainter lustre of the stars, there rose a sweet earth-odour, spicier than wine, the first alluring taste of the brimming cup of spring.

But Agnes drank not of it, or, drinking, found it bitter. On Tuesday evening, April 15, she came slowly downstairs to perform the unwelcome duty of aiding Mistress Campbell in entertaining a number of Sir Hugh's Whig acquaintances.

She was arranging the tea and scones with listless fingers, and thoughts travelling ceaselessly northward, when the outer door quivered under a ponderous knock which sent the startled blood in crimson to her temples, but left her paler than before.

When, at a glance from Mistress Campbell, she rose to answer the summons, she felt a tremor of weakness sweep through her from head to foot, and was conscious that her throat had grown strangely dry. It was like walking down the hallway of a dream, so endlessly long seemed the distance. When at last the door was open, she found herself facing a man in a dragoon's uniform, much muddied by fast riding,—a stalwart, swaggering fellow, greatly the worse for liquor, bold-eyed, boisterous and insolent.

"Oho, Mistress," was his greeting, "I bear sweet tidings for your pretty ears, and tidings that old Sir Campbell will give his fortune to ken; Cumberland has crossed the Spey, and follows hot on the Pretender's trail. The rebels are caught like a hare in the teeth o' the hounds! They are starving, while the Royal Duke has the fat o' the land. And the gibbet and axe will be fed full ere a sixmonth, for the Pretender's pretty game is up, and Cumberland holds the cards!"

The moonlight shimmered white as marble over the old mansion, but she was whiter far than the moonlight,—a pallor piteous to see upon a face so fair and young. For an instant both hands were clasped against her breast in a gesture of despair, the next she caught at the casement, swaying, like one stricken by a blow above the heart.

The tipsy messenger, who, as one of Gardiner's valiant troopers, had been captured at Prestonpans, and later had calmly broken his parole in order to join Cumberland, remembered hearing in tavern-gossip that the Prince had been much enamoured of some Highland beauty, who had somewhat resembled him in look and bearing. Now it occurred to his beer-befuddled brain that he faced the girl in question,

"The Broken Heart Kens Nae Spring" 171

and seeing the effect of his news, he attempted garrulous consolement.

"Ne'er mind, Mistress," he bellowed, "the Pretender's wondrous bonnie, but 'tis like he'll trip no more reels in Geordie's country, so ye'd best look ye out a Prince o' Whiggish colour. Just show that pretty face o' yours to our Royal Willie, an' he'll sooner kiss you than harm you."

The girl continuing to stare past him without answer, he was meditating whether he himself should not administer comfort by proxy, when he caught sight of Sir Hugh in the hallway, and was moved to change his policy.

"The evening's greetings to ye'r lor'ship," he shouted thickly, and proceeded to rehearse his message with many vivid additions. Sir Hugh drank it in like wine, and without a glance at the girl, standing white-faced and mute beside him, committed the reckless generosity of bestowing a sovereign on his maudlin benefactor, who muttered something of "the Pretender in the devil's claws," "his serene and Christian Majesty, George the Second, and the holy Hanover succession"; and staggered off to drink brimming bumpers in Cumberland's honour.

But when Sir Hugh had departed to gladden his fellow-Whigs, Agnes still lingered at the door, her hand clenched at her bosom, her body tense and quivering, her wide eyes gazing out on moonlit Holyrood. A burst of exultant laughter stung her to self-control. With lips compressed and head dauntlessly high she passed into the house. All the evening long she held fear at bay, though her hands clenched again and again, and her eyes grew ever darker and more stormy, and her heart raged against them,— these traitors who denied their lawful King!

It was nearly midnight when she at last was free to light her candle and climb the shadow-thronged stair. At her chamber-door she paused, shaken, like the flickering flame, by a very gust of terror. A waft of wind blew the candle out. She stood, seized suddenly by superstitious dread, afraid to enter. But she gathered her courage resolutely, and pushed open the door. Only a shimmer of moonshine lit the room, but she felt at once with the strange prescience of fear that something was changed therein. Impelled by unerring instinct, she swayed rather than ran across the room, gave one glance of shuddering comprehension, and sprang wildly back, with a low cry of anguish. For the space where the sword had hung was empty! There on the floor, gleaming faintly in the moonlight, lay the ancient claymore which Dundee had drawn for the King. She gazed upon it in despairing woe, as if a man lay stricken at her feet. "Oh, laddie!" she moaned, "oh, laddie! laddie!"

A black shadow passed over the moon, leaving the room in utter darkness. But deeper by far was the shadow that shrouded the girl's heavy heart, as she knelt before this fearful symbol of impending doom. With trembling fingers she raised the fallen broadsword, her face whiter than the ribbon upon its hilt had ever been.

"His doom is sealed," she murmured, "his doom and mine! For when was not a fallen sword the harbinger of death? Was it not so on the eve before my father died, and before Lachlan Leslie fell at Sherriffmuir, and before the great Montrose was slain upon the scaffold? O God! 'tis a sign unfailing." And stretching out her arms, she cried imploringly, "Oh, laddie, do you lie already upon some battlefield where love can never reach you? But I will come to you, laddie, I will come!"

Her spirit had been shaken to its very centre by a surge of superstitious horror. But anger mingled with her grief as lightning flashes through a sombre sky.

"I'll bide here no longer!" she cried bitterly, her bosom still heaving with the remembrance of the evening. 'Tis a' a nest o' traitors! An' I'm no' leal mysel' an' I tarry in their fause-hearted company!"

Her rage dispelled the apathy of grief, and roused her to thought and action. She sprang up, and with nervous yet noiseless haste began her preparations for flight. In a marvellously short time she had exchanged her gown for a dark riding-habit, and laid her hat and cloak in readiness. As on the evening of the dance, she lit no candle, trusting only to the fading moonlight to assist her search.

Again she drew from its corner the little brass-studded trunk, wherein she had once found so dear a treasure; and lifted the ancient lid where the moon could shine into its shadowy depths. Again she unrolled the wrappings of a shimmering satin gown, as yellow as amber, on which the moon glanced vividly. Something glittered among those splendid folds, mocking the lustre of the pearls that had once adorned them. Agnes quickly brushed it away, and restored the gown to its wrappings with trembling haste. From another part of the trunk she produced a silver-mounted pistol of her father's, which she laid on the floor beside her, and continued her search till she found powder and ball with which to load it. Desperate as was the impulse which drove her northward, she was calm enough to know that she must not go unarmed. To follow in the trail of Cumberland's ruthless army would require not only the greatest courage, but the utmost skill. For all the wildness of her woe she would leave no weapon unforged that could cleave the path to her object. She remembered that Dundee had ridden northward, "whither the spirit of Montrose should lead him." So would she ride.

With dexterity she collected the things she needed; —food, clothing, and the few treasures she could not part with—Lydia Leslie's gown, her mother's prayer-book, and a bit of velvet from Montrose's sword. The tears overflowed as she touched them; soon they would cease to flow, and grief would be dry-eyed.

This was the very ghost of that radiant girl who had knelt, exultant, in the moonlight, not seven months before, with shining eyes, and gaily curving mouth, and cheeks like red Lancaster roses. The hazel eyes had lost their laughter, and grown wide and haunting and piteous; the mouth was compressed and quivering, and the ecstasy of hope that once had lighted every feature, had vanished with the wild-rose bloom. The face she lifted to the moonlight was white with unspeakable woe.

"The Broken Heart Kens Nae Spring" 175

With an aching effort she roused herself from her lethargy, drew from the farthest corner of the trunk a slip of yellow paper, unfolded it, and counted out a number of sovereigns. Using the lid as a desk, she wrote a few words and directed them to Mistress Campbell.

"My uncle lies dead or dying, and I go to find him. You have been very kind; I shall never forget it! The money give Sir Hugh in payment of the debt I owe him. If I live, I will return to thank you, but I pray to die with those I love."

She signed it, "Agnes of Auchnacarry,"—nothing more.

The note finished, she wrapped it around the gold, and laid it in a conspicuous place upon the tall dresser, saying bitterly, "'Tis not for a Leslie to take a foeman's charity!"

With accustomed skill she buckled the fatal broadsword around her waist, and fastened her father's pistol in her belt. This accomplished, she sat down to wait, for not till the moon was low, and the entire household was wrapped in sleep, could she attempt her flight.

The deep bell of St. Giles's told the hour of one, told the hour of two, was very close to three, before she rose with a heavy sigh. She listened a moment at the window, hearing the watchmen crying along the streets; gazed a moment at the palace-front whose blackened walls the moon veiled with misty shimmer; then she lightly unbarred the door upon the balcony, and crept noiselessly to the latticed edge whence she had given Donald greeting one

September dawn. An iron trellis, set for climbing roses, supplied a slender ladder, by means of which she quickly reached the ground. Protected by the shadow of the house, she made her cautious way into the garden, so weirdly lighted by the setting moon.

As she stole silently along the deserted paths, her skirt brushed the bare twigs in her flight. Here, where she had so often strayed when joy was at full bloom, where she had plucked her Stuart roses for Donald and the Prince, all was dark and desolate. Yet in a few weeks more, summer would return to it; roses would blow and boughs be green again. But in her breast no impulse of spring was stirring; it had no hopes to blossom and unfold. There was no place more dreary than the dark autumn of an aching heart.

Agnes, saddling and bridling "Prince Charlie," pressed her lips to his snowy mane, whispering pet names in Gaelic, to which the horse replied with little whinnies of delight. When the watchman had passed out of view up the Canongate she led "Prince Charlie" through the shadowy garden, and out at the gate she had unlatched for Donald. She gave one mournful glance at Holyrood, more ghostly by far under the fitful April moonlight than in the September shadows. Edinburgh faded from sight as the Prince's namesake, his head turned northward took the road to Inverness.

CHAPTER XXI

"THERE ARE HILLS BEYOND PENTLAND, AND LANDS
BEYOND FORTH"

"There are hills beyond Pentland, and lands beyond Forth,
Be there lords in the south, there are chiefs in the north;
There are brave Duinnewassels three thousand times three,
Will cry, 'Hey for the bonnets of Bonnie Dundee!'"

ONCE the city lay behind her, and she found herself fully embarked upon her desperate errand, Agnes yielded to the reaction which follows moments of great stress, and wept with unrestrained bitterness of her utter desolation. The future lay before her like some pathless wilderness, for she had formed no plans beyond her unfaltering determination to reach the Scottish army, and learn what fate had befallen Norman Leslie. That it was a tragic one, she no more doubted than if she had seen him lying dead. Her Gaelic blood made her believe infallibly in signs and premonitions; the very air of the Highlands was peopled with gnomes and fairies. Each family had their attendant spirit, protective or malignant, to warn them of impending woe; or some unfailing portent of disaster to doubt which would be to doubt that there was a God in Heaven.

Dawn found Agnes on the highway to Linlithgow, a road skirting westward along the deep Firth of Forth. After leaving the sovereigns for Sir Hugh,

little money had remained, and she determined, should
the weather be warm, to spend several nights in the
open air with only her plaid for shelter, as she had
often done in her roamings through Lochaber when
darkness had overtaken her. This first evening she
feared she must part with one of her sovereigns, for
the day was bleak and wintry, and the snow fell in
bitter gusts. She found refuge for the night at the
inn at Linlithgow, whose keeper, however, himself a
Jacobite, refused any payment for his hospitality,
and wished her "godspeed, and better times for the
cause."

As she passed the ruined palace of Linlithgow
where, on a certain drear December morning, Mary
Stuart had first seen the light, Agnes wondered bitterly if the lovely, hapless Queen could know what
tragedy had haunted her descendants. If she did,
then the fatal scene at Fotheringay had not ended
her sufferings. The thought was but another vagrant
thread from the tangled weaving of which life was
spun; and the spinner broke it off, and wove no
more.

The second and third days crept by uneventfully.
Agnes made rapid progress, for her horse was a thoroughbred, and used to a more rugged country. The
sword and pistol were hidden beneath the folds of her
plaid, and she pursued her journey unquestioned and
undisturbed, though many a wayfarer turned repeatedly to gaze after this girl with the beautiful,
anxious face, who bore herself so proudly.

On the afternoon of the third day, Agnes found
herself entering the wild and wooded Pass of Killie

"*There Are Hills Beyond Pentland*" 179

Crankie, the scene of Dundee's immortal victory. She had traversed it on her way to Edinburgh, twenty months before, with oh, how changed a heart!

Night was very near; already dark Ben Vrackie and the sombre ramparts of the hills that walled the glen had lost the lingering gold of the afterglow, and had begun to clothe themselves in the mist of twilight. The wild waters of the Garry, foaming tempestuously over the jagged boulders with which the gorge was strewn, glimmered fitfully through the veiling trees like the wind-tossed mane of a white charger. Agnes, looking about her with a shrinking sense of loneliness, realised that she could go no further that evening, for even should the moon be bright enough to show the road, there was too much danger of encountering some of Cumberland's stragglers in the narrow pass.

As she sat drearily thinking, she observed not far away a small stone cottage, hardly larger than a hut, built against an enormous boulder which overshadowed and sheltered it. As she looked, a light gleamed from the window, and at this, and at the slender column of smoke which rose to mingle with the dusk, the darkening valley grew still more forbidding. She dismounted, and hastened eagerly toward the friendly beacon. As she approached, an old man emerged from the doorway, but, at sight of her, paused abruptly, as if he saw a spirit of mountain or of glen. He was very old, with long white hair and beard, and glittering blue eyes, which he fastened rigidly upon her face. He wore the Highland costume, and his shrunken knees, which the philabeg left bare,

bore witness to his extreme age; yet he stooped but
slightly, and except when he moved, appeared almost
vigorous. He did not move now, but stood, statue
like, and stared at the fair intruder; and Agnes saw
that she must accost him.

"Will you give me shelter for the night?" she
said beseechingly. "I am far from home, and it is
too dark for me to ride further."

He made no answer, nor did he cease to gaze at her.
Following an impulse, she repeated her question in
Gaelic. As if it were the magician's wand which
bade him speak, the old man replied gravely in the
same language: "Aye, ye are welcome; do ye enter.
But for the one ye seek, *ask of Drummossie Muir!*"

At these mysterious words, his aged features be
came strangely rapt; to Agnes's startled eyes, he
seemed a part of the surrounding weirdness. Indeed
his whole aspect was so wild that one less courageous
than this dauntless maiden of the Leslies might have
hesitated before accepting his proffered welcome.
But Agnes was too utterly weary to be deterred by
so slight an obstacle as an old man's vague utterance.
Besides, those possessing second sight were by no
means unknown to her, and she thought him of that
number. So she followed without hesitation as he
led the way into the firelit gloom of the hut.

Bare as the place was, it supplied warmth and
shelter, and Agnes breathed a weary sigh of content.
The meal he set before his guest consisted only of
bannocks of barley and spring-water, though he
gravely proffered his flask of usquebaugh, which the
girl courteously declined. The frugal supper ended

he replenished the fire, secured the door, and returning to where Agnes sat beside the hearth, again subjected her to a rigid scrutiny. Sinking to a seat near by, he began speaking slowly as if to himself.

"Fair as the white bells of the heather,—pure as the snow upon Ben Nevis ere it be trod by foot of man,—what fate has linked her with the lad of the fair hair and the King's face,—for I see them together!——The sea is black, and the waves leap above the boat——"

Here he broke off suddenly, then turned to her, exclaiming, "You are of kin to him who died yonder,"—he motioned up the pass,—"you have his eyes and his look, and the sword he drew hangs at your side. I saw him fall,—he was an angel to see,—aye, an archangel for beauty and for wrath." Again he bent his rapt gaze upon the girl— "But the clans sleep on Drummossie Muir, where the heather is red that should be green, wet with a crimson dew."

Agnes sprang up, shuddering at the horror thus foretold. "Why speak ye of Drummossie Muir?" she cried, "'tis a level heath beyond Inverness, near Culloden House, where Sir Duncan Forbes lives. Oft have I ridden across it. But what has this to do with Dundee and the fate of the clans?—Do you mean there will be a battle?"

But the old man muttered dreamily of a "broken vision," and did not explain his words.

A deep silence followed, in which the plaintive sobbing of the wind among the rocks, and the muffled roar of the stream that dashed beneath the windows produced an eerie monotone.

In the fitful pauses of the wind the old man spoke: "Three there are for whom your heart beats warm, with whom your fate is twined as harebells twine with heather,—one is your kinsman, the brave, sad heart, —of him my tongue has spoken,—and one is the fair-haired lad with the star upon his breast. The star of his life is sinking in thick clouds like those above Ben Vrackie when lightnings play and leap. —— And there is still another,—with eyes of the harebell's blue, and a tartan red as the sunset's flame and oak-leaves waving in his bonnet,—ah, you tremble, *for his fate sways your life, as the moon sways the sea.* Yet concerning him my ultimate sight is sealed,—and I see only a line of claymores in the midday-sun,—a wall of broadswords bent and crimson,—and the lad of the yellow hair is foremost in the charge;—and again I see a prison dark and grim and the lad of the oak-leaves walks between armed men, with fetters on his hands.—— And again I see——"

But Agnes could bear it no longer, and swaying like a wind-swept leaf, she seized the old man's withered fingers in a restraining clasp, crying distractedly, "Tell me no more—O God!—no more—of *Donald Cameron!*"

The old man met her shuddering appeal with the look of one awakened from a dream. He made a confused effort to collect his thoughts, and, failing, answered "All is dim,—the vision comes not,"—and lapsed into silence.

When Agnes climbed to the little chamber under the eaves, she was so wrought upon that every shadow

"Tell me no more ~ Oh God! ~ no more ~ of Donald Cameron!"

startled, and every sound alarmed. After a futile effort to regain her calmness, she gave way to a superstitious prompting, and drawing out a tiny Bible, opened it at random, and read with feverish haste the words her eyes fell upon:

"So the spirit lifted me up, and took me away, and I went in bitterness,——*but the hand of the Lord was strong upon me.*"

Vaguely comforted, she sank to her knees by the bedside, and poured out a supplicating prayer that the hovering peril be averted, that the sword of doom fall not as one had fallen. Soothed at last, she yielded to overpowering exhaustion, flung herself upon the rude bed, and found a brief forgetfulness in sleep.

At the first grey glimmer of dawn she awoke, bewildered by her strange surroundings, but most of all by the dull unwonted ache at her heart. As the bitter memory returned to her, she rose, sighing heavily, and began to dress. In the palid dawn-light her face showed startlingly wan and woeful,—the look of a creature helpless in the gauntlet grasp of Fate. "I must go," she murmured, "though I ride to certain doom!"

The sun had not yet mounted the hills, and the dark defile of the glen lay wrapped in shimmering robes of mist, as the white horse and his rider began to climb the pass. Ben Vrackie loomed a giant through the shifting curtain of bright vapour; already his frowning brow was crowned with early gold. The road, following the left bank of the Garry, wound in gradual ascent through woods of twilight gloom, hung thick with pearls of dew, and spread with radiant green of fern and heather.

The mist was curling up from the hills like smoke of battle, as Agnes drew rein and listened. Was it the Garry leaping over the rocks below, or the rush of warriors sweeping down the glen? This was the fateful spot! Here on a morning of midsummer sixty years agone, Dundee had fallen, fighting, for his King. This girl, in whom his life-blood flowed, in whom his spirit burned, had need of no magician's wand to conjure back the scene. She lingered breathless, and alone, and saw it all:—the Lowland army fleeing headlong before their plaided foes, the proud figure of Dundee—Ian Cath nan Dhu, or Dark John of the Battles, as the clansmen fondly called him,—upon his bold black horse, cheering his Highlanders to victory;—heard the fatal shot ring out and beheld him sinking mortally wounded in the arm of a clansman. A moment he is hidden by the smoke the next it lifts and shows the dying victor.

"How goes the day?" Dundee whispered.

"Well for King James," replied the soldier, "but I am sorry for your lordship."

And Dundee answered, "If it is well for him, matters the less for me!"

The vision passed, as the wind passes. The scene grew dim and faded into mist. But the spirit of it passed not, and it stirred the girl as flame is stirred. Instinctively, she lifted the sword at her side, and kissed it. Unconsciously, her lips repeated the dying whisper of the Graeme, "*If it is well for him, it matters the less for me!*"

CHAPTER XXII

"LOCHEIL, LOCHEIL! BEWARE OF THE DAY!"

"Locheil, Locheil! beware of the day
When the Lowlands shall meet thee in battle array!"

THE light of a dying fire flung splashes of vivid crimson on the group of plaided warriors lying within the circle of its radiance, lingering fitfully on the scarlet tartan of Cameron and Fraser, of Macintosh and MacLean, or glancing ruddily on the rich blue of Gordon and of Leslie. The polished blade of dirk and broadsword sent back the red reflection, and the brilliant cairngorms clasping plaid and bonnet flamed like topaz. The scene abounded in blended lights and shadows, through which the Scottish hues of gold and crimson were superbly dominant. But all the splendid glow of colour could not hide the deeply graven signs of want and suffering that marked the forms and faces of the clansmen. Their only food upon that eve of battle had been a small oat-bannock made of husks.

"There are those of us who will sleep to-morrow in plaids of a redder hue," said Alexander MacGillivray, touching, as he spoke, the rich folds of his tartan.

"'Tis the death we pray for!" cried Donald Cameron, his ardour flashing in his bright blue eyes,— "the death of glory!"

Apart from the rest, where the shadows lingered darkest, Norman Leslie, his head upon his hand, reclined beside Lochiel.

"The lad speaks the wish of my heart," said Leslie; "you know for what I pray."

"God forbid, Norman!" Lochiel answered. "And yet if the doom strikes, it will be those whose plaids become their shrouds to whom Heaven is kind. The Duke is in a cruel humour; no mercy will he know toward vanquished rebels!"

Beyond the crimson circle of the firelight, Drummossie Muir swept far into the shadows, brooding and bleak and grim, of one foreboding blackness with the sky. Out of this encompassing gloom appeared a figure in a bright plaid, whose slender stateliness and courtly grace proclaimed his royal blood. Prince Charlie stood before them, as pale and hunger-worn as any there, but still with eyes undaunted and undimmed, and voice yet vibrant.

"Lads!" he cried, "why starve we here, while Cumberland revels yonder? Let us march and attack him ere dawn! Therein lies our strongest chance!"

The wild devotion his voice and presence never failed to waken, rekindled all their dimly burning hopes. Ardently repeating the password, "James the Eighth," they sprang to arms, impatient to embark upon their desperate expedition. Charles solemnly embraced Lord Murray, who placed himself at the head of the first column, while the Prince assumed command of the second, and the advance began.

Who shall describe that wild night-march to Nairn! They could not follow the main road to Cumberland's camp, lest their approach be betrayed, and so were compelled to force a slow and painful way through heavy bogs and tangled woods. The night was of an utter, impenetrable blackness, unlit by moon or star; those who marched side by side could scarce discern each other. Men sank beside the road at every step, too spent with hunger and fatigue to keep their footing. Even Donald Cameron, whose buoyant youth had hitherto sustained him, began to stagger with exhaustion, and had it not been for Angus MacDonald's supporting arm, he must have fallen. Two o'clock found the Prince, with pitifully diminished force, far in the rear of Lord Murray, and still three miles distant from his destination. Dawn would break in an hour more, and with it hope would perish. Yet the Prince would have pressed on, had not Lord Murray, dreading discovery of their plans, insisted on retreat, to which Charles yielded, though reluctantly, exclaiming, " 'Tis no matter; we shall meet them, and behave like brave fellows." Yet Despair and he rode together through the drear, grey dawn, as his exhausted army staggered blindly back to Inverness to wait the cruel coming of the day.

. . . . .

While the unhappy Highlanders were making their futile march to Nairn, Cumberland was celebrating his birthday by a wild carousal. A group of officers—Kenneth among them—who were not disposed to join his riotous rejoicing, sat rather sullenly apart in a corner of the banquet-room, awaiting orders from their amiable commander.

About midnight, Kenneth, at Cumberland's maudlin behest, approached the gaming-table where he sat, and was presently astonished by the Duke's flinging him a playing-card with the order: "Obey it or die!"—which somewhat failed in force by being decidedly run together.

Kenneth, vainly endeavouring to hide his disgust, snatched the card from the floor, and retired abruptly. He held in his hand the nine-spot of diamonds,—forever after to be known as "The Curse of Scotland,"—on the unornamented back of which were scrawled these fiendish words: "Spare not as you value your life. No quarter to the rebels! No mercy to the Pretender! William, Duke of Cumberland."

As he read, Kenneth was shaken by a fierce surge of triumph. The sword of merciless power lay ready to his hand; grasping that deadly nine-spot, he grasped his longed-for vengeance! Here was the chance to requite in bitter measure for the insults he had received from the Prince, and for the heartless coquetry with which Agnes had repulsed his love. But a strong revulsion followed, as mighty as his thirst for vengeance, and he shuddered at that painted bit of pasteboard that must cost so many lives. He was by nature fiery, but not vindictive, and he knew he could never avenge his wrong upon those brave, devoted clansmen who had shown him such generosity. He was seized by an impulse to return, and dash the card in Cumberland's face with

"Locheil, Locheil! Beware of the Day!" 189

the advice to seek a butcher for the task. But such an act would be but useless rage; it would not avert the morrow's doom. Turning wildly, he sought an adjoining room, and flung down the fatal nine-spot before an English officer of gallant bearing.

"These orders," he cried fiercely, "are an insult to mercy and to manhood! I cannot—and I will not—obey them! Nor will *you* obey them, if you have a heart within your breast!"

Kenneth went out, and stood beside a window looking toward the east. The first grey gleam of dawn was flickering in the sky, like some low-burning lamp. He shuddered, hiding his face in his hands, in shrinking horror of the coming day. "God pity the clans!" he cried. A voice behind him echoed his words, "God pity the clans!"

He turned, astonished, unaware that he had spoken aloud, and faced the young English officer before whom he had flung the card:—a man whose name the New World honours, whose memory Westminster still enshrines.

"You are right," said Wolfe. "Cumberland is a fiend, and knows no mercy. He cannot revere a brave enemy. God pity the clans to-morrow,—no! —to-day!"

. . . . .

Whitely the sad dawn gleamed over the heath-clad slopes of green Drummossie Muir, upon the faint blue hills that fade to southward, the stately towers of Culloden House that rise against the background of the sea, and the walls of ancient Inverness that span the sunset sky. Silence brooded over the moor unbroken, as on eagle's wings; scarce a sign was seen of stir or movement. Those of the clansmen who were not lying in exhausted sleep, were scattered miles away in frantic search for food.

About eleven o'clock there appeared on the eastern horizon, where the green vastness of the moor was merged into the vaster sky, an object with the seeming of a cloud. But no cloud ever loomed so ominous, however black with thunder, however charged with shafted lightning, as did that wavering greyness. *It was Cumberland's army marching to the attack!*

Alarm-guns pealed over the moor, summoning the scattered troops to their position. Charles, who had eaten nothing but a bit of bread and whisky at Culloden House, galloped headlong to the field. Wildly and in haste the lines were formed;—five thousand starving and exhausted men to face an enemy ten thousand strong. Vainly did his officers suggest the prudence of retreat. Charles was so fully assured of the courage and devotion of his clansmen that he did not hesitate to offer battle, even against such odds.

The English army advanced in stately ranks, the fitful sunlight flashing on their bright accoutrements and scarlet trappings, the wind fluttering their gorgeous flags, and their drums sounding the thunderous notes of the charge.

Mute but undaunted stood the waiting clansmen. The blueness of the morning sky was gone, and the snow drove in blinding gusts from the northeast; even the wind, so favourable at Preston, had turned

"Locheil, Locheil! Beware of the Day!"

against them. The English troops approached to within five hundred paces, when they halted and formed in three deep lines, each protected by cannon.

It was at this moment, as the two armies faced each other, that Prince Charlie rode slowly along the front of the clans, to make his last appeal to their loyalty and courage. As he spoke his few brave, ringing words, as he gazed at them with mute entreaty, their eyes answered his with looks of unspeakable devotion; the passion of love they bore him inspired each heart with animating flame. The Prince had barely returned to his position behind the second line, when the Highlanders began the battle with a cannonade, which, owing to the scarcity and smallness of their field-pieces, worked little harm; while on the other hand, Cumberland, who soon brought his guns into play, made cruel furrows through the Scottish lines. Charles still delayed to attack in the vain hopes of compelling the Duke to make the first move; but at length, unable to endure the great destruction wrought among his ranks, he gave the signal for the charge.

The Highlanders had remained silent and motionless, patiently awaiting his coommand, although on every side they saw their comrades falling beneath the cannon's fire. But now a sudden thrill of fiery rapture glowed in every eye; the men poised, expectant, with bodies bent like tigers for the spring. Each clansman paused to "scrug" his blue bonnet upon his brow, grasp with firmer hand his gun and target, and murmur a last brief prayer to the God of Battles and of Hosts.

Donald Cameron, whose clan occupied a position on the extreme right of the foremost line, glanced along the tartaned ranks, and, stirred unutterably by the look on every face, felt his bosom heave with the fierce pulse of vengeance. The moment ended ere it had begun; for the next instant the gallant Macintoshes, led by the dauntless chief of the Mac-Gillivrays, sprang headlong from the centre of the line to meet the foe. Scarce a pace behind them rushed the Murrays and the Camerons, the Stuarts, Frasers, Maclachlans, and MacLeans,—one awful line of blended tartans, of lifted targets, and of broadswords' gleam. Darting within gunshot of the English, they rapidly discharged their muskets, unsheathed their claymores, and rushed with fearful impetus upon the shrouded foe. They hurled themselves through that grim cloud of mingled smoke and snow, where flashed the deadly lightning of the bayonet, like some stupendous and resistless wave, that shatters and is shattered where it strikes.

Yet still they paused not! Impelled by that sublime and desperate valour, unfalteringly on they swept,—a hurricane of flashing, blinding steel,—straight on and through that serried English line, sheathing those cruel bayonets in their devoted breasts. Yet the survivors recked not of their doom! Forward they surged, a shattered, reeling few, the broken crest of that once mighty wave, to whom fierce death in honour was a welcome fate.

In that first dreadful moment of contact with the foe, Donald Cameron found himself opposed to the Scots Fusiliers; and suddenly beheld, amid the blinding play of bayonet and broadsword, a young officer in the tartan of Argyle. Even through wreathing smoke, Donald recognised Kenneth Campbell. To the young clansman's eyes he seemed a very traitor, —this man who had left the Prince's standard to join its enemies. Donald sprang upon him as a wildcat springs, and bending his left knee, in the Highland manner of combat, presented his target to his foeman's point. But Kenneth, obeying Cumberland's command, thrust not at him, but at his left-hand comrade, Angus MacDonald, who, thus taken unawares, was wounded in the sword-arm. Ere he could repeat the thrust, Donald, with a single agile movement of his strong young body, darted between him and Angus, exclaiming, as Kenneth's sword sunk deep into his shield, "Nay, when you strike, strike fairly, son of Diarmid. [Son of the Mist—a Gaelic name given the Campbells.] If you be a traitor, false Campbell, may vengeance overtake you! But you have eaten my bread, and worn my tartan, and your blood shall not stain my sword!"

By a grassy well, in after years to bear his name ("The Well of the Dead" to-day bears the inscription: "Here the Chief of the MacGillivrays fell"), Alexander MacGillivray, the dauntless leader of Clan Macintosh, fought with desperate courage. Already his fatal prophecy was half fulfilled:—redder was his rich tartan than ever it had been dyed. Cruelly wounded, he sank at last, and lay amid his dead and dying clansmen, wrapped, like them, in the folds of a plaid deep-crimsoned with a hero's blood.

In the gap of a wall stood Gillies MacBane, a

giant in height and purpose, hewing down with the mighty sweep of his broadsword the foes who sought to enter. Thirteen fell before his deadly thrusts ere the doom closed over him, and he staggered, pierced with bayonets, to his death.

Donald Cameron had followed his father into the thickest of the fray, and was fighting valiantly beside him, when the brave Locheil received a severe wound through both ankles, and would have fallen had not Donald rushed forward to support him. Holding the enemy at bay, young Cameron cast a desperate glance about him, for the fate of prisoners seemed inevitably theirs. But his faithful foster-brother, Angus, his left hand wielding the claymore, cut a bloody path to their assistance, and, snatching the bridle-rein from a dead dragoon, lifted the wounded chieftain, with Donald's aid, into the empty saddle, and guiding the horse through one of the broken enclosures, accomplished Locheil's escape.

Donald and Angus again mingled with the shattered fragments of the clans, and a few Lowland and Irish troops, who, led by the desperate Prince, were making a last heroic stand against the deep-massed English lines. But all was futile! The reeling columns, wavered,—receded,—broke in full retreat. On every side was heard the Highlanders' despairing cry, —"Prions! Ochon! Ochon!" ("Oh, Woe is me!") Yet Charles would even yet have rushed upon the enemy, had not Donald caught his horse's rein, and forcibly restrained him.

"Let me go!" cried the Prince. "Better death than dishonour!"

"*Locheil, Locheil! Beware of the Day*"

But his officers interposed, and seizing his bridle between them, compelled him to withdraw. Never could Donald forget the look with which Charles left that fatal field. It was the look of a man stricken old, with all the buoyancy of youth and beauty crushed out by one fell blow, and in its stead a face so pale and desperate that it might have been sorrow's own. And as Charles gazed with horror-widened eyes upon the fallen clansmen, piled three and four tiers deep upon the blood-stained heather, he pressed his clenched hands to his temples, and one low shuddering cry burst from his lips:—"*My God! The clans! The clans!*"

The fatal die was cast, and the Stuart hopes lay trodden low amid that crimsoned heather. The clans had died, and died in vain, save that no death for love's sake has less than martyr's glory.

Donald, bleeding and exhausted, fleeing amid the wild retreat, heard a faint voice call his name, and saw Norman Leslie lying among the trampled heather, not far from that fatal well where the dead lay deep. Speechless the young man knelt and raised him in his arms. Blood flowed from the wound in his breast, and stained the blue folds of his belted plaid dark purple. His face, though white with death, was marked with neither suffering nor regret, but with a radiant peace,—nay, more,—a splendid triumph. And seeing Donald kneeling there beside him, he raised his head and smiled.

"God has been good to me," he said, low but unbrokenly;—"He has granted my prayer,—I have not outlived the cause I love! Were it not for

Agnes I would die content!—Care for my little lassie, Donald!—Oh, let no harm befall her!" He paused, and the old splendour shone from his eyes,— " God save Prince Charlie!" he whispered.

And Donald, looking at him through hot tears, saw that he had died with that prayer upon his lips.

. . . . . .

That evening, when the shadows shrouded that tragic field with peace, they laid him tenderly beneath the heather, wet with a deadlier dew than heaven had ever sprinkled; and on his breast they found— deep-crimsoned with his blood—the picture of a face,—a boy's face,—brown-eyed and brave and winsome,—upon whose laughing lips and ardent eyes the shadow of a fated race was cast. They laid it back upon his breast, to sleep with him beneath the heather, through the long, long years, till the angel of God should awaken the silent clansmen of Culloden!

CHAPTER XXIII

"THE FIELD OF THE DEAD"

"For the field of the dead rushes red on my sight,
And the clans of Culloden are scattered in flight."

WHEN Prince Charlie fled, broken-hearted, from the fatal moor, none but the dead and dying kept the field, and of the dying there were ever less, for by Cumberland's brutal orders his men traversed the heath, bent above each huddled group where life yet lingered, and with thrust of sword or bayonet, stilled that life forever. Never, in the history of civilisation, was any victory so foully sullied with cruelty as that of Cumberland at Culloden! Justly did he merit the odious title of the "Butcher Duke" with which history brands his name, for the horrible atrocities he inflicted upon his helpless foes were an outrage to England and Christianity! The road to Inverness was strewn with the victims of that merciless pursuit; while the prisoners met a doom, compared to which death had been a happy fate. The wanton cruelty of the Duke presented a glaring contrast to that of his unfortunate rival; for whatever his failings, Charles had never been lacking in pity, and at both Prestonpans and Falkirk had shown himself a merciful conqueror.

But Cumberland was not content with beholding

the execution of his barbarous vengeance; he, himself, accompanied by his officers, rode over the field directing, like some arch-demon, the fiendish effort of his men. In the midst of his progress, his eye fell upon a youthful Highlander, who, although wounded had raised himself on one elbow to gaze intently at the advancing horsemen.

"To whom do you belong?" the Duke demanded

"*To the Prince!*" came the unhesitating answer Cumberland, infuriated, turned to Major Wolfe exclaiming, "Shoot that scoundrel!"

Wolfe, his face pale with suppressed rage, replied coldly, "Your Grace may command my duty as soldier; but that of an executioner I decline."

Cumberland, grinding his teeth in fury at the sarcastic coldness of the reply, addressed the same command to Kenneth Campbell, who refused with equal indignation; whereupon the Duke, after trying his remaining officers with no better success, finally called a dragoon, inquired if his gun was loaded, and again repeated his savage order. He was at last obeyed the trooper fired, and the wounded Highlander sank back dead. Kenneth and Wolfe exchanged glances of bitter impotence. Kenneth had recognised the man so brutally murdered as young Charles Fraser a leader of that gallant clan, with whom he had been well acquainted in the Prince's army. To be compelled to sit passively by, powerless to save this victim of despotic vengeance, first chilled to ice the blood in Kenneth's veins, then sent it burning through his body like iron at white heat, with the splendid fire of indignant manhood.

Nor was his fury allayed by an incident which occurred that same evening at Inverness. An unfortunate youth of Clan Forbes, whose rash ardour for the White Rose had induced him to desert to the Prince, had been hanged by the Duke's orders, when an English officer, spurning the lifeless body of the deserter, exclaimed, with a brutal oath, "that every Scot was equally a traitor!" Kenneth could bear no more. He had heard insult after insult heaped upon Scotland and the clans, and his hot Gaelic blood flamed up in passionate defence. Though a Campbell and a Whig, he was of one race and one heritage with the brave Highlanders he had seen so foully slaughtered, so shamefully maligned. Wrenching out his sword, he sprang furiously upon the slanderer of Scotland, and dealt him a fiery blow. News of the combat spreading, every Scot within drum-beat rallied to Kenneth's aid, while his opponent was reinforced by a number of his own countrymen. The fray assumed large proportions; and again, as on a thousand battlefields, Scotsmen and English were opposed in deadly enmity. It was not till the insult had been retracted that Cumberland was able to restore peace, or even its outward semblance.

That evening, on Drummossie Muir, the lifeless bodies of the clansmen, enshrouded in their crimsoned plaids, were flung by the ruthless conquerors into a common grave, to lie where they had fallen, "in one and burial blent." Eightscore years after, those low, heath-mantled mounds—green with awakening springtime, or purple with deepening summer—yet guard in mournful vigil that field of tragic memory.

. . . . .

It had been early dawn of a mid-April morning when Agnes, ascending the Pass of Killiecrankie had lingered to create the scene of Dundee's heroic death; it was upon an afternoon three days later that the spires of Inverness first met her sight. With every passing mile she had kept more vigilant watch for it became increasingly evident that she was following the trail of an army; a fact to which trampled fields and deserted dwellings bore mournful testimony.

Yet not for fear, and not for danger, would she swerve from her path of despairing purpose. She sought Norman Leslie, living or dead, and seeking would not pause till her search was satisfied.

The "rose-red" town of Inverness, set between the azure sweep of the Moray Firth and the blue bend of the Ness like a ruby amid sapphires, nestled far and at seeming peace in the gold of the April sun shine. Its narrow streets had known the passing of Queen Mary; the ruined castle perched upon the hill had looked on good King Duncan's violent death; and thence Macbeth had gazed with murderous mind upon the distant peaks of blue Ben Wyvis and Strathconon.

How often had Agnes ridden hither with Donald or Norman Leslie in the happy days that were only haunting memory! But now she wished to avoid those quaint, familar streets, for she knew from tidings she had gathered on the road that the Duke held the town, and that to venture therein would be

to risk imprisonment, or at least delay. All her
questions as to the fate of the Prince's army had
been answered in the one way: there had been a terrible battle, and the Highlanders had been defeated
with great slaughter, and scattered far and wide.
She shrank instinctively from asking more, when
every word confirmed her fears.

Avoiding the town by a circuitous route, Agnes
followed the highway that wound in deep curves
along the Moray Firth. At length she left the sea
behind, and passing at a distance the grey walls of
Culloden House, where she and Norman Leslie had so
often dined with Sir Duncan, found her path emerging upon the green desolation of Drummossie Muir.
A sharp pang of horror clutched her heart, though
thus far she had seen no signs of struggle beyond
those which had already marked her way.

Yet it was with a dreadful sense of hovering evil
that she dismounted and led her horse toward a small
house which stood on the verge of the billowy heath
like a pebble cast by the sea. She had not approached unseen, however, for before she had gone
three steps, a woman with a child in her arms, and
another clinging to her dress, appeared in the doorway, and a sturdy lad of fourteen, who, at the sound
of the horse's hoofs, had snatched up a musket,
emerged from the tiny kail-yard.

Finding the intruder of her own sex, the woman's
apprehensions ceased, and she greeted Agnes with a
faint smile, quite transforming a face whose constant
expression, of late, had been one of grief and terror.
She was a comely person of thirty-five, with the simple dress and keen, alert features of the Scottish

peasant. She wore neither shoes nor stockings, and her short skirts were tucked up to afford free movement. But the most distinctive touch about her was a broad band of black ribbon tying the bright shawl in which she had wrapped her child. Agnes's eyes were resting mournfully upon this token when the woman spoke.

"Ye will be seeking someone, my lady?" she asked with solicitude, her quick discernment having already marked the stranger's gentle rank. "God help ye, an' ye had loved ones yonder!" she continued sadly, with a glance over her shoulder at the sea of heather.

"I seek my uncle, Colonel Norman Leslie," Agnes replied with an effort. "He is the only kinsman I have left on earth,—if indeed he be on earth!" And her voice sank in a despairing whisper.

"God grant he lie not wi' Davie MacLean!" wailed the woman,—"there was nae happier wife than I ten days syne, and now,—I am a widow, dowie and lane, and Sandy there is a puir orphan." She broke off, sobbing distractedly, clutching the child to her heart.

The boy, blue-eyed and yellow-haired, clad in a ragged kilt and jacket of the MacLean tartan, had stood silent hitherto, but at the mention of his father's death found speech.

"I wad ha'e fought alangside o' him, an' it hadna been for my mither!" he cried eagerly, "but she said I was ower young! I could bear a broadsword fu' stoutly, ne'ertheless, for 'twas my father taught me."

"And wad I ha'e let him gang,—the lad,—and

a' that was left me?" the woman appealed piteously; then, remembering Agnes's quest, exclaimed, "But sorrow mak's us ower selfish; ye maun forgi'e us. Sandy, lad, ken ye aught o' the leddy's kinsman? Ye were on the field that fearfu' e'en, I wat weel!"

"Wae's me, mither!" said Sandy, "when I foregithered wi' the young Locheil 'twas to lay——" here a look from his mother forestalled him, and he stopped confusedly,—"but—but I canna tell ye," he faltered, addressing Agnes.

"Oh, give me the truth," she entreated, her eyes upon his face, "the truth, cost what it will!"

"Sir Norman was killed i' the battle, lady," the boy responded to her wild appeal; "'twas I helped to bury him. When a' had fled the field, twa-three o' the leal Camerons, pretty [brave] men, forebye, cam' back the nicht, and we found puir Sir Norman lying cauld i' the heather,—ah, leddy, it waves noo aboon his grave."

Agnes heard the dreadful news with strange composure. Indeed, she had suffered so much in anticipation that this blow came with numbing power. The pallor swept her face, and her eyes grew wide with pain, but she met this utmost grief with mute endurance, too crushed for moan or outcry.

Mistress MacLean stared, appalled, at the girl's white face. "Sandy, ye will ha'e killed her!" she moaned. "Ah, Mistress, he shouldna ha'e told ye sus plainly."

But Agnes shook her head, then, with the low, measured tones of a dreamer spoke to Sandy:

"You know where he lies, you say. Take me to his grave! I will not rest till I find it!"

"Oh, Mistress, I daurna tak' ye. 'Tis a fearsome sight. And there's danger o' Cumberland——"

She interrupted him fiercely. "I'm not afraid o' Cumberland, or any o' his men! If he touches me I'll kill him!"

Her brown eyes had grown dark and ominous as a stormy sea.

"But it wadna be safe for a young lass like yoursel' to gang to that bluidy field," protested Mistress MacLean. "Wha kens how mony o' Cumberland's red corbies [crows] will be hovering yon? 'Twould be better to strike the dirk deep through that bonni white throat o' thine than meet wi' him or his hirelings!"

"I have no fear," said Agnes firmly. "But perhaps you fear for the lad, and I have no right to endanger him."

"Na, na," was the undaunted answer, "I've na fears for Sandy, and if your sad hairt is set on ganging, I'll no' prevent ye. But come ye in for a wee bit, whiles Sandy tak's heed to the horse."

At this repeated behest, Agnes entered the little cottage, but although she had tasted no food since early morning, she could eat nothing, and it was only to please her hostess that she swallowed a few mouthfuls of cordial. Before the tiny mirror, the girl tore the white snood from her hair and replaced it by a black ribbon of Mistress MacLean's.

So they set out upon their tragic errand. Before them to the north the wide moor swept in desolate waves of earth away to Culloden House and the sea, while on the south a low wall of mountains bounded the surges of green heath. Sandy MacLean strode along by the horse's side, stealing stealthy glances over the moor in search of red-coated soldiers. Agnes had grown very white; her sweet, once laughing lips were crushed into a hard line. As they slowly proceeded, Sandy described the battle, relating in quivering tones the foul deeds of "the Butcher." He told her how the dying had been murdered on the field, of how a hut where some wounded Highlanders sought refuge had been given to the flames, with all its inmates.

"Twa-and-thirty died sae, mistress, but that was nae the wurst, for at Culloden House, ye ken, the steward hid fu' nineteen o' our chieftains, wounded sair, and will ye believe it, lady, the Butcher had them a' dragged out anent the long park wa', and shot doon in cauld bluid like beasties,—Gude rest the puir sauls o' them! And when 'twas ower wi', for my ain een saw it a',—I was unco glad my father lay under sax feet o' airth whare the deils couldna touch him!" He spoke with frenzied vehemence, his cheeks burning hotly, and his hands clenched. Suddenly he sprang upon a flat boulder (it is called the Cumberland stone, because from its summit the Duke commanded the army. Sandy's act of execration is continued to this day by the Scottish wayfarers, who invariably stand upon it and curse "the Butcher") beside the road, and stamped furiously upon it, muttering fierce Gaelic curses beneath his panting breath.

Not far beyond the stone, they came upon the low, bare outlines of the graves,—ghastly islands dotting that desolate sea. Agnes gazed at them with wide-eyed shuddering. "O God!" she moaned below her breath,—and again, "O God!"

Presently they reached the fatal well, now a huge burial-cairn heaped above the slain. Pausing beside it, Sandy began to recount the tale of Alexander MacGillivray's tragic fate: the dreadful wounds he had received, the long, cold night of rain through which he lay upon the field, and then the ending of the hero's life by a sword-thrust from Cumberland's fellow-fiends. Suddenly, Agnes, whose eyes were fastened on the fearful spot, seized the boy's hand convulsively. She had caught sight of something stirring near the scattered stones by the well. The next instant she had sprung from her horse, and was kneeling beside a man who lay, half-hidden, in the trampled heather. *It was Alexander MacGillivray!*

Frightfully wounded in a dozen places, his tartans black with mingled blood and rain, he lay upon the verge of death, and yet his eyes were open, and fixed in seeming recognition on her face. Unconsciously she slipped her arm beneath him, and supported his head.

The dark cloak shrouded her figure completely, hiding all its girlish outlines, save where it parted at the waist to show the claymore fastened at her side. Her loose curls had slipped from their ribbon, and lay strewn over her shoulders; her face was rigid and colourless, all its warm young beauty frozen in the marble of despair. The dying man marked these tokens, and a faint smile flickered over his pallid features. With a mighty effort he raised the hand upon her arm, and bore it to his lips: "*My God! the Prince!*" he gasped.

A look of pitying wonder lit her face as she realised for whom he had taken her.

"Oh, Sir Alexander," she sobbed, "don't you know me,—Agnes of Auchnacarry, the foster-daughter of Locheil,—little Agnes whom you carried as a child?"

But the dying chieftain gave no heed. "Stay not here, your Majesty!" he urged in failing tones,—"Flee for your life! Think not of me;—for me it matters not!" His voice ceased, but the soul of a deathless ardour shone from his eyes. The final words came whispered, low but clear,—"God keep your Majesty! God give thee the throne of thy fathers!"

The fingers loosed their clasp upon her hand; the head drooped heavily against her breast. To Agnes's lips sprang a shuddering sob. "Oh, it is death!" she cried.

CHAPTER XXIV

"THE HELMET IS CLEFT ON THE BROW OF THE BRAVE"

"The target is torn from the arm of the just,
　The helmet is cleft on the brow of the brave;
The claymore forever in darkness must rust,
　But red is the sword of the stranger and slave."

IT was Sandy's touch upon her arm that startled Agnes from her trance of horror.

"Mistress," he whispered timidly, as if he feared to wake the dead, "ye can do nae mair. Will ye no' come wi' me?"

Agnes gently covered the figure with its plaid, and rose without speaking. Fifty yards more of trampled heath and rudely fashioned mounds, and Sandy paused. He did not speak, but simply pointed downward.

It was a solitary grave, scarce raised above the level of the moor, and marked only by a cross drawn in the earth. Here the heather throve undisturbed, as in some sheltered garden, where the fierce tide of war had never swept. The place was set apart from those huddled mounds of death, and guarded by its very isolation. Agnes gazed down upon it, motionless, speechless, with yearning eyes, unvisited by tears. Suddenly she turned to Sandy.

"Go ye back to your mother, lad," she whispered;

she will be waiting for sight of you. And tell
them at Culloden House that they must dig another
grave. There is no danger here,—and I—I would
be alone!"

When he had gone, and hers was the only figure
that breathed on the moor, she moved, and with a
low, wailing cry flung herself upon Norman Leslie's
grave.

Night crept on apace; lengthening shadows trailed
across the heath, or cast their solemn purple athwart
the distant hills. A sunset, crimson as the blood
poured out upon Culloden, was staining the sky
over Inverness; it bathed the field of death in that
ensanguined flame; and wrapped the lonely mounds
in a radiance ruddier than red tartan.

But Agnes recked not of the splendour. She lay
face downward in the heather in the utter abandonment of grief; shaken by agonised, tearless sobs that
strove convulsively for some relief, till at last the
tears came, mercifully,—mad and blinding. Ever
afterward, till her life ended, the fragrance of wet
heather recalled the desolate billows of Drummossie
Muir, and the bitterest anguish—save one—she ever
was called upon to endure.

When her passion of woe was spent, she lay exhausted utterly, as far removed from time and space
as the quiet form beneath the heather. The sunset-
fires faded;—gave place to ashes of pale amethyst.
A sudden feeling of remoteness from every living
thing,—a shrinking dread of the ghost-peopled
moor, smote on her aroused consciousness. She
started to her feet, trembling with the superstitious

terror of her Highland blood. It was then she became aware that a figure was coming toward her, a figure which paused the while she regarded it. The fear she might have felt was banished, for she saw that he wore the Highland dress. A moment more and the pale after-glow wrought a mutual revelation. Agnes Leslie and Donald Cameron gazed upon each other, like the ghosts of those companions of the garden,—the sunlit garden opposite Holyrood.

Then Donald seized her hands in the passionate clasp of his, holding her fast as if he doubted her reality, devouring those fair, loved features with wistful unbelief. Sorrow was writ upon him, in his worn and faded tartans, in his drawn and pallid face, in the hunted vigilance of his glance. Changed he was, but not more changed than she! For the tears were wet on lashes that had oftener gleamed through smiles, and the eyes were grave and piteous, that had flashed triumphant fire, and the scarlet lips, that had curled in mischievous mirth, were set in lines of woe.

"Can you guess for whom I took you, Agnes?" Donald asked. "When you rose from the heather and stood, so strangely tall, with that black cloak about you, 'twas of Prince Charlie I thought. I never saw the likeness so before. You are a beautiful woman, and he is a handsome man; but for that difference you might almost pass for each other."

"Tell me, is the Prince safe?" she cried with anxious eagerness.

"God grant so!" replied Donald. "He has foiled his enemies thus far; but the price of £30,000 which the Usurper offered for his capture in the beginning, now threatens him more darkly than ever. He has some wild plan of reaching France, and bringing aid to renew the war. Pray Heaven he prosper! But as for me, I think the last blow for Scottish liberty was struck here on Culloden, and how it failed these graves bear witness!"

His last words recalled to Agnes a sense of their present peril. "Oh, Donald, why came you hither?" she cried reproachfully. "Is not your life endangered here?"

Donald gave a bitter laugh. "There is not a place in Scotland where I am free to breathe the air! What matter where I challenge fate? A mighty impulse brought me here to-night, and have I not found *you*, Agnes?—is not that worth all hazard?" His voice, his look, alike bespoke emotion.

"Yet you did wisely, Agnes, to remind me what perils haunt this place, for on my life depends my father's fate, and that of many another gallant chief. Already we have tarried here too long. 'Tis time we reached the hiding-place. Will you share the lot of a fugitive, little playmate?"

"We are all 'fugitives' now," she answered mournfully. "Yes, let us go! For him who lies sleeping here,—he needs not our aid! *You*, Donald, risked your life to give him Christian burial; what avails *my* grief?"

"I loved him," said Donald simply. "His heart and Locheil's were as one! And better had a Cameron be dead, than faithless to his friend in life or death!"

Under cover of the rapidly darkening sky, they left the tragic field to its lone graves and deep enfolding shadows, and made their silent way toward the sheltering hills of Ross that rose, themselves like mighty shadows, beyond the level heath. Donald kept ceaseless outlook for any foe, the while he told, with the swift dramatic utterance of the Gael, the wild, heroic story of Drummossie Muir. And Agnes listened sadly, aglow with mournful ardour.

But although Donald's speech was of fierce death in battle, his thoughts were not of battle nor of death, but of a power mightier than both. The love he had never spoken lighted all the toilsome way. To him it was enough to gaze through the twilight gloom at the dim outlines of that lovely face, to walk, as her protector, by her side, and feel the light, warm pressure of her hand upon his arm. Strange that love should kindle her lamp at such a wayside altar, where the rude wind of circumstance would blow so roughly on the unguarded flame! And yet the torches of love's lighting, though blown by many a hostile gale, burn ever stronger, and with purer glow.

Agnes and Donald, each assured of a sympathetic listener, relieved their weary journey by an interchange of confidence. Agnes had always confided in Donald as freely as in a brother, and despite the latent warmth of feeling with which she regarded the handsome young Scot, she found the habit of past years too strong to conquer. Yet it is worthy of note that although she mentioned the quarrel between herself and Kenneth, she carfully omitted the part the Prince had played, and very unjustly imputed Kenneth's change of allegiance to zeal for the House of Hanover.

Locheil's hiding-place since that fatal 16th of April had been a cave in Glen Urquhart, a deep and lovely valley opening on Loch Ness. It was a distance of twenty miles from Culloden, wild and inaccessible, and therefore well adapted for a place of refuge. To the hunted chieftain, who knew the glen as he knew his own Lochaber, it was by no means difficult to elude discovery, surrounded as he was by clansmen whose loyalty would end only with life.

To this retreat came Agnes and Donald after a wild night journey through the rugged glen. Agnes found the place, however rude, a very sanctuary, and the meeting with her beloved foster-father, a deep though painful joy. Severely wounded in both ankles, and unable to stand without aid, Locheil could not come to meet her, but was forced to remain seated on his pallet, while she, forgetful of all weariness, ran swiftly through the cave, and sank, convulsed with mingled woe and rapture, at his side.

He gathered the girl into his arms, and she hid her face against his shoulder, and shook with tearless sobbing.

"My child, my poor child!" he moaned repeatedly, and "Norman, Norman Leslie!"

Startling as was the change in him, it was less of the body, than of the mind. His face wore the pallor of pain, and the deeper pallor of despair. Yet a dauntless fire still lit the sad blue eyes; a lofty courage, nurtured in defeat.

When both were a little calmer, Agnes spoke of Alexander MacGillivray, and the pathetic fallacy which had seen in her the beloved Prince. Locheil listened with painful interest.

"It was no fantasy of death, dear child. I, too, have seen the resemblance, and wondered at it. You are more alike than ever in these days of sorrow," he added, sighing, "for you have grown to wear the Stuart look,—the woe that haunted Mary's eyes, and now looks out from his,—poor fated Prince!"

"But if he reach France, Cousin Donald—" began Agnes with the quickly awakened hope of youth.

"France?" cried Locheil almost fiercely: "France? How has France helped us? Did France save Mary of Scotland when she lay at Elizabeth's mercy? Did France stay the hands of the Regicides in the days of the martyr Charles, even though the Queen who shared his throne was a French princess. And what support gave she to James the Eighth when he sought to win his crown? And what of our own Prince Charlie, whom France has deceived and trifled with, promising gold she never gave till all was over, and men and arms that ne'er saw Scottish soil! France is a false coquette, buying us with vain favour, flinging us smiles and kisses, when her fancy pleases;—frowning on our ventures, leaving us to battle with despair, when that fancy veers!"

He made an effort to rise, then sank back, burying his head in his hands.

"To think of Scotland lying at her foemen's mercy—trodden beneath the heel of that demon

Cumberland!" He staggered up and stretched his hands toward Heaven in desperate appeal. "If I escape his clutches I vow I will never rest till Scotland has regained her ancient glory!"

What fate was theirs,—these men of noble hearts, —whom even foes must reverence and admire,—to see their high hopes trodden in the dust,—the roses of defeat,—to see their ancient honours blotted out, like stars at midnight. They were martyrs of destiny, faithful to a fated memory. Was their devotion less because so futile? Great is the courage of victory;—greater beyond words is the courage of defeat!

CHAPTER XXV

"THE SUN IN HIS GLORY HAS LOOK'D ON OUR SORROW"

"The sun in his glory has look'd on our sorrow,
  The stars have wept blood over hamlet and lea."

THE three weeks which Agnes spent at Locheil's retreat were set in such peaceful contrast to the days that followed and preceded them, that they seemed like isles of rest in the midst of a turbulent sea. Bereft of her natural kinsmen, Agnes's heart clung with heightened affection to those whom Highland custom had made close as kin. Her one desire was to remain with her foster-father, and share his destiny, however darksome. But to this, Locheil refused to listen. Over his head fate hovered sable-winged; at any hour might the vulture swoop. To keep Agnes with him might be to risk for her imprisonment or worse.

"No, my child, it cannot be!" he said insistently, "though parting will wring this sad heart of mine to breaking. I must find for you a safer refuge than the cavern of an outlawed chief, who is forced to skulk in his den like a hunted wolf." The last words came bitterly, from the wounded depths of his proud spirit.

Agnes raised her eyes beseechingly to his; instinctively her fingers clasped each other.

"Oh, Cousin Donald, do not compel me to leave

you," she entreated piteously, "for my heart tells me that if I do I shall never see you more!"

"Ah, Agnes, Agnes," murmured Locheil sadly, "why will you double my distress by seeking to dissuade me! I could not sleep one hour in peace, with the knowledge that my black doom overshadowed you. Listen, dear child, and make no resistance, for all is purposed for your good. One of two courses lies before you: you must either return to Edinburgh, or seek refuge with some of our kinsmen in Skye. There is yet another way,—Sir Duncan Forbes would gladly receive you at Culloden House, but—God pity me!—I would not send you there!"

"I will not go to Edinburgh!" cried Agnes. "And surely it were better for me to stay here, Cousin Donald, than to attempt a journey through the Highlands. Who knows but a ship from France——"

"One chance in a thousand!—Do not torture me, child, by tempting me to keep you! Scotland is a conquered country, and Cumberland a fiend incarnate. In a month no woman—no child—will be safe in all this northland!" He broke off, gazing at her in horror, his face dark with misgiving. A doubt had seized him as to whether he ought to send her from him. But he quickly mastered it, and continued: "The safest way, dear child, is for you to seek refuge with the MacDonalds of Kingburgh, in Skye. They are kinsmen and true to the cause; and with them, if God be willing, you may dwell safely." He sighed deeply, and murmured: "Yea, in the shadow of Thy wings will I make my refuge, till these calamities be overpast."

Presently he roused himself from the reverie into which he had fallen, and said with decision: " Angus MacDonald shall go with you; he knows every mountain and glen in Scotland. The journey will not be arduous; at worst you cannot encounter the dangers and privations with which my path is strewn. Follow the Great Glen to Lochaber, strike northward through Loch Arkaig to Knoydart,—it is all the MacDonalds' country,—and from thence you may easily embark for Skye. But you must be supplied with a pass,—that I will find means to secure from Sir Duncan. He will not refuse that kindness to the child of his old-time friend."

Donald, for manifold reasons, opposed his father's decision, and Agnes, finding him a strong advocate, began to nourish faint hopes of ultimate triumph. It was not until she became convinced that her opposition increased Locheil's suffering, that she yielded to his wish.

Donald then proposed to accompany Agnes on her westward journey.

" She shall not go with only Angus for protector!" he insisted hotly.

" You seem to forget, my son," said Locheil rather sternly, " that a man with a heavy price on his head would hardly afford a maiden much protection." To himself he said: " If fortune should relent, if I reach France in safety, perhaps Agnes and Donald may yet wed and live in happiness, for all that is past and gone."

He had said more than he had intended, for at the mention of Donald's danger, Agnes turned very pale, and uttered a stifled cry. Nor would all Donald's dissuasions allay her fears.

When the moment for parting came, and the three were alone in the cave, Agnes clung wildly to Locheil, unable to tear herself from the clasp of those fatherly arms. With a breaking heart she turned from him to Donald, whose eyes met hers with a strange hesitation in which pleading mingled.

"Oh, Donald!" she cried, taking his hand, "it is only God above knows when we shall meet again. Will you not kiss me, Donald?"

That moment all the barriers were swept away. Donald was kneeling beside her, passionately kissing the hands he held.

"Agnes!" he cried, "I cannot give you a brother's kiss, and a lover's kiss I have no right to give."

For answer she raised her lovely face, and he pressed upon her lips the only caress of his they had ever known since the days of a child's unconscious kisses.

In the solemn memory of that kiss they parted.

. . . . .

Besides Angus for body-guard, Agnes had for company Angus's sister, Jeanie, a girl of seventeen, who spoke only Gaelic. As Locheil had advised, they followed the Great Glen, not along the highway built by General Wade, but through devious paths well known to Angus, threading that lovely chain of lakes which clasps the Highlands like a band of pearls.

On the afternoon of the second day they passed

Fort Augustus,—now garrisoned by the enemy, and well beyond it, ventured into the highway. Suddenly, Agnes was startled by a Gaelic oath from Angus, who, with Jeanie, rode respectfully behind her, and, turning, beheld him struggling in the grip of a dozen red-coats. Angus, faithful to the last, cried in Gaelic: "Fly! Fly, my lady! Give ''Phrionnsa' his head; he will carry you free!"

Powerless to aid him, Agnes obeyed, and with Jeanie's terrified screams in her ears, urged the "Prince" to his utmost speed. "'Phrionnsa! 'Phrionnsa Teàrlach, save me!" she cried imploringly, and the noble horse responded eagerly.

When she was sufficiently beyond pursuit to pause and consider her course, she stood appalled at her plight. Save for three sovereigns, Angus had all her money, though fortunately she wore the passport stitched in her gown. Her first impulse was to return to Locheil, but she had learned that there were troops between her and Glen Urquhart. The only choice remaining was to pursue her solitary course toward Skye.

Accordingly, she continued on her way, though with increasing fears, and deep anxiety for Angus's uncertain fate.

By sunset she had reached Locheil's country, the scene of her birth, and of her happiest years. As in a dream she approached Loch Arkaig, and with leaping heart beheld the ancient walls of Auchnacarry lifted between her and the setting sun. Lone and deserted though it stood, she was strongly tempted to venture thither to catch one last glimpse of the loved hearth-stone, twined with hallowed memories. But a curious instinct restrained her, and instead, she made a cautious circuit of the castle, and finally climbed a lofty hill behind it. Half-way to the summit she dismounted, and knelt amid the heather to gaze her long farewell. The castle below her was merging darkly into the mist of twilight; she could barely distinguish it from its wall of trees.

Suddenly she started forward, quivering,—with horror-quickened breath. A crimson flicker leaped athwart the ivied battlements, sprang aloft, and cast its deadly glow afar. *They had fired the castle!* Agnes uttered one stricken cry, and then grew strangely still! The red destruction reared its giant horror, flung out demon arms to clasp the mighty walls, and leaping balefully toward heaven, defied the stars.

This castle, where her eyes had opened to the light, whence had passed her father's parting soul, where she and Donald had been happy children,—whose ancient hearth had once made all her world,—Merciful Father!—must this be the end,—this cruel pyre of devouring flame!

The night air in the Highlands was chill with mist, but Agnes hardly felt the cold, so held was she by fearful fascination of the scene. She knew that the Duke's soldiers must be close at hand,—perhaps around her in the woods, yet she was hardly conscious of any fear; she was spell-bound as in some frightful dream.

Now and then she saw forms, silhouetted black against the red glare of the flames, and caught the glint of gold lace on a scarlet coat. She gazed fixedly at the work of destruction, her eyes aching with unshed tears,—the tears that would not fall, although her heart was breaking. At last the roof of the castle crashed inward with tremendous force, flinging upward a shower of golden sparks like shattered stars. Its fall was greeted by an exultant cheer from the English soldiery, who hailed the ruin of this mountain eyry with shouts of "Destruction to the rebels," and "Death to the Pretender!"

Agnes could bear no more; she sank to her knees among the heather, and covered her tearless eyes to hide the fearful sight.

As she crouched there, shivering, her trembling fingers shutting out the glare, her muffled ears caught the sound of footsteps crackling through the underbrush. She sprang up, with raised pistol, but the approaching feet were too light for a man's; an instant later a small figure ran toward her through the brightening moonlight,—a little boy of seven or eight, with flaxen hair and terrified blue eyes.

"O mither, mither," he wailed, "where gang ye, mither, that I canna find ye?"

The girl caught him to her, crying softly, "Hush, thee, laddie, dinna ye see the soldiers?"

Even in that dim light her quick eyes had distinguished the Cameron tartan. She had recognised him as the little son of Locheil's brother, Dr. Archibald, whom she had not seen since his babyhood.

"Ye'll be ane o' Locheil's clansmen, laddie?" she questioned tenderly, soothing his passionate sobs.

"Aye, that I am," he burst out, still weeping, though more from rage than grief. "What wadna I gi'e to be a man grown, and ha'e a shot at them! When they fired the castle 'twas 'Death to the Camerons!' they cried!"

Then, suddenly freeing himself from the girl's detaining hold, he faced round, and shook his small clenched fist at the flaming ruins. "Ye deils!" he cried, his small voice almost choked with passion, "ye deils!"

Then grief drowned his anger like a quenched flame, and he clung again to Agnes, whispering:

"O mither! mither! She fled the nicht with the wee bairnie, and whare I dinna ken! O mither! mither!"

"Dinna ye greet, Malcolm, Cousin Agnes winna leave ye," she whispered, "we'll gang fin' your mither, and we'll gang awa now, before the red soldiers find us."

Without another word she caught his hand in hers, and casting one last shuddering glance at the glowing ruins, mounted and lifted the boy to a seat behind her; then put the horse to a gallop, nor paused till full five miles of shadowy forest lay between them and the fell destroyers. By aid of the full moon Agnes descried a small pathway, branching from the road and winding steeply up the mountainside. She instantly recognised the path as one which she and Donald Cameron had climbed years before in order to reach a little clearing near the mountaintop. She knew the place would afford a safe shelter for the night, for it was too high to be easily reached by marauders. She therefore dismounted and, leading "Prince Charlie," began the steep ascent, arriving after some half-an-hour's climb at the sylvan refuge, a tiny open space, thick-carpeted with heather, and closely rimmed with firs. Here they could spend the night with small fear of disturbance, since their enemies were far below them, and there was no reason to think they would climb so high.

The boy lay down in the heather, with his head in her lap, and Agnes unwound her plaid and covered him with it.

The stars shone down upon the mountain's face, and their golden lustre recalled the starry sparks that had risen from burning Auchnacarry. The boy sobbed in his sleep, but to Agnes's aching eyes there came no tears. It was not till three o'clock, when the moon was setting, and the mist was creeping up over the mountain, that she wearily fell asleep, to be awakened less than an hour later by the first rays of the rising sun.

And the sun rose upon a scene of desolation! Where but a week before, peaceful hamlets, mountain farms, and rugged castles had decked the matchless picture, now the cruel smoke streamed upward from a thousand ruined hearth-stones! All the natural beauty of this glorious land remained unaltered;—loch and burn rippled silver, field and brae glistened green, the lower mountains towered dark with pines, and Ben Nevis raised his coronet of snow;—but the homes of men had perished like flowers of the forest before a merciless storm. The desolation was complete! Dust and ashes, and the brooding spirit of pitiless destruction! But not yet complete was the sacrifice of Scotland for her hunted king! For the merciless sword of her conquerors was stretched out still; there was yet more to suffer and to dare!

CHAPTER XXVI

"BEHOLD, WHERE HE FLIES ON HIS DESOLATE PATH!"

"Lo! anointed by Heaven with the vials of wrath,
Behold, where he flies on his desolate path!"

THE curse invoked on Scotland by an earlier age had been fulfilled. The traveller might ride for days through that unhappy country *without seeing a chimney smoke, or hearing a cock crow!* Agnes and the boy, after a week of disconsolate wandering, found a clansman of Glengarry, who knew the hiding-place of Mistress Archibald Cameron, and Agnes entrusted Malcolm to his keeping, and proceeded on her westward way. Had it not been for the food she carried with her, she would have suffered serious want, for the few dwellings that had escaped the flames had been utterly stripped of all means of sustenance, and their inmates driven out, at Cumberland's fiendish command, to starve on the barren mountains.

. . . . .

Agnes sat on the steps of Ormaclade House, in the island of South Uist, and gazed at the sparkling sea. After her adventure at Auchnacarry her journey had been comparatively uneventful. She had easily secured passage for Skye, but, owing to war ships in the channel in wait for the hunted Prince, had been obliged to land on South Uist. Here she had been warmly welcomed by Lord and Lady Clan ranald, who, like the MacDonalds of Skye, were her distant kinsmen.

It was now late in June, and she had been at Ormaclade House for two weeks. Her weary wandering was ended, yet the ache at her heart was no less poignant; rather, it throbbed the more painfully, unassuaged by excitement or danger.

As she withdrew her eyes from their dreary contemplation of the sea, they fell upon the figure of an old man, who was approaching the house. Recognising him as Donald MacLeod of Skye, the pilot who had brought her to South Uist, Agnes rose to accost him, astonished as she did so, to see him beckon her toward him with a look of extreme solicitude. Obeying his wary gesture, she went to meet him, and was still further startled by his slipping a bit of paper into her hand, and whispering hurriedly in Gaelic: "Fail not, for the sake of one you love!"

An instant later he had disappeared.

In the secrecy of her room she read these words: "Follow MacLeod to the hill-top at moonrise to-night. *A life depends upon your loyalty!*"

Agnes's heart leaped with wild emotion. Could it be Donald she was thus to meet? Or the "gentle Lochiel"? It could not be the Prince, for he was known to be concealed in Skye. She spent the day in excited ponderings over the mystery.

Agnes retired early to her chamber. The moon rose at ten, and a little before that hour she stole quietly out into the late June twilight. Behind Ormaclade House stretched the rocky uplands, destitute of trees, which in summer afforded pasturage for vast herds of cattle. For their own convenience the shepherds lived in tiny huts, or sheilings, erected on the hills, and it was to one of these that MacLeod conducted Agnes. It had taken an hour's climb to reach the spot, along a path imperfectly lighted by the summer gloaming, and the bright disc of the rising moon.

Arrived at the sheiling, MacLeod threw open the door, and bidding Agnes wait within, vanished outside. The girl cast a single glance around the hut, and, finding it empty, sank with a weary sigh of disappointment into a seat by the rude table. Forsaken enough seemed the place at that midnight hour. The moonbeams, streaming in at the low window, lit with melancholy splendour the girl's pale, pensive face and sable dress. Either to banish a sense of desolation, or to relieve the pent-up passion of her heart, Agnes began to sing,—softly, and half below her breath:

> "Come boat me owre, come row me owre,
>   Come boat me owre to Charlie;
> I'll gi'e John Ross anither bawbee
>   To boat me owre to Charlie.
> We'll owre the water, we'll owre the sea,
>   We'll owre the water to Charlie;
> Come weal, come woe, we'll gather and go,
>   And live or die wi' Charlie."

A figure had stolen into the hut, and lurked in the deepest shadow, but the girl was unaware of its presence. The fervent self-devotion of her song absorbed her wholly.

> "I swear by moon and stars sae bright,
>   And the sun that glances early,
> If I had twenty thousand lives,
>   I'd gi'e them a' for Charlie.
>
> . . . . .
>
> "I ance had sons, I now ha'e nane,
>   I bred them toiling sairly,
> But I would bear them a' again,
>   And lose them a'—*for Charlie!*"

On the last line the voice broke in a gasping sob, and the next instant the low sound of weeping filled the room. Those soft, suppressed sobs were a thousand times more piteous than any violent grief, and after listening to them for a moment or two the Prince could endure it no longer. Noiselessly he came forward into the brilliant square of moonlight in which Agnes sat. Her golden head was bowed upon her outstretched hands, and her slender body heaved with broken sobs. Half-hesitant, Charles drew near, and touched her softly.

"*Agnes!*" he whispered, "*Agnes!*"

She lifted her head from her hands, and gazed at him intently, though without surprise, the tear-drops on her lashes shining like bright pearls. From head to foot he was forlornly ragged, his face pale and haggard, his long fair hair falling in wild disorder about his shoulders, but she had recognised him instantly.

"Prince Charlie! Prince Charlie!" she sobbed aloud, in a rapture of despairing joy.

Before he could prevent her, she had flung herself at his feet, and kissed the hand with which he sought to raise her.

He gazed with a shudder at her sombre gown, and at the black ribbon binding her bright hair, for he knew they were worn because of him. He touched despondently a dark fold of her dress; "Sir Norman?" he whispered, and at the title her eyes brightened, and a little colour crept into her face. She felt a thrill of mournful pride that he should name her uncle thus; yet it was only the crumbling ashes of honour on a dead hearth-stone,—the faded roses of that glory that had bloomed so fair at Holyrood!

. . . . .

Although by miraculous fortune the Prince had thus far eluded every foe, he was now surrounded on all sides, and capture appeared inevitable. But fate had not reckoned upon Agnes Leslie; her wit and courage were weapons yet to be drawn for his defence. Charles had barely finished relating his dilemma before Agnes's fertile mind had concocted a plan of escape, to which, before leaving the hut, she secured the Prince's consent.

It was long past twelve when she set out for Ormacade House to confide in Lady Clanranald, and the two spent the rest of the night in excited discussion. Agnes's passport insured not only free passage for herself, but for her man-servant and maid as well, and Agnes proposed that the Prince, suitably disguised, should accompany her as maid on the voyage to Skye. To this Lady Clanranald assented eagerly and suggested that Neil MacEachain, who was tutor at Ormaclade House, should both act as guide and supply the part of man-servant.

The next six days were passed in secret prepara

ions, but by the evening of June 27 the plan was
so far perfected that Agnes and Lady Clanranald
betook themselves with the necessary articles of disguise to the Prince's hiding-place,—a cave on the
neighboring island of Benbecula. Charles was in
the act of cooking his own dinner, a circumstance
which moved to tears both his fair spectators. The
Prince, observing their distress, exclaimed cheerily:
"Oh, I must occasionally doff my crown, and perhaps 'twould be as well for all kings to endure the
same ordeal."

Presently he pronounced the dinner ready, and
they all sat down to partake of it. Hardly had they
begun, however, when the alarming news arrived that
a party of Hanoverian troops, in pursuit of the
Prince, had landed on the island, and that another
detachment had reached Ormaclade. Lady Clanranald, thoroughly frightened, hastened homeward to
divert suspicion, while the rest, aroused and anxious,
were left to face the coming night.

A tiny fire was kindled on the stone floor of the
cavern, and before it Agnes sat, half-kneeling, a
loaded pistol lying in her lap, her head, alert and
lifted, turned toward the opening where Neil MacEachain, Donald MacLeod, and their two companions, kept silent watch. Beside her, so near that
her outstretched hand could touch him, lay the royal
fugitive, sunk in exhausted slumber. After much
persuasion Charles had been induced to occupy the
bed of bracken prepared for him, and had
hardly stretched himself upon it before sleep came.
The girl's eyes lingered, with the firelight, upon his

upturned face, from which the fair hair fell away, showing that look of rare distinction, which neither suffering nor defeat could hide. A sigh almost a sob heaved Agnes's bosom at the memory of a pictured face,—how like this, yet how different, that slept on Norman Leslie's breast beneath Culloden's heather.

At dawn the wanderers left the kindly cave, and proceeded to the beach, where they ensconced themselves behind a giant rock to wait for sundown. Before leaving the cave, however, Agnes aided Charles to don his disguise: a gown of flowered linen, a light-coloured quilted petticoat, a white apron, and a mantle of dun camlet made with a hood after the Irish fashion. He was now appropriately attired in maid's costume, but as garments do not make the man, they did not,—in this case,—make the woman and Agnes remarked to herself somewhat ruefully his unfeminine appearance. "Nothing will ever make him resemble a woman, much less a servant He has the king writ so clearly on his face that I marvel if others see it not." But she did not impart this reflection to Charles.

In the lee of the rock the day wore slowly on Once they were seized with alarm at beholding four wherries, manned by soldiers, approaching the shore but by the time they had hidden themselves in the heather, the boats had passed out of sight.

The lingering summer daylight at last began to fade, and in the gathering darkness they embarked for Skye.

CHAPTER XXVII

"OVER THE SEA TO SKYE"

"Speed, bonnie boat, like a bird on the wing,
  Onward the sailors cry;
Carry the lad that's born to be king,
  Over the sea to Skye."

THE little boat, with its precious freight, had not sailed far from shore, before the waves, already ruffled, became darkly agitated, and the wind, blowing fiercely from the northwest, foretold a tempest. But the fugitives preferred to trust themselves to the mercy of the sea, choosing rather a grave beneath its waters, than the cruel fate man held in store. Agnes and the disguised Prince sat upon the gunwale of the boat, and gazed across the heaving ocean, fast shrouding itself in the dismal pall of darkness. Agnes, looking down into those seething billows, whose salt spray wet her face, would gladly have prayed, save for the Prince, that those wild surges might close over her, and still forever the weary aching of her heart.

As if he guessed at her despondent thoughts, Charles began to sing a spirited ballad called, "The Restoration," and followed it by several humorous tales, which restored the little company to at least a semblance of cheerfulness. And great was their need of encouragement, for the prospect was grim enough; foes behind them, foes around them, and, doubtless, foes before them.

As the night advanced, and the storm increased in fury, Charles urged Agnes to shelter herself in the bottom of the boat, and this, after some demur, she was induced to do. The comparative warmth of her refuge, and the regular rise and fall of the vessel combined to lull her into drowsiness, and presently into sleep.*

Disturbed by a noise in the boat, she awoke in alarm, and started from her recumbent posture to find the Prince bending over her, with his hands extended above her head to protect her from injury during the movements of the boatmen. He soothed her alarm with tender solicitude, and gently arranging her plaid about her, bade her continue her slumber. But sleep would not come again, and seeing her shivering in the chill wind, the Prince produced a small flask of wine, which Lady Clanranald had given him, and insisted that she should drink it, although himself refusing to touch a drop.

"Do you think I would deprive you of the few comforts procurable in the wretched situation in which I have placed you? They are yours, Mistress Leslie, not only by right of sex, but by right of courage and devotion!"

---

* All who know the history of the "'45" will observe that from this point the adventures of Agnes Leslie coincide with those of Flora MacDonald, the heroic preserver of Prince Charlie. But those who doubt the reality of Agnes Leslie may find her name inscribed on the pages of an old Bible in Dundee.

"Over the Sea to Skye"

And to this chivalrous regard she could only murmur a confused acknowledgment.

Fearing lest any light should attract a hostile ship, the crew were soon compelled to row in utter darkness; when black midnight fell they drew in their oars, and left the boat to toss at will in the wild cradle of the Atlantic.

. . . . .

The first faint flicker of returning day was tinting the vast horizon with pale primrose. Beneath it lay the ocean, the hue of polished steel, save where the curling billows caught the glow of sunrise. There was no land in sight, nor did they know how far they might have drifted from their course. But they continued to row onward, and soon beheld, as in some dim mirage, the lofty peaks and rugged cliffs of Skye. Agnes and her "handmaid" stood in the bow, and scanned the shore with anxious eyes. Slowly the oarsmen commenced to pull the boat toward a deep bay not far ahead. Timely indeed was their caution, for they had hardly approached the strand when they caught sight of a number of soldiers in hostile uniform, who, on beholding the little vessel, shouted, "Land, or we fire!" and followed this command by snatching up their guns. The boatmen bent to their oars with all speed, but before they could row out of range, the bullets began to hum about them, and to clip the water on every side.

"Never mind the villains!" cried the dauntless Prince to the boatmen, and received the devoted answer, "We care not for ourselves, but for your Royal Highness."

"Oh, no fear for me!" he responded gaily, then seizing the girl's arm, exclaimed, "In God's name, Agnes, do not stand here! Lie down out of reach of those missiles! I would a thousand times rather resign myself into the enemy's hands than any hurt should befall *you!*"

But Agnes, quite as obdurate as he, returned unflinchingly, "Not one inch will I move, your Majesty, till *you* are safe! Your life is immeasurably more valuable than mine!"

A second shower of bullets put an end to this lively argument, and Charles stretched himself flat in the boat, compelling Agnes, with gentle force, to accompany him, nor did he allow her to move till they were well out at sea. As he aided her to rise, he said laughingly, "You are a rebellious subject, guilty of high treason to your sovereign. What penalty shall I impose upon you?"

"I must throw myself upon your Majesty's mercy!" she replied in the same playful vein.

"As your king is a Scot, you shall go *scot* free this once. But remember, beauteous rebel, the next time I shall exact heavier punishment."

He spoke lightly, and yet he sighed, perhaps recalling the tempting forfeit he had longed to claim from those fair lips so lately near his own.

Skirting the island northward for several miles, they again turned shoreward, and finally succeeded in landing not far from Monkstat House, the home of Sir Alexander MacDonald.

Sir Alexander, a zealous Hanoverian, was even now with Cumberland at Fort Augustus, but his wife, Lady Margaret, was quite differently inclined, and in fact had already communicated with the royal refugee during his wanderings. Agnes, who knew Lady Margaret well, and indeed had visited at her house, determined to confide to her the perilous secret. Accordingly, she left the Prince on the beach, seated upon the trunk she had brought from Ormaclade, and set off for Lady Margaret's abode.

Upon arriving she was straightway ushered into the long parlour, where she found Mistress MacDonald entertaining *Lieutenant MacLeod of the militia.* This disagreeable surprise was somewhat counteracted, however, by the presence of MacDonald of Kingsburgh, the ardent Jacobite at whose house she had intended to seek refuge. If she could but draw him apart, and communicate her startling intelligence! But she must first greet Lady Margaret, be introduced to the Lieutenant, and exchange with him several idle platitudes, the while her mind was racked by keen solicitude for "Betty Burke."

The Lieutenant, on his part, much impressed by the beauty of this chance acquaintance, had no desire to end the conversation, and found a means of continuing it,—his duty being to search every boat that landed,—by asking her a vast variety of questions as to her journey and her destination. These she answered with becoming readiness, and without betraying the least embarrassment, although meantime conscious of a hysterical desire to laugh.

At length dinner was announced, without the slightest chance for confidence having arrived. Lady MacDonald, unsuspecting, urged the Lieutenant to to remain, and Agnes, powerless to escape without exciting suspicion, found herself escorted out on the Lieutenant's arm. At table she exerted every effort to amuse her companion, and so far succeeded as to keep him in constant laughter at her brilliant sallies, little guessing for what purpose they were framed.

In the midst of the meal, while Lady Margaret and the Lieutenant were engaged in a merry altercation, Kingsburgh beckoned Agnes into one of the deep windows, for the ostensible purpose of showing her a wonderful rose in the garden. Bending to look at it, Agnes leaned close to her kinsman, whispering, "The Prince is on the beach in woman's clothes. For Heaven's sake, Cousin Kingsburgh, hide him!"

Kingsburgh, with rare composure, answered only by pressing her hand, and turned toward the table, observing merrily, "Well, we cannot live on the sight of beauteous flowers; have you left us any viands?"

Immediately dinner was over, the Lieutenant took his departure, remarking with an ardent glance at Agnes that he should not forget their pleasant meeting, a sentiment,—barring the adjective,—which the girl could reciprocate.

He had hardly vanished, when Kingsburgh hurried Lady Margaret aside, and informed her of the startling intelligence. Alarmed beyond measure, she uttered a loud scream, exclaiming, "Merciful Heaven, we are all ruined!" But Kingsburgh, naturally firm and fearless, speedily soothed her terror.

"You shall incur no danger, Lady Margaret," he said, "for I myself will hide the Prince at Kingsburgh House. I am an old man, and I would rather die for my king with a rope about my neck, than await death in my bed."

With these heroic words he left her, and supplying himself with provisions, set out in search of the disguised Prince. After Charles had partaken of food, the two proceeded on foot along the highway, directing their steps toward Kingsburgh House, which stood several miles to the southward.

Meanwhile Agnes and Neil MacEachain, taking reluctant farewell of Lady Margaret, turned their horses' heads in the same direction. As they rode rapidly, they soon overtook Kingsburgh and his "female" companion, and passing them with a casual bow to the gentleman, continued onward at the same swift pace, as if their destination were quite different from that of the wayfarers.

When the riders had disappeared, Kingsburgh and the Prince left the main road, and took a bypath leading through the fields. In truth, they both felt immensely relieved at thus escaping further notice, for during their walk they had been greatly annoyed by the people coming from church, who had stared open-mouthed at the extraordinary woman, and commented audibly upon her unusual height and clumsiness. Some of them, in fact, went so far as to question Kingsburgh on the subject, but he skilfully parried their inquiries, and finally dismissed the inquisitors with the well-calculated remark: "Oh, sirs, cannot you let alone talking of worldly affairs on the Sabbath, and have patience till another day?"

Charles, indeed, quite forgot the part he was playing;—bowed when he should have curtsied, held up his skirts too high, or let them hang too low, and altogether presented anything but a womanly appearance. As they followed the unfrequented path, Kingsburgh could not refrain from remarking, "Your enemies call you a pretender; but if you be, I can tell you you are the worst at your trade I ever saw," to which the Prince, much amused, responded merrily: "Why, I believe my enemies do me as great injustice in this as in some more important particulars. I have all my life despised assumed characters, and am, perhaps, the worst dissimulator in the world."

It was nearly midnight when Charles and his protector, joined by Agnes, reached Kingsburgh House, which was situated in the centre of the island, on the shores of a small lake. The mansion was somewhat in need of repair, and presented a still more gloomy aspect from the fact that all its occupants had long since retired to bed. Kingsburgh conducted Agnes and the Prince into the great hall and despatched a sleepy servant to waken his wife. Lady Kingsburgh, however, supposing the new-comers to be intimate friends, did not rise, but having given directions for the comfort of the guests, was about to fall asleep again, when her little daughter ran into the room crying excitedly, "My father has brought home the strangest woman I ever saw. He says she is Mistress Leslie's maid, but I don't believe it."

Kingsburgh himself now entered, and in anxious tones bade her dress immediately. Alarmed by his manner, she hastily obeyed, and descended to the hall to greet the travellers. Having warmly welcomed Agnes, she turned with hesitation toward the suspicious stranger. To her astonishment, the so-called maid advanced, and, bending, pressed to hers a cheek roughly unfeminine. Speechless with fright, Lady Kingsburgh disengaged herself, and rushed from the room to seek her husband.

"Alexander, this is no maid!" she cried, "'tis some poor exiled nobleman in disguise. Think you he can know aught of the Prince?"

But Kingsburgh, taking her hands, said gravely: "My dear, *this is the Prince himself!*"

CHAPTER XXVIII

"WITH THE BLOODHOUNDS THAT BARK FOR THY FUGITIVE KING"

"I tell thee Culloden's dread echoes shall ring
  With the bloodhounds that bark for thy fugitive king."

"GRACIOUS Heaven, the Prince! Then we'll all be hanged!" gasped Lady Kingsburgh at this alarming revelation.

"We can die but once," said Kingsburgh with composure. "Could we ever die in a better cause? We are only doing an act of humanity such as our Christian faith enjoins toward prince or beggar. Besides, look at Mistress Leslie,—a lass not long out of her teens. 'Twas she proposed this project, and willingly engaged in all this danger, and yet she bears herself as fearlessly as if 'twere but a jest. There," he continued, "make haste with the supper;—eggs, butter, cheese, anything that can be quickly prepared."

"Eggs, butter, cheese!" echoed Lady Kingsburgh with scorn. "A fine supper for a prince,—he'll never look at it!"

"Alas, wife," said Kingsburgh, "you little know how this poor Prince has fared of late! Our supper will seem a banquet to him. Besides, to make a formal dinner would cause suspicion. So make haste and join us at table."

Completely overawed by such a prospect, Lady Kingsburgh ejaculated: "Do you expect *me* to come to supper? I know not how to behave in the presence of majesty!"

"But you *must* come," Kingsburgh insisted; "the Prince would not touch a mouthful without you; and you'll find it no difficult matter to behave before him, —he is so kindly and gracious."

The private drawing-room in which supper was speedily served, presented a curious scene. The strangely attired Prince, who occupied the place of honour, seated Agnes, toward whom he always observed the etiquette due a princess, on his right hand, and Lady Kingsburgh on his left. The impromptu feast progressed merrily, in outward guise at least, for each one strove for cheerfulness, although the laughter on the lips belied the fear at the heart. In the midst of the banquet Charles rose, and drank with princely grace: "To the health and prosperity of Kingsburgh House."

The supper ended, Agnes and Lady MacDonald withdrew, leaving the Prince and his host to converse over their wine till toward morning. The girl followed her kinswoman upstairs into the great chamber, used only upon state occasions, and there assisted in spreading the massive, curtained bed with the finest linen the house afforded for the Prince's reception. Having completed their task, Lady Kingsburgh glanced anxiously about the room, and took up her candle.

"Think you that all is as it should be?" she questioned doubtfully. "This house is no fit place to entertain a prince,—above all one so bonnie as he! But now we must to bed ourselves. You shall sleep with me, Agnes, and tell me every word of your adventures."

But so exhausted was Agnes, and so much relieved by the Prince's temporary safety, that she fell asleep before Lady Kingsburgh could extinguish the candle, and the tale of her adventures was necessarily postponed till morning.

．　．　．　．　．

Charles, who for two long months had hardly known the luxury of a comfortable bed, or more than four hours' consecutive slumber, did not waken till he was aroused at one o'clock by Kingsburgh himself, who inquired solicitously how his guest had rested.

"I never had a sweeter slumber in my life," the Prince exclaimed, "not even in Holyrood, nor before my hopes of glory set me dreaming of the throne." He sighed as he concluded, perhaps in memory of his careless boyhood, or of the golden dreams which had gilded the sombre shadows of Holyrood.

Kingsburgh dispelled this reverie by observing "You must wear your female attire until you have left the house, in order that no suspicion be aroused among the servants, but lest the secret of your disguise should have been disclosed, I should counsel you to change it at the first opportunity. Yet there is one article I think you may shift with safety,—and that is your shoes,—or what is left of them. Here are a pair I have never worn, which I vow will fit you finely."

"I shall hardly miss my old ones," cried the Prince, laughing,—"they and my toes had long forsworn company. But what are you going to do with them?" he inquired suddenly, for Kingsburgh, picking up the tattered footgear, was hanging them in a corner of the room.

"Why," he responded, "when you are fairly settled at St. James's, I shall introduce myself by shaking these shoes at you, to remind you of your night's entertainment and protection under my roof."

Charles smiled, though rather mournfully, at the good man's vagary, and bade him keep his promise.

It was after Kingsburgh had left his guest, that Mistress MacDonald, pausing outside the Prince's door, said wistfully: "If I could but get a lock of his Royal Highness's hair for a keepsake, how happy should be! Will you not entreat him for me, Agnes? You know him so much better than I."

"But I think his Royal Highness is not yet awake," Agnes objected, "and I could not think of disturbing his rest."

At that moment the Prince himself exclaimed, "I am awake, ladies, and prepared to grant any wish in my power."

Accordingly he threw open the door and showed himself attired in a velvet dress of Kingsburgh's.

"'Richard's himself again,' for a short hour," he announced to them merrily. "This is my morning-room, and you are my court come to offer your homage. State your petition, fair damsel," he added, addressing Agnes.

Responding to his playful mood, the girl dropped lightly on one knee, and repeated Lady Kingsburgh's request.

Charles took her hand, and raised her with grave ceremony, saying, " Since you desire this token, your monarch grants it, though knowing that 'tis only your devotion that makes a thing so worthless aught of value."

As he spoke he handed her to a chair, and kneeling bowed upon her lap that royal golden head upon which so great a price was set.

" Cut any lock you will, sweet lady, in token of more substantial favours. I hardly think the House of Hanover,—should I be captured,—will miss a lock or two."

He felt the fingers tremble that rested on his head, and a quick shudder agitate the figure.

" God forbid! your Highness," the girl cried tremulously. " God forbid that such a fate befall you."

" Well, one lock will be safe, come what may," Charles assured her, as he rose, and smilingly surveyed the long fair curl which lay in Agnes's lap. " And now, alas, the King must disappear, and ' Betty Burke,' for whom I have no liking, must speedily return. So my levee is ended."

Agnes divided the treasured lock between Lady Kingsburgh and herself, and her own share found shelter in her bosom.

To aid the Prince in the difficult task of dressing Mistress MacDonald despatched her daughter, who found her assistance greatly needed, since, as afterwards declared, " not a pin could he put in

Both Agnes and Lady Kingsburgh were soon summoned to advise concerning his various garments, and all were instantly convulsed with laughter at the ludicrous scene. Indeed, Charles behaved more like one who had donned the dress in sheer mischief, than like an outlaw, fleeing for his life.

When at last his costume seemed complete, he sent the company into fresh merriment by exclaiming anxiously: "Oh, Miss, you have forgot my apron. Where is my apron? Oh, get me my apron, for it is a principal part of my dress."

When supper was over, the refugees prepared to resume their journey, with the understanding that Agnes, having seen Charles safe at Portree, should return to Kingsburgh House. Lady MacDonald, with tearful eyes, took leave of her royal guest, begging him to accept, as a slight remembrance, a snuff-box which she owned, and saying it was fitting he should take it, because the design on the cover,—a pair of clasped hands and the words "Rob Gib,"—had reference to one of his ancestors. "Rob Gib," she explained, was the court-fool of Scotland in the days of James the Fifth, and it was a favourite remark of his that all the other courtiers served the king for what they got, but he, alone, out of "stark love and kindness," and therefore ever since, she added, the name had been a symbol of true friendship.

Charles responded gallantly: "I assure your ladyship that I sincerely admire that maxim, which has been most nobly fulfilled by you and your brave husband. I shall keep this box as long as I live, and I pray I shall never outlive the memory of your kindness."

When the Prince had departed, Lady Kingsburgh repaired to his bed-chamber, and tenderly wrapped in lavender the sheets which he had used, declaring that they should never be touched till her death, when they should compose her shroud.

. . . . .

Kingsburgh, "Betty Burke," and her mistress set out for Portree, the principal harbour of Skye,—a walk of fully fourteen miles. When they were safely beyond the house, Kingsburgh escorted Charles in the woods, and there aided him to don a man's attire. When they emerged, the Prince wore the Highland costume,—tartan coat, philabeg, plaid and bonnet, and "Betty Burke" was henceforth seen no more.

Kingsburgh and his royal protégé were now obliged to part, the Prince, joined by faithful N MacEachain, proceeding by one road to Portree, and Agnes by another. Malcolm MacLeod, who lived Raasay, a small island between Skye and the mainland, had been summoned by Donald Roy, a kinsman of Lady Margaret's, to aid the Prince, and five met in the little tavern at Portree, all shivering and thoroughly drenched with rain.

"I am sorry your Royal Highness should endure such discomfort," remarked Donald Roy, observing the water dripping from the Prince's plaid.

"I am more sorry that *our lady*,"—the title which he always referred to Agnes,—" should be exposed to such an evening," Charles replied.

After the Prince had changed his wet garments

dry, and partaken of food, he was told that the boat was in waiting to carry him to Raasay. The hour of parting had come, and however reluctant, Charles could postpone it no longer. He advanced to where Agnes stood apart, and taking a tiny packet from his breast, closed her fingers over it, saying earnestly, "Accept this as a slight token of my debt of gratitude."

But the girl caught the gleam of gems between her fingers, and demurred.

"Your Majesty, I must refuse a gift of so great value. The service is as nothing,—is but your lawful due. The ring I cannot take!"

But the Prince whispered with insistent pleading, "Agnes, Agnes, keep it for my sake, then; at least till I return to Scotland to claim it from your hand."

More he could not say without rousing suspicion, for the landlord was watching them attentively. Pale with agitation, he raised her hands and kissed them twice; cast one despairing glance at her tear-laden eyes and quivering lips, and murmuring, "We shall meet at St. James's yet!" followed Donald Roy into the night.

CHAPTER XXIX

"TO DRAW THE SWORD FOR SCOTLAND'S LORD"

"To draw the sword for Scotland's lord,
  The young Chevalier."

ALTHOUGH Agnes fiercely resented the inquisitive looks of the landlord, who had evidently half-suspected the royal quality of his guest, she was obliged to spend the night at the inn, for it was out of the question to return to Kingsburgh House at such an hour. Heavy-hearted, she slept late, and the morning was well advanced before she set out to retrace her journey.

Her road lay now along the stretch of moor, whose verdant heather would soon wear hue of purple, now upward through the hills, where ferns and birches flourished, and water-falls flashed glimmering down the rocks from some clear mountain-tarn. On one hand rolled the sea, sparkling and sapphire-blue, whose wide salt-water lochs ran deep into the land; on the other rose the rugged wall of mountains, grey, cloud-swept and awesome. The way was lonely and untravelled, and, finding herself in utter solitude, she flung the bridle loose over the horse's neck, and burst into a passion of wild sobs. Again, as on the road to Inverness, the desolation of

"To Draw the Sword for Scotland's Lord" 251

her grief possessed her, but now in parting from the Prince, the height of wretchedness seemed reached, and she wept as she had not wept,—save for that midnight in the hut,—since the eve when she had lain, convulsed by sorrow, on Norman Leslie's grave.

The horse pursued his way, but his rider, blinded by her tears, took heed of nothing. Even when a ragged form in kilts of the Murray tartan emerged from out the towering bracken and laid a hand upon her rein, she did not start, but only wondered listlessly why an Athole man should be in far-off Skye, for the Athole-men (Murrays) held the district north of Killiecrankie in central Scotland. It was not until he had twice repeated his muttered Gaelic message that she seemed to comprehend its meaning, and firmly whispering, "I will come," prepared to follow where he led. With a nod of satisfaction, the man took her rein, and turned the horse out of the highway. Stealthy and vigilant, he glided forward upon unshod feet, and the girl yielded freely to his guidance.

They had begun to climb the foot-hills which mounted like a giant's stepping-stones toward the loftier summits; and, as they ascended, valley and loch and sapphire reach of sea, lay spread below them like some mighty scroll. Instinctively, Agnes paused, and looking eastward over those blue straits which sunder Scotland from her sister-isles, sought with feverish intensity for sight of some stray boat.

The afternoon was far spent when they arrived at a mountain sheiling, similar to that in which she had met the Prince. Her Highland guide informed her that this was their destination, and an old woman, emerging hastily, gave her an eager Gaelic welcome. Tense with excitement, Agnes entered the hut. It surely could not be the Prince with whom she was to meet a second time;—the Prince with whom she had parted only the night before. Again her thoughts flew wistfully, like a homing bird, to Donald and Locheil! But no! the chieftain with the dark stern face, who came to meet her, was neither of these. Memory showed the oaken hall at Auchnacarry, a table spread as for a banquet, and an eager company assembled round a bowl of snow-white roses. It was Lord George Murray who confronted her, and bent on her an anxious, searching gaze.

"So you received my message, Mistress Agnes? I might have known you would not fail me. You are of the 'leal Leslies,' to whom loyalty is religion. And well have you proved your kinship, for twice have you obeyed me without question."

"Twice?" Agnes echoed, utterly perplexed.

Murray smiled grimly. "Aye, twice, for 'twas my hand penned the missive you took from MacLeod —'twas I arranged your meeting with the Prince near Ormaclade."

"I did not know!" cried Agnes. "I could not guess from whom it came. I had never seen your writing, my lord."

"But now," continued Murray, "I have a plan far more desperate than your midnight voyage to Skye."

He began to pace the room, conversing in low keyed, agitated tones.

"The Prince is now, as you know, in hiding

Raasay; but he cannot remain there. Remote as it is, the place will be searched sooner or later,—and then! 'Tis true Cumberland has given orders to stab the Prince if taken, but yet 'tis not swift death I dread for him, but capture!" He paused, and eyed her intently. "Were you never told you resembled Charles Edward as closely as maid can resemble man? Suppose that you assume a man's dress, and guide him to a safe retreat upon the mainland?"

Agnes had risen, breathing quickly, with lips apart, and eyes intent upon his face.

"Oh," she cried appealingly. "There's naught on earth I would not do to save him,—naught that lay within my power; but I fear I could never make a proper man, and none would ever take me for Prince Charlie!"

"Nay," cried Murray feverishly, "it could be done!—If you but had something belonging to the Prince——" he pondered.

Agnes regarded him with hesitation, reluctant to reveal the cherished gift.

"I have—a ring," she faltered shyly. "His Royal Highness gave it me at parting, and bade me keep it for his sake till he returned to Scotland to reclaim it."

Thus speaking, she drew from her bosom the treasured ring, wrapped in a bit of plaid, and held it out toward Murray, the circle of rare diamonds flashing coloured fire. He uttered an exclamation.

"Aye!—the topaz ring,—one of the Sobieski jewels,—the one he saved when he sold the rest for arms. I wonder that he parted from it, for he prized it above all else as his mother's ring, and would never take it from his finger." (The Prince's mother, Clementina Sobieski, granddaughter of the heroic King of Poland, possessed a costly number of jewels at the time of her marriage to James VIII.)

Suddenly Murray's dark brows grew stern, as his mind recalled a scene in Holyrood; and he subjected Agnes to a rigid scrutiny. But her eyes met his so frankly that his own gaze cleared.

"Look ye, lassie," he said, his tone softening, "ye've not lost your heart to the Prince?"

The colour surged into her face, but her wide brown eyes still met his with the same sweetly childlike regard.

"'Tis true I would give my life for him," she answered simply, "but my love for him must be only what a maid may give to one so far above her. I think of him as every leal Scotsman should think of his lawful king."

Murray was seized by misgivings. The girl's beauty or her helplessness smote his heart. He went to where she stood, with the Prince's ring between her fingers, and put his hands upon her shoulders, regarding her steadily.

"Lass," he said huskily, "it's right ye should see the matter clearly ere ye choose. 'Tis no light task lies before you,—ye will be risking life and honour, and that's all ye've left to give."

She straightened herself rather haughtily, her clear eyes flashing at his words.

"My life I hold not dear when one far dearer is at stake; and as for honour, why, I think in denying duty lies the shame!"

A silence followed her words. Murray released her, and going to the table, seated himself and took up a pen, before he trusted himself to speak.

"Ye're a brave lass," he said hoarsely. "God pity me, I must send you, for no other way remains to me. Before the Prince lies certain doom. Every moment draws the net more closely; every moment may mean his capture,—and—ye ken the rest—*high treason and Tower Hill!*"

She gave a sharp gasp of horror. "Oh, why in God's name will you delay, when every instant threatens such a doom? Think not of me, nor of a thousand like me, in such a need as this! Only show me how to save him!"

The passion of loyalty broke through the calm of words like a fire through some frail barrier of twigs.

"Lord Murray," she cried, "you see this broadsword? My kinsman, Dundee, bore it to the last against the foes of his monarch, King James the Seventh; my father drew it in defence of King James the Eighth; and I, maid though I am, will wear it, as long as the steel holds true, as long as my heart-blood flows,—in the cause of *King Charles the Third!*"

And with the last, low, passion-breathing words, she raised the broadsword hanging at her side, and kissed the worn blade and the faded ribbon.

"Perhaps 'twas not for naught that I learned to use sword and gun. Perhaps 'tis not for naught that the blood of heroes runs in my girl's veins, if I may thrust my life—a weak but willing target—between the King and death!"

Murray turned to her with kindling eyes. "Lass," he cried, "ye are brave beyond all words. There spoke the *spirit of the Cavaliers!*"

He remembered mournfully the pretty, mischievous maid of Auchnacarry, with her green-kilted skirt and scarlet-laced bodice. He looked now into the beautiful, fervent face before him, lifted white above the sable gown, and wondered if the two could be the same. The gay and careless maid his memory held, had become a man for courage, a woman for devotion.

"Agnes," said Murray, "since you have chosen to perform this mission, hark to this: In yonder room ye will find all things needful for the disguise. When ye have donned them, and have tied those golden locks like the Prince's, I'll warrant 'twill take sharper eyes than the auld carle o' Hanover's, or the Butcher's, either, to tell you from our 'Bonnie Charlie.' At midnight come MacLeod and his fellow-clansmen, to take ye to the Prince. Till then, lass, seek what rest ye can."

With the words he handed her a candle, and opened the door of a tiny bed-room.

Strangely enough, it was not with the thought of her desperate enterprise that Agnes's mind was filled, when she found herself alone. Perhaps it was the reaction from the passionate heights of the previous hour that left her with only a longing for repose. She made some hurried preparations, then flung herself upon the rude bed, and, wearied, slept.

When Murray's knock aroused her, she rose, refreshed; and began to struggle into the male attire which besprinkled the bed:—the blue coat, philabeg,

"To Draw the Sword for Scotland's Lord" 257

tartan stockings, and low-heeled Highland brogues. She buckled on her broadsword, and fastened in her belt the silver-handled dirk that had actually been Prince Charlie's. When at last she stood fully arrayed, she paused, and glanced down ruefully at her pretty, bare knees, but there was no time to waste in blushes.

She shook her hair out of its ribbon, and let it fall in a gleaming mass to her waist. With an involuntary sigh she took up the scissors and severed the long locks till the shorn curls reached only to her shoulders. When the destruction was ended, she viewed with satisfaction the image in the mirror, caught up the plaid, wrapped it round her, Highland-fashion, and buckled it on the shoulder, and perched the blue, plumed bonnet on her yellow curls.

The transformation was complete. In the broken glass she beheld the bright brown eyes, the scarlet lips, and mournful smile;—in fine—the *haughty, handsome, melancholy face of the last Stuart!*

CHAPTER XXX

"ON HILLS THAT ARE BY RIGHT HIS AIN"

"On hills that are by right his ain,
 He roams, a lonely stranger;
On ilka hand he's pressed by want,
 On ilka side by danger!"

MURRAY approached the door, whispering "Come forth, Prince Charlie," and the next instant his mandate seemed obeyed, for there stepped into the room the Prince's very counterpart. The figure advanced a few paces with stately tread, then halting, presented itself for Murray's keen inspection. The body, slight, yet rounded into curves, the delicately fashioned hands and feet, the haughty lift of the fair head, and above all, the royal air of dignity that marked both face and form, made the resemblance one to brave detection. Even Murray, sternly averse to praise, uttered a word of approval. He studied critically the girl's erect figure, commenting audibly as he did so.

"Yes, you will pass, I think. You are not tall enough by several inches, but you make the most of your height. And, besides, your feet and hands are too small, but then the Prince's are not over large. The resemblance between you is superficial, of course —anyone knowing you both as well as I do, would not be tricked for a moment, but they'll scarce have time to observe at their leisure if my plan carries, and, seen at a glance, you will do very well. Th

Duke himself is not so closely acquainted with his cousin Charles that he may not be open to deception."

Having completed this rapid criticism, Murray again scanned the girl rigidly, and continued: "Remember you go by the name of MacNeil,—Malcolm MacNeil,—your plaid is of that tartan,—and for safety the Prince is Dugald McCluny;—always address him thus. If capture or other danger threaten, —to you I say it needlessly,—*shield him at all costs!* And if he objects, as 'tis like he will, being chivalrous, you must find means to deceive him. Above all, keep watch for a French ship to carry him from this doomed country."

The " gentle Locheil " would not have sent the girl upon so desperate a mission even to save the Prince he adored; but Murray, relentless toward others as toward himself, would have sacrificed her and a thousand more, to save a single lock of Prince Charlie's golden hair. He had chosen Agnes with the unerring penetration which marked the man. Besides her remarkable resemblance to the Prince, she knew the country well, having roamed it from a child;—moreover, she was keen-witted, high-spirited, dauntlessly brave,—above all,—loyal to the death!

Murray was on the point of concluding his instructions, when the old woman appeared, followed by Donald MacLeod and his fellow-Highlanders, all of whom halted, spell-bound, at sight of Malcolm MacNeil. That gentleman endured their looks composedly, with the ease of one born to the purple, gracefully resting one hand on his broadsword, and allowing the other to fall by his side.

"Heaven defend us, if it's no' the Prince himsel'!" gasped the astonished old woman.

"Nae, nae, guidwife," said MacLeod, who was in the secret, "it'll no' be the Prince ava,—only a fair bit lassie wha bears him an unco likeness, and, belike, if the guid God wills, may save the puir laddie's life.

"Dinna hold your head sae haughty, lassie," he objected, "the Prince, wi' a' his royal bluid, doesna tilt his chin sae high. Aye, he's stately enow, I ken, but he isna half sae saucy."

Agnes smiled at this curious protest, realising that the pose in question was indeed more natural to herself than to the Prince. Determined to show them her powers of imitation, she wheeled suddenly, drew herself up, and cried in a commanding tone: "Advance, Clan Cameron! Take the right flank, Glengarry!"

Fairly astounded, the Highlanders sprang to their feet. "The Prince! The Prince!" they shouted in wild delight.

"Ye're a witch, lassie," cried MacLeod, "'tis the Prince's very tone!" while Murray smiled a stern approval.

MacLeod now inquired of Agnes if she were willing to bind her fealty to the Prince in the Highland fashion of oath upon the dirk, which was considered the most solemn of all oaths among the Highlanders, and corresponded to our oath upon the Bible.

To this Murray objected that it was needless waste of time. "The girl is true as the broadsword's steel." But Agnes, coming quickly forward, announced her willingness to seal the compact as MacLeod desired.

Accordingly, Murray unsheathed his dirk, and, gathering the Highlanders in a circle round him, commanded Agnes to declare her purpose. The girl responded with composure, and laying her hand on the bared steel, repeated with resolution the solemn and awful words of the oath: " That my back shall be to God and my face to the devil, that all the curses the Scriptures do pronounce may come upon me, and upon all my posterity, if I shield not the Prince in the hour of utmost danger, and if I disclose to any being,—man, woman, or child,—the secret that I bear."

In tones low yet vibrant the words were spoken, and they rang with the clear ring of steel. A stifled murmur of applause broke from the clansmen; they gazed with profound awe at the look of sublime devotion which lit that youthful face.

Agnes turned to Murray, saying simply, " I am ready to go; need we delay longer?"

She advanced toward the door as she spoke, but Murray followed her, and caught her hands, whispering feverishly: " Harken, lass;—fling not your heart away; remember princes may not wed beneath them; though he's a gentleman, and honourable, which is more than they all are. And now, God keep you safe, and save him from his foes!"

But when the receding hoof-beats had ceased to sound, Murray dropped his head upon his hands, murmuring bitterly: " A grievous shame it is that we must drag a slip of a maid to ruin with us! God forgive me! God forgive me! There was no other way!"

Through the early dawning of mid-summer, a little boat crept on its cautious way, befriended by the fog which wrapped the channel. Once, from out this mantle of protection, they caught the voices on a frigate's deck, and heard the sentry's challenge smite the heavy air. But they stole by, unheeded, upon muffled oars, and sought the kindly gloom beyond.

It was upon a midnight three days later, that a little company of travellers, proceeding anxiously along the shore at Moidart, halted in agitation at the sound of approaching horsemen. But the two new-comers drew rein some paces distant, and the foremost, whom the moon showed to be young, inquired for "one Malcolm MacNeil."

Immediately a horseman left the opposite group, and rode forward into the imperfect moonlight, which glistened faintly on his bonnet's plume and loosely flowing plaid. He, too, was young, and his face revealed an almost feminine delicacy of outline. Swiftly he reined his horse beside his questioner. "*I am Malcolm MacNeil*," he said.

The moon emerged from the engulfing clouds, and poured its undimmed light upon the two. He that was Dugald McCluny started violently, with a sharp-drawn breath of unconvinced amazement. "Merciful Heaven, Agnes!" he exclaimed.

A deep blush overspread the youth's face; he retained his composure with an effort.

"Nay, I am Malcolm MacNeil," he said, "and your most obedient, humble servant, Dugald McCluny."

CHAPTER XXXI

"THERE GREW IN BONNIE SCOTLAND A THISTLE AND
A BRIER"

"There grew in bonnie Scotland a thistle and a brier,
And aye they twined and clasped like sisters kind and dear;
The rose it was sae bonnie, it could ilk bosom charm;
The thistle spread its thorny leaf to keep the rose from
   harm."

I VOW you are my very counterpart," the Prince declared, "although a most transfigured counterpart. But in Heaven's name tell me, how came you to assume this dangerous disguise? MacLeod told me nothing, save that I should meet a youth called Malcolm MacNeil who would guide me into safety. How little I guessed, Agnes, that it would be *you!* But this sacrifice is too great,—I will never accept of it!—You do not realise what you are doing!— You are hazarding life and honour,—and for *me!*" He ceased abruptly, inexpressibly stirred by this undreamed-of loyalty which withheld nothing from the object of its devotion.

"You exaggerate the danger, sir," she answered lightly. "I am safer in this dress than in any other; —it is *you*, Dugald, the *real* Prince, who incur the danger; for whatever likeness I bear you, is not enough to deceive any save the credulous,—of whom your cousin Cumberland is not one." And with this argument, and others similar, did she strive to quiet his misgivings.

That midnight meeting upon the beach at Moidart was but the beginning of vicissitudes;—weary wanderings, hiding in caves and sheilings, hairbreadth escapes, and strange encounters, in which night became day, and day masqueraded as night, and peril was a thing to play with like a child's toy. Hunted upon every side,—menaced by ruthless foes,—hunger, and want, and man's most deadly hate,—never knowing at what moment the lifted doom might strike, they learned to look fear in the face and smile.

They had not long embarked upon these hardships when Malcolm proposed that Dugald, for a few days at least, should appear in the capacity of his servant. To this Dugald demurred, on the ground that the master of the aforesaid servant would incur additional danger.

But as usual, the artful Malcolm brought weight to bear upon the dissenter, and the matter ended in Dugald's acquiescence.

Accordingly, Charles doffed his tartan coat, exchanged his shoe-buckles for strings, pulled the ruffles out of his shirt, and fastening a soiled white napkin about his head in pretence of a wound, inquired of Malcolm if he were not suitably disguised.

But Malcolm shook his head. "I think your Highness might even yet be recognised," he admitted ruefully, whereupon Charles exclaimed: "This is an odd, remarkable face I have got, that nothing can disguise it."

"It is a king's face," Malcolm answered, "how

can that be concealed? And, furthermore, 'tis not the face alone,—'tis your Majesty's whole air of dignity;—and that you can never dissemble!"

Their journey was now continued on foot, MacLeod and Malcolm in the lead, and Dugald following at a respectful distance, with his master's bundle over his shoulders. In the course of time they arrived at the home of MacDonald of Morar, whose wife was a sister of Locheil's. MacLeod, who knew the lady well, introduced young Malcolm as a friend lately come from abroad, and anxious to leave this unhappy country as quickly as possible. Fortunately, the former Mistress Cameron had not seen her brother's foster-child in years, or Agnes would not have escaped recognition; but in her rôle of foreign traveller, she was welcomed without suspicion.

An ample meal was spread for them, to which Malcolm and MacLeod applied themselves with zeal, necessarily consigning their hapless servant to a distant seat, and less dainty fare. Malcolm, indeed, almost betrayed their secret by the deep solicitude of the looks he cast in Dugald's direction.

Their dinner ended, the wayfarers fell asleep, but the buoyant Dugald did not slumber long, and his astonished fellow-travellers awoke to find him gaily employed with Mistress MacDonald's baby. The little fellow, throned high on the Prince's shoulder, was laughing in childish glee at the merry songs and antics of his strange companion, while an aged woman, who had the child in charge, sat watching the scene with amusement. Charles, his part of servant quite forgotten, exclaimed mirthfully, "Who knows but this little fellow may be a captain in my service yet?"

"Or you rather an old sergeant in his company," amended the aged nurse.

. . . .

The next refuge of the wanderers was a tiny hut of turf, so skilfully constructed—with the grass side outward, in a deep cleft in the rocks, that it seemed a part of the verdure-clad bank. It was Malcolm who first arrived at this retreat, for, as occasionally happened, the party had been obliged to separate upon the road; and Dugald, having doffed his menial garments, approached the hut alone. The night was wild and dreary, and the rain drove in torrents from the sea; but enough of the grey gloaming still lingered to show the path. Following it, Charles reached the tiny doorstep, when suddenly his entering feet were stayed by the sound of low-toned singing from within.

Mutely the door unlatched beneath his fingers, and there floated out to him the sweetest and most plaintive melody his ears had ever heard; borne on the tender cadence of that voice which had touched his heart so deeply upon another threshold,—months—nay, *years*—ago. It was the very whisper of a song that stirred his memory now,—a very ghost of melody that mingled with the air as softly as rain or wind might mingle.

"By yon bonnie banks, and by yon bonnie braes,
  Where the sun shines bright on Loch Lomond;
Where we ha'e passed sae mony happy days,
  On the bonnie, bonnie banks o' Loch Lomond.

> "We'll meet where we pairted in yon shady glen,
>   On the steep, steep side o' Ben Lomond;
> Where in purple hue the Hieland hills we view,
>   An' the moon comin' oot frae the gloamin'.
>
> "Still fair is the scene, but ah, how changed
>   Are the hopes we sae fondly cherished;
> Like a wat'ry gleam, like a mornin' dream,
>   On Culloden's field they ha'e perished!
>
> "Oh, ye'll tak' the high road, an' I'll tak' the low road,
>   An' I'll be in Scotland afore ye;
> But trouble it is there, and mony hearts are sair,
>   On the bonnie, bonnie banks o' Loch Lomond."

The soul of a tragic pathos breathed through the haunting sweetness of the song, as the overflowing heart poured forth its pent-up sorrow. The singer sat beside the hearth, with a face, whose girlish loveliness belied the man's attire, illumined clearly by the leaping flames, and eyes that lingered woefully upon their ruddy splendour, to see a castle crashing to its fall.

It was not till the last plaintive note had melted into silence that the unhappy listener sought to break the all-pervading hush; and even then, it was with downcast eyes, and hesitating step, that he ventured to intrude upon the singer.

She started from her seat like one awakened from a dream; and turned to meet him with a look of self-reproach.

"I would I had not sung," she said regretfully, "since I have saddened you, not cheered you;—I knew not I was minstrel to the King."

And then, with that swift change of speech and feeling that marked the Agnes of the happier days:

"I ha'e left my harp behind me, as your Royal Highness observes," she cried lightly. "Has his *dis*-Grace o' Cumberland ta'en it, I wonder? 'Twill ne'er sound a chord for him! If 'tis e'en so, I maun ask a favour of your Majesty at St. James's itsel'. It maun be for a harp whereon to sing the King's triumph."

"How well you have played the man!" Charles exclaimed, "and I failed so completely as a woman."

"'Tis rather bewildering," admitted Agnes. "I sometimes forget which I am! 'Tis well I had a masculine education since I must 'quit me like a man'!"

There was that in his intensity of gaze which made her eyes droop suddenly, and caused her to be painfully aware of her unfeminine apparel. Instinctively, she suddenly drew the kindly plaid more closely, and put the hearth between her and the Prince before she spoke again.

"I would ask your Royal Highness not to look at me so attentively, an' it please you. I am not yet accustomed to this dress," she murmured, blushing, though with childlike naïveté of speech, while the Prince hastened to pour out profuse apologies for his inadvertent rudeness.

So moving was the beauty of her face, that only with a mighty effort did Charles subdue the passion of his heart. This need of self-suppression had grown to the stature of a giant, who daily must be battled with and mastered;—opposed at every point lest he break through and conquer. To live constantly in her company, and yet to keep unmoved a cool and even dignity of manner, required all his power of will. Lonely and defenceless, and wholly at his mercy as she was,—this girl who had risked the utmost for his sake;—he was constrained by every bond of honour, to bear himself, in all his conduct toward her,—with the perfect chivalry which beseemed a prince.

They were presently joined by MacLeod, who entered, dripping and disconsolate, and straightway knelt beside the hearth to dry his streaming plaid. The wind cried down the chimney, and the rain beat at door and casement with the din of armed men.

"The prince o' the powers o' the air and a' his deils, in the shape o' the Duke o' Cumberland an' his dragoons might ride abroad the nicht, an' we ken na a blink o't!" muttered Donald MacLeod, as he crouched by the fire and mumbled a curse on the royal personage in question.

Having eaten their scanty supper, Agnes and Charles "foregathered," as was their wont, about the blazing hearth, and told whatever tales their memory could produce, to the weird accompaniment of rain and sea and sombre moan of wind.

On this particular evening, the Prince, after gazing dreamily into the fire, turned suddenly to Agnes, saying:

"Will you think me foolish, I wonder, if I tell you the curious omen that first embarked me on my wild expedition to Scotland? 'Tis a fanciful tale, in truth, and yet, perhaps, *you*, my little Highlander, a firm believer in all signs and visions, will not deem me credulous, for having laid such faith in the occurrence:

"My brother, Henry, and myself attended prayers one day in Rome at the little English chapel. Now I was ever a restless boy, and so, while my head was bowed, my eyes were partly open, and you may picture my surprise when suddenly a bit of bright mosaic, fashioned like a *Thistle*, dropped into my lap. Astonished, I raised my head to scan the inlaid ceiling, whither it had fallen, and as I gazed, another fragment, wrought into a *Rose*, fell likewise. They crumbled quickly in my eager fingers; but so did not the hope they had inspired. The Rose for merry England,—the Thistle for dear Scotland,—set the boy of ten to dreaming of glorious things to be,—embattled fields of conquest, and the golden highway to a three-fold throne;—they sent the reckless youth of four-and-twenty across the hostile seas, resolved to hazard all things for that glittering crown."

CHAPTER XXXII

"WE WATCH'D THEE IN THE GLOAMIN' HOUR"

"We watch'd thee in the gloamin' hour,
  We watch'd thee in the mornin' grey;
Tho' thirty thousand pounds they gi'e,
  O there is nane wha wad betray!"

DUGALD and Malcolm beguiled long days of dread, and weary nights of watching, with manifold diversions. The Prince related merry tales of his childhood in Rome, and his stirring boyhood in the Spanish camp. Of the days at Holyrood he never spoke, for the memories they invoked were too sacred to be uttered lightly, and moreover they stirred feelings that must lie sleeping still for many a day. He and Agnes would converse in French, and he would teach her verses in Italian from Michael Angelo or Dante; while in return, she would have the Prince repeat some Gaelic sentences, or, which he liked much better, would herself recite long passages from the poems of Ossian, translating them for his benefit.

At other times they practised fencing, in which the Prince found Agnes an apt and eager pupil. The girl possessed the litheness and dexterity so requisite for a skilful swordsman, and with the alert perception which marks an adept in the art. For the moment they grew almost gay as they rehearsed each varied form of thrust and parry to the low tinkle of steel against steel, and their own quick-breathed comments. Had it not been for that black shadow of danger that ever loomed so grimly, and for that yet more sombre shadow of Scotland's woe, they had been well-nigh buoyant in spite of hunger and distress.

Again, they made gay mockery around their ill-spread board, pretending they were seated at a royal banquet, with costly viands served on silver dishes. The Prince would offer Agnes a slice of bread and cheese, with an air of the utmost dignity, while she, her goblet brimming with no richer wine than spring-water, would gravely drink the King's health in the Gaelic words of: "Deoch slaint an Righ." When, as chanced but rarely, they had the luxury of wheaten bread, the Prince refused to touch it, declaring, as he cut the oaten loaf: "Why, 'tis my own country bread, and I, as a true Scot, will eat no other." Once, when for days they had tasted nothing but dry oatmeal, Charles observed humorously: "I think I have learned what a quart of meal is, having lived on that quantity for nearly a week."

At frequent intervals, MacLeod or a fellow-Highlander went boldly into Fort Augustus, and, at infinite risk of capture, secured for the Prince's benefit the newspapers of the day. Charles, however impatient for tidings, always insisted courteously that Agnes should read them first. Sick with dread, she would scan the lengthening columns of trials and executions for the names of Donald and Locheil, then, reassured for the moment, would draw a long sigh of relief, and hand the paper to the Prince.

He would sit and absorb them madly, devouring

"We Watch'd Thee In the Gloamin' Hour"   273

every tale of cruelty and outrage, with burning eyes and bitterly compressed lips.

And yet amid these days of fearful danger the reverence due to God was not forgotten by these strange comrades of misfortune. Each evening at a certain hour, the Prince, withdrawing from the rest, would kneel and tell his beads with Catholic devotion; while Agnes, equally zealous in the tenets of the Scottish-Episcopal Church, knelt by the hearthstone and opened a small worn prayer-book that had been her mother's, its once beautiful binding marred by the vicissitudes of that earlier Agnes.

. . . . .

On a certain starlit evening the fugitives were journeying on horseback along a rocky road that swept aloft into the mountain shadows;—the very road that Charles had followed to his fleeting hour of glory at Glenfinnan, one tragic year ago. Tortured by that bright memory,—how bright against his present gloomy fate!—the Prince communed a while in bitter silence. However great his hardships and privations, he had never failed to meet them with both cheer and courage; but the cruel doom that had pierced, because of him, through the souls of his devoted subjects, had shattered the last bulwark between him and gaunt despair. Memory spoke accusingly, and peopled all that moonlit road with haunting shadows,—the shadows of those who had bled for his honour;—the willing victims of his wild ambition. Nor were the dead his sole accusers! He remembered this beautiful girl beside him, so ruthlessly engulfed in the whirlpool of his devouring destinies, and, overwhelmed with self-reproach, he touched her bridle-rein.

"Agnes," he whispered brokenly, and she saw his eyes were wet, "do you not see them,—those men who marched to battle at my call? This road is thronged with them. Yonder I see Sir Norman,—and they all went to their death for love of me! 'Twas but a dream-crown, yet it cost the lives of brave men none the less." He broke off, sighing deeply. "What matters it what hardships *I* endure," he murmured, half-aloud,—"I am only one out of many, but when I think of the heroes who suffered for my sake,—*that* stabs me to the heart,—*that* strikes me deep!"

Agnes, the Prince and MacLeod spent the night in a ruined sheiling between shadowy hills, each mounting guard by turns, although it must be confessed that Dugald and MacLeod conspired to give young Malcolm the shortest watch, even though the act required a slight perversion of the truth.

Agnes, completely exhausted, fell asleep on her couch of heather as quickly as a weary child. Her face, half in light, half in shadow, now darkened and now illumined, by the fitful glow, wore a pathetic beauty. MacLeod stood guard at the door, and was out of vision; therefore the Prince was free to regard, unperceived, that beautiful dreaming face. His own was obscured by shadows far more sombre than those the firelight cast;— shadows of bitterness and baffled hopes, and an ever deepening desperation;—the cruelest of all spectres that haunt the human breast! In later years they were to throng his soul with sinister intent, an warp it beyond recognition. And though to-night their demons' work was yet to do, they clung to him with dread persistency.

Agnes stirred in her sleep, and drew a plaintive sobbing breath that merged into a shuddering moan. A single word fell from those dreaming lips,—one word, but thrice repeated,—a word the wretched listener shrank to hear:—"*Culloden!*" Trembling as from some pang of bodily distress, the Prince sprang up, pressing convulsive hands to his throbbing temples as if he even yet beheld that field of death, and trod the crimson sepulchre of the clans. Death had been very near to him of late;—so near, that he had often seen its ghastly beckoning; and yet he had never shuddered as he shuddered now to hear this unconscious condemnation from the lips of the woman he loved.

Again the dreamer stirred, and murmured mournfully of one who slept on that red field;—of Norman Leslie, last of all her race. And straightway, he who listened caught the whispered name of "*Donald Cameron.*" Again Charles started, bending forward in an attitude of eager expectation. Would she not breathe *his* name also? If she did, it should be a felicitous omen! He listened with fierce intensity, holding his breath in feverish agitation. But vainly did he harken;—the girl's rest had grown dreamless, and boding silence reigned unbroken till two o'clock, when Charles himself lay down to a brief and troubled sleep.

. . . . . .

The wanderers spent the succeeding day in this

refuge of comparative security, but they did not seek to speed the lingering hours with any of their former buoyant pastimes. A silence and constraint lay heavy on them all, unsolved and undispelled. But when the second evening came, Charles could endure no longer the burden of his grief, and, to lighten it, he spoke.

"Agnes," he whispered mournfully, "why do you never reproach me for all the suffering I have brought you? The cause of it lies wholly at my door:—'twas I that made you homeless and forlorn; that rent from you your last remaining relative, and sent your foster-kindred into exile, and wrung your heart with utter anguish!—'Twas I that made of you—*you*, a lovely, delicate woman—a hunted wanderer, clad in man's attire,—enduring all the misery and woe that makes the outlaw's fate a very hell! And yet you utter not one word of blame,—O God, 'twere easier to endure, an' you but did!—It is your sweet forbearance that torments me!—O what am I, that I should have such love!"

Twice amid this outpouring of his weighted spirit had Agnes made a gesture of remonstrance; now she was swept to her feet by a torrent of passionate feeling.

"Say not so, your Majesty!—Better it were that every Scotsman slumbered low in dust, aye, and that Scotland should be known no more, than we should stain our honour, and forfeit our allegiance!"

The power was hers—above all others—to re-inspire his despairing soul. "Had all men been as loyal," he cried passionately,—"loyal to the last drop of blood,—to the last throb of the heart,—*there had been no Culloden!*"

He had struck a bitter chord too strongly. Her lips trembled piteously, and the shadows gathered in her eyes. "Culloden!" she moaned in a sobbing breath, as she had moaned in her sleep, and in that one sad word there breathed all the tragedy of Scotland.

"Braver men than those of the gallant clans can ne'er be found on earth! I dreamt not that there could be valour mightier than theirs! But for courage!"—he broke off abruptly, to gaze at her with wondering eyes,—"for courage,—one woman,—one maid,—has excelled them all!"

"Ah, your Majesty!" Agnes cried protestingly, the vivid colour flashing to her face at this warm praise,—"you judge me far too highly! None are braver than—" she faltered; tears were in her eyes and voice.— "None are braver than the clans! I am but the daughter of the clans!"

The royal "bed of state" to which Charles presently retired, was made of flowering heather, arranged,—in ancient Highland fashion,—with the rosy sprays erect as when it grew. It thus composed a comfortable couch, whereon any sovereign, above all, one so weary, would gladly rest.

Agnes, declaring that she felt no need of sleep, had taken her place as sentry by the fire, although in truth she was compelled to struggle constantly against alluring drowsiness. Kneeling there alone, in the utter stillness of the midnight-hour, her present dangers and vicissitudes grew shadowy and remote, and the past possessed her wholly. She closed her eyes for a moment, and let the flood of memories enfold her, as mist enfolds the mountains. They came in magic multitudes, serene and sweet and hallowed, and she locked them safely in that mystic chamber of the mind where peace alone can enter. Again she trod the braes of dear Lochaber, and saw the ivied walls of Auchnacarry rise grey athwart the burning gold of sunset. . . . And Donald walked beside her,—his hand lay warm in hers;—the love-light dwelt in his blue eyes, and spoke in his low tones and tender glance. . . .

But not Donald's was the voice that smote her vagrant dreaming and startled all her sweet, illusive fancies to bewildered flight. It was the Prince whose voice had thus recalled her. He was moaning in his sleep, and presently she caught low words and broken phrases, clothed now in French, now in Italian. The girl, with hands clasped on one knee, and wistful gaze upon that troubled face, continued motionless. Suddenly Charles flung his arm across his brow, like one who shrinks appalled at what he sees; then let it fall inertly at his side in an unconscious gesture of despair. "O God!" he sobbed, "O God! *poor Scotland!*"

CHAPTER XXXIII

"LONE PLACES OF THE DEER"

"Lone places of the deer,
 Corrie, and loch, and ben,
  Fount that wells in the cave,
  Voice of the burn and the wave,
 Softly you sing and clear
  Of Charlie and his men!"

THE refugees had wandered far to northward of the Great Glen, among wild corries looking on the sea, and barren mountains, stern and desolate, and tenanted by herds of deer, who lurked, like them, remote from man's abode;—a weird, forsaken land, possessed of sombre beauty that laid its touch of awe upon the soul. But now they turned their footsteps toward a kindlier country,—kindlier, at least, in natural aspect and in human presence, and yet for these same reasons, a thousand-fold more dangerous to hunted exiles such as they. Still, venture hence they must, for Cumberland's cruel soldiers were scouring every inch of the region they had lately roamed. Moreover, a wary Highland messenger had lately brought intelligence from Locheil to the effect that he and a few of his fellow-fugitives were securely concealed in the very heart of the enemy's country; concluding with the earnest entreaty that Charles should immediately join him, little imagining how closely the fortunes of his sovereign were intertwined with those of his fair foster-daughter.

Accordingly, the last days of July found the Prince and his attendants travelling southward toward the lovely, fateful country of Lochaber, and the line of hostile forts that guarded the Great Glen. Agnes's heart leaped constantly at the thought of meeting Donald and Locheil, although the prospect of appearing in the guise of Malcolm was hardly to her liking.

It befell upon a sultry afternoon that the fugitives approached a partly ruined castle on the beautiful shores of Loch Arkaig. It was wholly unfit for habitation, but not far from it stood a small stone dairy, which promised at least a shelter from the heat, and here they halted for a brief rest and refreshment. MacLeod, who had observed some cattle browsing at a distance, set off in search of milk wherewith to quench his comrades' thirst, leaving Charles and Agnes alone together.

MacLeod had no sooner departed than the Prince came to the window where she stood, and suddenly taking her hand, demanded anxiously: "Agnes, will you promise to do the thing I ask you? I am convinced that danger is approaching,—that at last our foes have found where we are hid. Agnes, you *must*—you *will*—pledge me your solemn word to escape while there is yet time?"

But the girl eluded an answer by turning quickly to the window and exclaiming, "Look, look, your Majesty!—hither comes a stranger!"

Charles, following her eager gesture, saw a man in

Highland costume advancing slowly toward the hut.
"Why," he declared, astonished, "I vow 'tis none
other than young Robert Mackenzie, who served so
faithfully in my bodyguard. What strange fortune
brings him here? But stay! I will disclose myself
to him,—he is of my leal Highlanders."

Holding his plaid as a screen before his face,
Charles stepped to the door and accosted the newcomer.

"Come you in, Robert Mackenzie; there is one
here who would hold converse with you."

The stranger, although he started at the Prince's
voice, complied without the slightest hesitation. But
just as he crossed the threshold, Charles let fall his
tartan covering, and stood unmasked before his loyal
partisan.

"My God! the Prince!" Mackenzie cried, becoming ashen-pale, and he fell upon his knees to kiss the
outstretched hand.

As he rose, his gaze met Agnes's, and the two stood
spell-bound in mute amazement. Then Mackenzie
turned again to Charles.

"What! are there *three* of us!" he ejaculated.

Despite the graveness of the situation, a gleam of
amusement lighted the Prince's face, and Agnes
barely repressed a nervous desire to laugh. For in
Robert Mackenzie a vivid portrait of the Prince appeared before their eyes. In height and figure, in
hue of hair and tint of skin, in attitude and mien,
another Charles apparently confronted them:—*apparently*, for the likeness was by no means so striking
as that which existed between Prince Charlie and his

fair preserver. Still, it was quite pronounced enough to deceive a chance beholder.

The Prince seized this opportune moment to acquaint Mackenzie with the heroic part which Agnes had assumed for his deliverance. The young man listened with enthusiasm, and when the tale was ended, he cast upon its heroine a look of heightened wonder. Meantime, Agnes stood apart, her face averted and suffused with crimson, but Mackenzie, undeterred by her timidity, advanced, and bent over the hand which the blushing young clansman reluctantly offered.

"'Tis a lion's heart you wear in your bosom!" he cried with ardour. "How great must be your courage, Mistress Leslie,—for 'Malcolm MacNeil' I cannot call you,—yet of equal greatness your reward will be,—to know that you have saved your King! As for me, I ask no happier fate of Heaven than to die,—if need be,—for my lawful Prince!"

Barely had the devoted words been spoken when MacLeod, spent with running, burst headlong into the hut. "God help us! the militia!" he gasped wildly; "the deils are on the way to tak' the Prince alive or dead,—a'ready they're aboon yon hill! Ane path alane is left,—flee, flee, your Majesty!"

"Aye," said Mackenzie calmly, "go, your Majesty, waste not an instant! You are the King, but we are the parliament, and you must do our bidding. The rest of us will cover your retreat. MacLeod, do you defend the hut, while I go forth to meet them, and, perchance, divert them from their mission."

And without waiting for the Prince's answer, he rushed upon his desperate errand.

A moment of appalling stillness trod on his departure. MacLeod, beckoning Charles to depart, unslung his musket, and placed himself before the tiny slit that served as window. But the Prince, with no movement toward flight, loosed the pistol from his belt, and turned to Malcolm.

"Agnes, in God's name leave me, and escape. Nay, do not seek to urge me!—Honour forbids that *I* should fly, but *you* shall not remain to face an unknown fate. Go, as you love me,—I implore you!"

But Agnes made no pretence of complying. Calmly she drew her claymore from its sheath, and spoke with a decision as final as his own.

"Your Majesty, that will I never do! No power on earth,—not even your command,—will make me leave you in the face of danger!"

It was a daring challenge, but Charles opposed it with an equal resolution.

"It is decided, then," he answered with composure; "your sacrifice and suffering shall be ended. I will straightway surrender myself to the Elector!"

With the words he flung aside his pistol, and advanced toward the doorway. But quicker than he was Agnes! In the flash of a dirk she sprang forward, and the next instant her sword formed a shining barrier athwart his path,—a bar of gleaming steel between him and his purpose.

"Your Majesty!" she cried, and her head was high, and her eyes looked dauntlessly into his, "I had thought to draw this sword *against* your foes, but now,—O Heaven forgive me!—you compel me to *draw it against yourself!*"

Charles would have spoken, but she stayed him with a commanding gesture.

"Listen to me! for I must speak, although time presses hard. If you think that by yielding yourself to those Whig traitors yonder you will end my sufferings, how greatly are you deceived! For though I doff this male attire, my sex will not protect me. This very moment there are women of noble birth foully confined in Edinburgh Castle, *for no other reason* than that their kinsfolk fought to save the House of Stuart. What think you, then, will be the penalty awarded *me* for having thus connived at your escape? Faith, something more than prison-walls, I trow! How dealt the 'Butcher' Cumberland with women when he ravaged the Highlands? Let Lochaber say!"

"No, no, in God's name, no!" burst out Charles, a fierce light leaping in his eyes. "They would not—nay—they *dare not*—harm a woman!"

She laughed, a light, defiant laugh of bitter mirth as she replied:

"'Dare not!' 'a woman!' why, look you, 'tis bu sixty years since Monmouth's time, and women suffered then in fearful fashion;—aye, at the whipping post, in prison, on the scaffold;—so will it be again your Highness, if you resign yourself into these vil lains' hands. I shall not go scot-free; there wait for me a doom!"

She lowered her drawn blade, and held out plead ing hands. "Better to die as dies a man, as die my kinsmen and my father, fighting sword in han beside my lawful King!"

With cheeks like ashes and eyes like flame did Charles receive her passionate defence. Convulsed with an appalling fear, he caught her hands, and murmured, half-distraught: "Agnes, Agnes, in God's mercy cease! Oh, you have wrung my heart with words of horror,—with shuddering at the picture you have painted! Speak of it no more! Cumberland shall yet requite a thousand-fold for all the woe and outrage he has inflicted upon my loyal subjects! Agnes, dearest clansman, you have conquered!—If die we must, then die we here with sword in hand,— *a Leslie and a Stuart*,—heart to heart."

"Yon come the deils o' Hanover!" cried MacLeod from the window, and Agnes turned to the Prince with a dauntless smile.

"Now may we prove the metal of our steel," she whispered low, and fingered lovingly the ancient sword.

She was white to the lips, but her eyes shone with unchanging and unfaltering fire, and the hand that grasped the sword-hilt hardly trembled. Her fears were not for herself, but for the Prince, and *his* eyes she would not meet, though they were constantly bent upon her.

So did they wait, claymore in hand,—courage at heart,—amid a deathly stillness,—for that approaching doom.

· · · · ·

The soldiers had covered half the distance between the hill and the dairy when a man sprang out of the heather directly in their path. It was Robert Mackenzie! He stood erect and unshrinking, although a dozen muskets were levelled at his heart, as the cry of "The Pretender!" burst from a dozen throats. A flashing line of fire rent the air, and the hills around Loch Arkaig flung back the fatal echo. Robert Mackenzie, faithful to his last breath to the King he died to save, sank, bleeding, to the ground, the bullets piercing his devoted breast, and the cry of "*Villains, you have slain your Prince!*" upon his dying lips.

* * * * *

The tragic close of this heroic drama was mercifully hidden from the anxious watchers in the dairy, although the ominous crash of muskets made them fear the worst. But so appalling was the silence that followed on the jarring echo, that when the lapse of several minutes revealed no sign of foemen,—no sight of Robert Mackenzie's returning figure,—MacLeod made bold to venture forth in search of him. A moment later he came reeling back, and his exclamation of affright drew the Prince and Agnes to the doorway.

"Oh, Gude be mercifu'," the old man wailed, the tears streaming down his furrowed cheeks, "the lad is dead, but 'tis ony the puir body o' him that will be lying yonder, for the deils ha'e ta'en his head!"

Dugald and Malcolm caught each other's hands in an unconscious clasp of horror. Then Charles, as on Drummossie Muir, pressed his temples in a fit of violent shuddering, and cried: "O God! another life for mine! Another life for mine!"

The twilight was now falling fast, and the threatening clouds that had hung all day above Loch Ar kaig were massed in sable tiers athwart the heavens. When the long, grey gloaming deepened into darkness, the muttering of the thunder spoke its low-toned menace, and bright arrows of the lightning darted fitfully across the zenith.

" 'Tis a nicht fit for goblins' frolic," quoth old MacLeod. " And yet ye twa maun ride. For though the deils i' Fort Augustus will dootless be keekin' [peeking] at puir Mackenzie's head, an' takin' it for the Prince's ain, I winna trust them to lie quiet lang, an' wha kens whither they'll be ganging!"

When Dugald and Malcolm left the dairy to mount the horses which MacLeod had brought, the night seemed to have gathered blackness, and to fold the fugitives within its shrouding mantle.

" 'Tis a foul eve for traveling, little comrade," said the Prince to his lovely companion, and he pressed the hand that held his bridle-rein.

" Alas!" she answered, " our journey's end is twelve Scots miles from here."

" We Scots must have an abundance of land since we measure it so lavishly," Charles observed.

Agnes laughed. " 'Tis true, your Majesty, that we have more land than money, since our miles are twice those of the English, while our pounds only equal their shillings."

They mounted and wrapped themselves in their plaids. MacLeod, who had stood at the Prince's stirrup, stepped aside, and the fugitives plunged into the black chaos of lowering night and brooding tempest. Their horses, well-acquainted with every steep-browed ben, with every rugged brae, and heathery hillock, bore them swiftly onward. No chance was there of speech, for Nature's voices drowned all others, but now and then Charles stretched out his hand in the darkness, and touched his comrade's.

Strange pageant this, for the progress of a monarch through his own domains;—with thunder-roll for beat of drum, and moaning of the wind for softer music, and blinding flare of lightning in lieu of streaming torches,—a spectral Cross of Fire lit by demons, that blazed full luridly above the heather.

The girl, with the unerring instinct of a Highlander, held to the northward without a star to guide, with naught but the deceptive play of lightning to reveal the path. Soon they found themselves again in the wilder country they so late had roamed. Dark Ben Doe reared his misty head from the storm-clouds, and the forest-shadows of Glen Clunie lay waiting to receive them. Whether they had left their foes behind they could not know; it might be that the Glen itself held foes among its shadows.

Agnes rode with every nerve at tension;—one hand grasped the rein and the hilt of a dirk, and the other a pistol at half-cock. Yet caution was of no avail. They had just begun to descend a thickly wooded hill, of so gradual a slope that they did not need to check their horses, when danger sprang upon them like a tiger from ambush. A broad flare of lightning revealed directly in their path two soldiers in King George's scarlet;—it lit their faces with a vivid glare, and showed to the girl's terrified gaze,—a sergeant of the guard, and *Kenneth Campbell!*

CHAPTER XXXIV

"THE BONNIE, THE BRAVE, THE DEAR"

> "Here has he lurked, and here
> The heather has been his bed,
> The wastes of the islands knew,
> And the Highland hearts were true
> To the bonnie, the brave, the dear,
> The royal, the hunted head."

THE horses, frightened by the glare and the sudden obstacles in the path, crowded together till their flanks touched. In that one awful instant of lurid revelation the memories of the past made frantic revel in the girl's benumbed brain;—her eyes met Kenneth's in one look of mutual recognition. But the lightning was hostile if Fate was not. A second flash leaped close upon the first, wrapping the fugitives in its baleful fire, and forcing them into wild relief against the darkness.

Agnes, freeing herself from the stirrups, seized the Prince's bridle-rein, else they had fairly plunged upon their enemies. She saw the sergeant's musket levelled at the Prince, and springing with a single dexterous movement from her horse to the other, flung herself across Charles's breast, a shield between him and that deadly danger. In the same breath she saw Kenneth spring forward,—just one second too late,—and strike up the raised musket, saw a flash of flame cleave the air, and heard the deafening crash go pealing off among the mountains.

She felt the Prince's arm about her, caught his frenzied whisper, "Agnes, Agnes, are you hurt?" then, swiftly escaping his clasp, regained her own saddle, wheeled the horses out of the road, and in a trice was plunging with the Prince through the hovering shadows of the storm-swept glen.

The rain came at last to their relief. Torrents fell about them, drenching them to the skin. Blindly the horses fought their way against the flood, stumbling over fallen trees and rolling fragments of stone.

They had not ridden far, when Charles repeated his insistent query, "Agnes, swear to me you are not hurt?"

"Why, how could that be, your Highness?" she responded; "the shot was turned aside by that young officer."

She showed no sign of having recognised Kenneth, and the Prince wondered if she had really done so.

"Yet you perilled your life to shield me, none the less," Charles exclaimed. "O Heaven, had he fired sooner!—Had the shot gone home——"

"But the shot went not home, your Highness, and so how near it sped, need not disturb us. Think no more of it, your Majesty!"

She laughed lightly as she spoke; perhaps to conceal a slight tremble in her voice.

Agnes had hitherto ridden upon the Prince's right now, for some reason, she abruptly changed her position, and rode upon his left. And from time to time she adjusted the folds of her plaid in such fashion as to cover her left arm.

The road they followed had begun to lead steeply upward along the hills that rimmed the glen, bordered by tall Scotch firs and wild luxuriance of heather. Suddenly, from out this heather sounded a low, clear whistle, " The March of the Cameron Men," and Agnes drew in her horse, crying softly, " Angus! Angus MacDonald!"

" Who comes? " cried a voice from the darkness.

" 'Tis only I, Malcolm MacNeil, a friend to the King, and one Dugald McCluny."

" O Dugald McCluny! " wailed the voice in a burst of joy or woe, adding in the same breath, " May the Lord God protect His anointed! "

The next moment a man in plaid and bonnet sprang from the shadows, and kneeled down in the road, raining passionate kisses upon the Prince's stirrup.

"Oh, for God's sake, cease, my good fellow!" besought Charles, vainly endeavouring to raise his devoted subject. " This place is too dangerous; there may be spies abroad."

" An' it please your Majesty, there is not a traitor in the Highlands! " cried Angus, rising, and standing, unbonneted, by the horse's side.

The loyal Angus, after his capture near Fort Augustus, had suffered barbarous captivity on board a British prison-ship, which lay at anchor in the Moray Firth. After existing for eight weeks, herded with his fellow-sufferers in the vessel's hold, with water and oat-husks for their sole subsistence, the indomitable Angus had escaped by swimming ashore, and had straightway sought the mistress from whom he had been sundered.

He now led the shivering refugees up the mountain to a sheiling near the summit. The thunder-clouds had parted, and a pale moon rode mid-heaven like a ghostly watcher. Agnes kept her face averted from the Prince, and several times during the ascent she sharply caught her breath as if in pain. When she dismounted she swayed, though slightly, and compelled herself, with an effort, to stand erect.

Within, there was food laid ready, and scarlet radiance of dancing flames to cheer the heart and body. Charles scanned the girl's face intently, alarmed at her growing pallor.

"Why, Agnes, you are almost fainting with exhaustion; you need care and quiet, and there is nothing but this rude place for you to rest in, and naught but my awkward ministrations to assist you."

He sank into a seat and, resting his arms on the table, covered his face with his hands.

"Oh, if I dared but tell you,—yet honour still forbids me." He turned to her where she stood, with her appealing eyes upon him. "Agnes, why did you trust yourself to my companionship? I am no saint, no hero; were you not afraid?"

She had sunk slowly to one knee, and though the colour faintly tinged her face at his strange question her eyes, so clear and childlike, still met his unfalteringly.

"Why should I fear?" she answered in a voice that quivered slightly. "Where should I be safe than under the protection of my King?"

Charles dropped his head upon his arms, and his shoulders shook with dry but dreadful sobs.

"I am not worthy the worship of a pure heart like yours!" he cried in tones of anguish.

A soft hand touched his plaid entreatingly. "Oh, your Majesty," besought a trembling voice,—"how can you thus malign yourself? *You*, so chivalrous, so noble——"

The voice ceased suddenly. Agnes, kneeling there, felt a fiery spasm of pain sweep over her,—was conscious that the room was wavering through a darkened mist of sight. Vainly she strove to conquer that overwhelming faintness,—vainly strove to raise herself. The Prince had risen and was coming toward her, and now his gaze was fixed upon her plaid. Then all the world went black before her eyes, and Charles, springing forward, caught her in his arms as she swayed backward, swooning, with the blood streaming from a wound in her left shoulder.

. . . . .

"Agnes, Agnes, in Christ's name speak to me! *Mother of God! she is dying!*" were the words that greeted her dawning consciousness.

She opened her eyes to find the Prince kneeling beside her, with her head resting against his knee. He had cut away her sleeve with his dirk, and had been engaged in bandaging her arm, when her deathly pallor had wrung from him the passionate appeal she had heard. As she stirred faintly, and her eyes unclosed, he gave a quick sigh of relief, and exclaimed, "Thank God, she is reviving!" With skilful hands he secured the bandage, and supporting her head against his shoulder, began to fan her with a fold of his plaid, while Angus MacDonald, himself not a little alarmed, held some brandy-and-water to the girl's reluctant lips. She took one burning swallow, then, as he urged another, she pushed it away with a faint gesture of abhorrence. After a moment's hesitation, Angus settled the matter by swallowing the mixture himself, with a curse upon its weakness.

He had hardly completed this performance when the Prince bade him depart, "and see if you can find any food besides oatmeal!"

As soon as Angus had gone, Agnes made a desperate effort to rise, but weakness conquered, and she sank back feebly against the supporting arm. "I am sorry to have put your Royal Highness to so great a trouble," were the first words she found strength to murmur.

"Trouble!" he ejaculated, "when you so nearly gave your life for mine, no service I could render would repay the debt by so much as a millionth part!"

"I hope your Royal Highness does not think that we Highland maids are like the Lowland lassies and faint from a mere scratch," the girl protested, gathering strength.

"A mere scratch!" cried the Prince, who, as a boy of thirteen, serving with the Spanish army at the siege of Gaeta, had fearlessly exposed himself in dangerous positions and learned something of wounds. "Why, Heaven knows, the ball plowed so deep a furrow from the shoulder down that your plaid was soaked in blood. 'Tis fortunate I learned a little of the surgeon's art at Gaeta. Yet I think, little Spartan, that you would have hid the hurt altogether had it not been for this swoon! That God should let you suffer so for me!"

"Ah, your Majesty!" she whispered, "I think He knows that there is none for whom I would suffer more willingly!"

Choked with emotion, Charles dared not reply. The sublime heights of her devotion overwhelmed him with their grandeur. He had known much of loyalty in his short life, yet he had not dreamed there could be such devotion upon earth as this.

After a lengthened absence, Angus returned unsuccessful. Charles, resigning Agnes to his care, arranged some heather in one corner, and spread his plaid upon it. He then lifted the girl in his arms, despite her protests, and gently deposited her upon his sylvan couch. Exhausted by pain and loss of blood, and lulled by the comparative comfort of her resting-place, Agnes yielded to a delightful sense of drowsiness, and soon drifted into a light doze, through which she was dimly conscious that Charles had left the hut. She finally wakened to see the Prince kneeling beside her. He held a cup of milk in his hands, which he had filled from a pail near by, and gently raised it to her lips. Faint with hunger, the girl drank it eagerly, finding the warmth and delicious flavour grateful indeed. But when she had finished the second cup, she turned to him, with startled look.

"What peril did you risk to get me this comfort? There are no cattle near this place; you must have ventured near some house. Oh, tell me, why will you hazard your life,—your royal person,—for so slight a thing as a draught of milk?" Then in a passion of gratitude: "This you did for *me*,—your Majesty,—for me, who would rather hunger,—who would rather die,—than one hair of your head should be endangered!"

But the Prince met her reproaches lightly.

"The danger was not so great as you think it, fair lady. I had roamed but a mile down the mountain when my ear caught the tinkling of cow-bells. One animal I seized, muffled her bell for precaution, and led her aside from the rest. I am no adept at milking, and the creature did not assist me, but somehow I managed to fill my pail, and escape unseen. The moon was low enough to afford me light, and yet cast deep shadows in which I could lurk, and I followed a roundabout path to baffle detection. So vex not your mind with fear for my adventures, my gallant little comrade, but compose yourself to sleep, if sleep you can, from pain."

The warming drink produced the effect of an opiate, and the girl slept fitfully. But whenever she started into fleeting wakefulness, the Prince was always near to murmur words of comfort, and watch over her with the tenderness of a mother for her child.

Toward morning Agnes sank into a feverish slumber, disturbed by troubled dreams, whose fragile substance shifted ere she could grasp their meaning, and yet continually tormented her with a sense of impending calamity. She was in Edinburgh, behold ing from her window the triumphant entrance of the Camerons, but the music suddenly altered, and the brilliant pibroch changed to a wailing coronach. She walked with Donald in the garden, but the sun no longer shone, and the flowers she plucked were withered, and as often as she strove to fix a snow-white rose in Donald's bonnet, it turned to ashes in her very grasp. And again, Norman Leslie stood before her in all his garb of war, as on the day they parted, but there was deeper anguish in his face than ever she had seen thereon, and the broadsword that he wore was broken quite in twain. But as she gazed at him in terror, and questioned what his grief might be, his face, in the fickle fashion of dreams, became that of Donald Cameron, and Donald Cameron, in like manner, changed to Charles himself.

This last vision was no fancy, for the Prince was really bending over her, and had gently aroused her by drawing one of her curls across her face.

"It is sheer brutality to wake you," he exclaimed, "but we have just been warned that a band of militia is ascending the lake, and that we must flee. MacDonald has gone for the horses, but will return forthwith. Do you think you can endure a short journey? If your condition forbids it, I will stay here with you, and risk what comes. They *may* search elsewhere after all."

But Agnes, terrified at such a prospect, swayed to her feet, declaring wildly, "No, no, I am strong again! I can ride; I can travel anywhere! Only let us leave this dangerous place! See,"—she took a few steps forward,—"I can walk right sturdily."

"But you must not attempt it without assistance," the Prince protested. "Forgive me for taking an unwarrantable liberty,—I cannot let you stand alone."

So saying, he passed his arm around her, in such a manner as to avoid injuring her wounded shoulder. In this position they began to walk slowly up and down.

When Angus returned with the horses, Charles gently lifted Agnes to the saddle, and kept close beside her on the journey lest she sway or faint.

The next three days the girl remembered through a strange blur of pain, like a vision in a dimmed mirror. She knew that they rode and hid and ventured as at other times, but she could recall nothing clearly, save that the Prince was constant in his sympathy, and constant in his care for her.

"Agnes, you must let me examine your arm," Charles urged repeatedly, but Agnes as steadily refused.

"Nay, nay, your Highness, 'tis not needful,—the wound is healing fast," while to herself she murmured, "Heaven forgive me for the falsehood,—the pain is well-nigh unendurable,—but *he* must not know it!"

On the third evening, the little party, consisting, as formerly, of Dugald, Malcolm, and MacLeod, gathered around a camp-fire for their nightly bivouac. Angus had returned that afternoon with a message from "the Seven Men of Morriston,"—a band of involuntary Ishmaels, who were to arrive at midnight and take the Prince under their protection, until he could join Locheil. Of her own intent Agnes said nothing, but as she lay in the firelight, beneath the stars, with the mountains rising dark on either hand, her half-formed purpose grew to strong decision, and waited but the fitting moment for fulfilment. Her presence was no longer needful to the Prince's safety, and she would disappear from his horizon,—at least until she was again required—and in the manner of her going would save him any futile pain.

MacLeod, the sentinel, paced slowly up and down outside the band of light, while Charles, reclining by the fire, his head propped on his hand, drew out a pack of crumpled cards, and, spreading them on the ground, essayed to tell his fortune, glancing from time to time at the fair, shadowed face of the sleeping girl. But the *king* and *queen* refused to take their proper places; the fate-cards were all sombre-coloured, and the cruel nine of diamonds intruded its fatal hue, till at length, with a heavy sigh, Charles tossed the cards together, and drawing his plaid about him, fell asleep.

The fire had sunken into orange embers when Agnes, rising noiselessly, stood listening till the low, regular breathing of the Prince convinced her of the soundness of his slumber. With a last regretful glance, she stole to where MacLeod sat, watching, and bending, whispered something in his ear. The old man shook his head in disapproval, but finally yielded to her persistent pleading, and, with a look of deep misgiving, saw her disappear into the shadows.

CHAPTER XXXV

"THE CROWN OF THY FATHERS IS TORN FROM THY BROW!"

"Fareweel, my young hero! the gallant and good;
The crown of thy fathers is torn from thy brow!"

THE red mid-summer moon was high, and all Glen Morriston was wrapped in dream-light, when Agnes crept warily down the mountain. It was a night too fair, too calm, to shelter any foes; a night whose beauty held the foretaste of a happier world. The Glen was a very paradise, with its soft, velvet shadows, and gleaming pearls of moonlight strung thick among the heather. The liquid lilt of a thrush floated down through the woodland, and the dainty tinkle of a waterfall scattered elfin music.

Agnes brushed lightly through a fairy world of shade and shimmer, and well it was that she trod lightly as a fawn. For on the confines of a little dell, in whose unshadowed heart the moonbeams lay like marble, there met her eyes a scene that made the night's rich splendour a hollow mockery, and smote its silver music dumb.

A man in Highland dress was bound by his wrists to the trunk of a rowan tree; and beside him stood two men in uniform, one of whom wielded a heavy cat-o'-nine-tails with brutal force, while the other repeatedly struck the prisoner with his clenched fist, exclaiming fiercely: "Curse you, confess, you devil of a Scot! or I'll take every drop in your veins!"

The lash, already crimsoned, fell with cruel hisses on its victim, but he, the blood streaming from his bared shoulders, hardly stirred, nor heeded his tormentor's questions. A vagrant moonbeam pierced the rowan-leaves, and lit his pallid face. *It was Angus MacDonald!*

Agnes, shuddering lest a breath betray her, crouched within the protecting shadow of a tree, and gazed in a horror of helplessness upon the dreadful scene. She wrung her hands against her breast, and cowered piteously, as if the red blows fell on her as well. That Angus, the playmate and protector of her childhood,—Angus, dearer to her because dear to Donald, should be tortured so, was unendurable; and she knew that he was suffering thus because of his fidelity to the Prince.

But duty laid on her insistent hands;—she could not linger here in futile woe. With indrawn breath, and muffled heart-throbs, she crept on hands and knees through the friendly heather till she was beyond the sound of those torturing blows; then leaped to her feet, and fled, like a hunted maukin (hare) through the forest. But the night was fair no longer; the very moon seemed cruel to shine, unmoved, on such a sight.

. . . . . .

It was perhaps two in the morning, and the moon

was throwing rays aslant across the valley, when Agnes reached a little cottage, from whose uncurtained window a candle glimmered forth to mock the moonlight. Swiftly she stole to the casement and peered in. By the tallow dip an old man sat with tears upon his furrowed cheeks,—great tears that fell unheeded upon the Bible in his lap. Without hesitation the girl tapped lightly on the pane, and instantly the old man rose and approached the window. At sight of the youthful stranger he started violently, and hardly waiting for her whispered, "I would speak with you," unbarred the door, and came to meet her.

The graceful figure in the moonlight gazed fixedly upon him, and held out a hand to him, saying meaningly: "Do you know me, Neil Ogilvie?"

With an inarticulate cry the old man sank on his knees, and fell to kissing rapturously the slender hand.

"Oh, my lord, my lord!" he sobbed, when his words found intelligible utterance, "how good is God! 'Tis even as I read this very night,—'Now know I that the Lord saveth His anointed: He will hear him from His holy heaven with the saving strength of His right hand.'"

"Can you hide me here for a few weeks without endangering yourself, Neil?" inquired the masquerader.

"Aye, that I can, your Majesty," cried the old man eagerly. "No greater honour would I ask, than ye should bide beneath our roof. The British bluid-hounds canna fin' ye here!"

"The Crown of Thy Fathers"

"So be it then," murmured the counterfeit Prince with royal dignity. "When I have reached St. James's, your loyalty shall meet its due reward."

. . . . .

On the evening of the 19th of September, Prince Charlie sat alone in a little cottage on the coast of Moidart, not far from the scene of his landing but fourteen months before. On the deep bay of Loch na Nuagh, whose waters rippled scarce a bow-shot off, two frigates rode at anchor, their masts and rigging rising black against the orange sunset. They were the ships from France to bear him safe beyond the sea. After weary months of hunted wandering, deliverance opened arms to him at last. Yet tonight he thought not of his wonderful escape, nor of his buoyant hopes of swift return to rescue Scotland from her conquerors. He sat with head on hand and gaze intent, like one who listens for a footstep, nor knows if he shall ever catch the sound of it.

Yet the footstep fell so lightly that even he who listened heard it not. A hand was on the latch, and on the threshold stood a slender figure, concealed from head to foot in its black cloak. "Your Royal Highness," said a girlish voice, "I have obeyed your bidding." Charles started up with shining eyes, elated by the joy of hope fulfilled. The cry of his heart sprang to his lips in her whispered name: "*Agnes! Agnes!*"

Then the two ran to meet each other, clasping hand in hand, like friends long separated.

"How could you thus have left me, Agnes?" Charles exclaimed reproachfully. "Save for your message I could not have borne it, for I thought that I had lost you evermore."

He paused, and then continued: "Did you not think me strangely forgetful, Agnes, strangely heartless and indifferent, never to mention during all our comradeship the hallowed days that lay behind us?—That night at Holyrood when the ancient kings looked down upon our triumph;—that hour in Queen Mary's chamber, when we bewitched the sombre memories of the place, and made of them fair golden visions. Did you not deem it strange for me to leave these things unspoken? But it was honour held me dumb;—to-night the spell is lifted. Will you hearken, Agnes, while I speak?"

Her wide eyes gave a wondering assent as he led her to a chair, and turned to her.

"Agnes," he said, "do you know whereof I dreamt at Holyrood? Oh, they were youthful dreams,— of conquest and of glory,—but one dream of them all was dearest to my heart! Ah, 'twas of *you*, Agnes, you alone of all the world! I used to see you Queen,—the Queen of Scotland, and *my* Queen!"

He paused, with eyes like stars for radiance, as if he saw again those cherished visions.

But Agnes rose, half-frightened, the startled colour springing to her cheeks, and eyes, amazed, incredulous.

"Your Highness!" she exclaimed, "what mean these words? You do not—no!—you cannot— realise what you have said!—These words to *me*— to *me*,—your Majesty?"

To her the words seemed little less than madness

—perhaps his mind had been unbalanced by protracted suffering.

"Nay, nay, believe me,—'tis my heart that speaks! You, only, did I love at Holyrood;—you, only—Agnes Leslie, *do* I love! Nay, call me king no longer,—kneel to me no more! To-night we stand here equal before God! Once it might have been King Charles that wooed you, that would have sought you for his Queen. That is passed,—perhaps forever! To-night it is Charles Stuart who seeks you for his wife!"

It was he who knelt now, though she tried vainly to prevent him,—knelt there at her feet, and clasped her hands in his, and kissed them with a tender reverence.

"Oh, your Majesty,—do not kneel to me!" she cried imploringly. "Who am I,—your subject,—that you should thus entreat me?"

"Ah, why will you resist my homage? Are you not Agnes Leslie,—the only woman that my soul enshrines,—or ever shall enshrine!—you,—pure as purest snow upon the mountains,—steadfast as stars that guide,—true as Heaven is true! Yet think not that 'tis gratitude alone I feel, though how you offered your sweet life for mine will thrill my heart so long as it shall beat! No, love has overcome all else, and gratitude is lost in love! O Agnes, Agnes,—fair as Scotland's heather,—brave as Scotland's heart,—my guardian angel and my better spirit,—go not from me;—with you the world is mine! We will conquer it together! Without you I shall sink in darkness deep as night without a star!"

He had risen and had loosed her hands, and as he ended, he stretched out his arms to her in a gesture of supreme appeal.

Her brown eyes rested, wistful and dismayed, upon his supplicating face; her lips were quivering with intense emotion.

"I pray your Majesty to listen, although I plead with you against yourself. Remember of what rank you are, and for what destiny you are reserved. The Leslies are of noble blood, 'tis true, it is but justice to their name to speak it;—six hundred years ago 'tis written, the King of Scotland's sister did not disdain to wed with one, Bartholf of Leslie, the founder of their line. Yet to the King alone they owe their honours; to-day, with all their pride, they claim no royal blood,—no right to mate with royalty. Ah your Majesty, consider!—a prince weds only with a princess!"

"But if the Prince have found the Princess?" whispered Charles.

He took her hand again, and leading her to the window, pointed out upon the wavering lanterns at the frigate's bow.

"Agnes, there lies the ship that is to carry me to France. *L'Heureux*, 'the Happy,' is the frigate's name. Richly will she deserve it, and happy above all men will I be,—although a fugitive,—an exile,— if *you*, my only love, go with me! . . . The frigate sails at midnight, and ere we leave the land the priest upon that ship shall have wedded us, Agnes —shall have linked in holy union the lives that were linked by fate. Agnes, Agnes, come with me,—a uncrowned Queen, an unacknowledged sovereign, in the world's eyes,—but in my heart how crowned,—O Heaven!—how loved and honoured!"

But at his words a shadow crossed her face, and with a look of infinite regret she forced herself to speak:

"I must entreat your Highness to hear me with forbearance. Forgive me if I utter words which pain you; but greatly would I wrong you if I spoke not the truth. None could be more deeply sensible than I of the lofty honour you have conferred upon me in asking me to be your wife. It is an honour I shall hold as sacred, close-locked within my heart, until the day I die. But oh! what can I give you in return? Alas! the love I bear you is not the love a maiden gives to him who is to be her wedded husband,—though 'tis a love as mighty and as deep! I thought of you as glorious, honoured Scotland, embodied in a man, and he a prince, a hero! I saw you far above me on the throne!—I dreamed not that that throne would be for *me* to share!

"This honour you have proffered me is great,—too great for such as I,—yet if I loved in that one way, I would accept of it,—that wondrous gift,—and wear so great a dignity as best I might. But—*that way* I love not,—O forgive me!—and so, your Majesty, I cannot go with you,—I cannot be your wife! . . .

"And yet to help you win the throne, I would gladly sacrifice all that is mine,—and I would give my life, as you have known, to save your royal life. And if, hereafter, you should e'er have need of me,

I would go through land and sea to bring you succour! . . . But that *one thing*—that one—it is not mine to give!"

She ceased to speak, as pale as ashes, with eyes that shone like woeful stars. But the Prince was paler than she, and his head was bowed like one who hears the sentence of his doom. Suddenly he moved to the table, and cast his arms upon it, and hid his face between them, as on the night when Agnes knelt before him, fainting.

"You do not know how deeply you have stricken!" he whispered in a voice that strove for calmness.— "*With* you I could have won the world to my resolve —could have retrieved my failures, and wrested Scotland from her foeman's clutch! I could have battled through a thousand perils, and won the throne at last! *Without* you I can never conquer The fatal weakness that I know is in me will prevail Nay, *without you* I shall return no more!"

His voice broke; from his lips came the heavy stifled sobs of a strong man crushed completely by the ultimate blow of Fate.

With a mighty effort he controlled himself, rose and turned slowly toward her.

"Agnes, I blame you not;—you could not be untrue to your own self. But, ah! to me,—the sun has set upon my life! And since we now must part forever, I may kiss you—may I not—one last farewell?"

She bowed her head in mute assent, for she was powerless to speak, nor could she look at him, for burning tears. She closed her eyes a moment in dim maze of anguish,—wherein the sorrows of a hundred years seemed met and gathered into one,—and at his touch a thrill of bitter woe ran through her,—the poignant anguish of a tragic past! Holding her hands in his feverish grasp, he bent and kissed her twice upon the forehead,—gently, reverently,—with a tender, mournful passion, and she heard him murmur: "Farewell, *Scotland!*"

CHAPTER XXXVI

"THERE'S NOUGHT LEFT BUT SORROW FOR SCOTLAND AND ME!"

> "The conflict is past, and our name is no more;
> There's nought left but sorrow for Scotland and me!"

AFTERWARD, Agnes recalled nothing clearly of how she left the cottage, so much did her emotion eclipse all minor incidents. She had blurred remembrance of the Prince, standing, with bended head, beside the window;—of the entrance of a Highland sentry, and of a question asked and answered; then, when perception cleared, she found herself outside the cottage, and looking back upon the lighted windows. A poignant sense of loss possessed her,—an aching in her breast that would not cease. There smote on her the realisation that she had left, in that dim room behind her, the strongest motive of her life,—the motive of the lives from which her own was drawn,—the dear, personified ideal for which her race had battled and had died He was king,—a *Stuart*,—how had she dared forsake him thus when he had cried to her in mortal need? It was as if she saw him lying wounded, and yet withheld the succour she might give. One moment pity had her in its thrall;—should she return and yield to his entreaty,—yield out of very shame at her disloyalty

"Nought Left But Sorrow for Scotland" 311

An impulse even mightier than her zeal forbade her. —As he had said:—to herself she could not be untrue;—her heart was Donald's, and would ever be. No power on earth could give it to another!

Yet she must steal back once again,—must gaze on him once more in mute farewell,—unknown to him,—or else the spirit in her breast that cried out "Traitor!" would not be laid in peace.

"His Highness sleeps," the sentinel objected, but she whispered him in Gaelic: "Let me enter.—I would touch his plaid before I go—forever!"

The single light burned low; the room was grey with shadows. Charles slept indeed,—a slumber born of sorrow,—with now and then a sob of uncontrollable despair. A fringed fold of his plaid lay on the floor beside him, and Agnes, kneeling, pressed her lips to it, with the same touch of passionate tenderness that she had given the sacred claymore of Dundee. Then, trembling lest he wake and know, she rose, and went, as she had come, in silence and in shadow.

Without, beneath the curtain of the night, she stood awhile, and pondered, looking on the sea. "There is but one thing left wherein to aid him," she said at last, "and that—God helping—I will do!" When she had found and mounted her faithful horse, "'Phrionnsa," she turned him to the east and gave him rein. And all night long she rode, unfaltering, inland, nor once looked back upon the sea.

. . . . .

It was past noon on the following day when a youthful Highlander drew rein before a humble cottage on the banks of beautiful Loch Oich. He had barely alighted from his horse, when a pale-faced woman ran from the cottage, exclaiming wildly "Alas! what do you here? In God's name, come within and hide yourself!"

The youth obeyed her passionate command, and entering, took the chimney-seat to which she pointed him.

"Oh, your Majesty!" the woman cried, "why will ye risk your life in this dangerous spot? For Augustus lies scarce eight miles distant, and there the 'Butcher' waits to murder you. Oh, wherefore cam' ye hither, my ain bonnie laddie?"

She had come forward, trembling, and fallen on her knees, and now she laid a thin, work-hardened hand upon his plaid.

"Four sons o' mine fought for your Royal Highness; ane sleeps upon Drummossie Muir. Will ye no' hearken to their mother's pleading?"

"Ah, madam," cried the Prince appealingly "how can you bear the sight of one who has been the cause to you of such distress?"

With unfaltering devotion came the answer: "Your Highness, I would still be glad to serve you, though a' my sons had perished in your service, for they would then ha'e done nae mair than was their rightful duty!"

With a heavy sigh the Prince rose, exclaiming "'Tis a loyalty that passes knowledge."

The woman set what food she had prepared before her honoured guest, and waited eagerly upon his wants. When he had finished, she addressed him

"Nought Left But Sorrow for Scotland" 313

timidly, "Your Highness hasna said what purpose brought ye here amang your foes?"

He answered her with face turned toward the window. "Madam, I go to Fort Augustus, there to surrender myself to Cumberland, in the hope that this woeful country, cursed because of me, may have relief at last."

She uttered a piteous cry, and started toward him. "Your Highness, in God's mercy, dinna speak it! Let Scotland bear the cost an' it maun be, but dinna show that bonnie face before the deils o' Brunswick! Better,—a thousand times,—that we should die, whase puir lives arena worth a plack compared wi' your dear life, your Highness!"

"'Tis cruel to deceive her thus," the Prince reflected, "and yet confide in her I dare not!"

This reverie was interrupted by his hostess, who had wrapped a plaid about her with the evident intention of leaving the house.

"Your Highness," she said anxiously, "if I gang to tak' counsel o' Patrick Macpherson, will ye e'en promise me ye winna pass oot yon door while I'm awa?"

With a flash of inspiration he responded: "Madam, I promise you my foot shall not cross that threshold till you return."

When she had departed the Prince sprang up, exclaiming: "'Tis really a falsehood I was forced to tell her;—I will go by the window, and not by the door;—if I stayed she would prevent me, poor loyal soul!—Perhaps the soldiers yonder will kill me at sight;—those were Cumberland's orders;—but I pray God they will not, for I would deceive them as long as possible."

Having convinced himself that the way was free of travellers, Charles climbed warily out at the low back window, which opened on the garden, and, loosing his horse from the tiny cow-shed, rode resolutely toward Fort Augustus.

. . . . .

Less than an hour later, the sentry, pacing to and fro before the gates, beheld a Highland horseman advancing at a gallop. So striking was the traveller's appearance, that it was not till he had halted at the gate, and accosted the sentry, that the minion of martial law recovered sufficiently from his astonishment to summon the guard. As a file of soldiers issued from the Fort, the Highlander sprang from his horse, and, advancing to meet them, drew his pistol, and offered it to the officer in command.

"I surrender!" he said briefly, and then, in his clear, ringing tones: "Tell the Duke of Cumberland that Charles Stuart yields himself a prisoner; and that he will surrender his sword to his Grace alone."

Even the hardened soldiers recoiled, amazed, at this temerity, and surrounded their royal captive with a look akin to deference; observing, to their further stupefaction, that this Bonnie Charlie was as slim and fair as a girl, and had also a girl's trick of blushing.

. . . . .

William of Cumberland sat alone, communing savagely with his own vindictive spirit. It seemed to him that the series of irritating events which had recently occurred would justify any degree of fury. First, there had been this utterly fruitless searching for the royal fugitive,—the more tantalising because so constantly deluded by hopes of ultimate success; —and then this baffling loyalty with which the oppressed and despoiled Scotsmen,—many of them the poorest peasants,—had concealed the secret of his whereabouts. Affairs had reached a really hopeless state, when neither torture nor the reward of £30,000 could wring the secret from the lips of starving and hunted men!

Next, he had heard of Kingsburgh's part in aiding the disguised Prince, and had not rested till the perpetrator of so monstrous a crime against his serene and "German" Majesty, George the Second, was fast in chains in the dungeons of Fort Augustus, thus securing "a whole year's safe lodging for affording that of one night." But even this prompt act of righteous anger had not met its due reward, for Kingsburgh, though a poor and aged man, had proved as stubborn as his fellow-Scots, and, when Cumberland had tauntingly reminded him how noble an opportunity he had lost of enriching himself and his family forever, had replied with scathing dignity: "Had I gold and silver piled heaps upon heaps to the bulk of yon huge mountain, that mass could not afford me half the satisfaction I find in my own breast from doing what I have done!" Truly, such efforts were discouraging!

He had barely despatched the obstinate old traitor to Edinburgh Castle when a new alarm had roused him. Some soldiers, roaming the Braes of Loch

Arkaig, had killed a man whom they claimed to be the Prince, and, in witness thereof, brought the severed head for Cumberland's scrutiny. Several weeks had elapsed before the Duke became aware that the real head, on which so tempting a reward was set, still remained undisturbed on the Prince's shoulders; and, in the meanwhile, the search for its rightful owner had been much delayed. Naturally, these repeated annoyances had not improved the Duke's disposition, as his soldiers might have testified.

Accordingly, when an officer appeared, and delivered the extraordinary message with which the Prince had charged him, Cumberland rose with an exclamation of impatient triumph. "The Pretender! By the gods, we've got the right man at last!" It was with a sense of fierce elation that he descended to the dungeon wherein his prisoner awaited him.

CHAPTER XXXVII

"RISE, SPIRITS OF YORE!"

"Rise, spirits of yore,
 Ever dauntless in danger!"

AS the Duke entered the dungeon, the prisoner rose with dignity, stood haughtily erect, and faced his captor with a coldly tranquil air. Cumberland, in his turn, surveyed with mingled scorn and exultation the graceful figure of his foe. He could not fail to notice how fair and slender was this Stuart Prince who had so aroused Great Britain. But his Grace was not remarkable for penetration, and no faintest suspicion of the truth dawned upon him. For a full minute the two remained thus, each confronting the other in a gaze of mutual defiance. Then the Duke advanced a step, exclaiming with a sneer:

"So you thought best to abandon your game of hide-and-seek, my aspiring young cousin?"

"By my honour, your Grace, 'twas a right pretty game, and one of which I did not seem to weary, but you played so losing a hand that, in truth, I came hither in sheer pity, to relieve you of further anxiety on my behalf."

The words were composed and careless,—deliberately tantalising,—with just the suspicion of a drawl underlying their cool indifference.

"You dare taunt me, do you, you upstart of spurious blood?" menaced Cumberland, reddening with fury. "Save your gibes for Tower Hill, where they'll sound to more advantage."

"Your Grace anticipates," observed the unruffled prisoner. "I believe some at Falkirk and at Prestonpans did likewise, and were a trifle disappointed. You know the scripture: 'Boast not thyself of tomorrow.' The blind goddess has been known to turn her scales."

"Curse your glib tongue,—you devil of a Stuart! —'tis a rope's end befits your effrontery more than the headsman's axe.—My faith!—a pretty sight for all these traitor-Scots to look upon!—but better still, to see the Old Pretender feast his eyes upon the Young Pretender's head!"

The Prince stood quite unmoved, and simply raised his eyebrows in gentle amazement. But suddenly he turned to Cumberland, and said imperiously:

"Sir, for myself I care nothing for your idle threats and malicious curses,—I do not charge my mind with them;—but I would have you know that when you offer insult to my royal father, you do so at your peril!"

The Duke had writhed his heavy features into an evil smile.

"You take too much upon yourself, my dear young kinsman. James Stuart is a dastard,— a rebel,—a usurper;—a dastard, for he slunk from Scotland like a hunted thief after the failure of 'the '15';—a rebel to his Majesty, King George the

First; and a usurper, because he tried to steal away the throne like the base pretender that he is! If this be not a speaking likeness——"

He was fiercely interrupted by the Prince, who, springing forward, struck him across the breast, exclaiming furiously:

"Foul slanderer of the just! Red Butcher of the brave!—take this, in token of the scorn in which all true men hold you!"

Cumberland's face grew ghastly with excess of rage. He sputtered rather than spoke:

"You shall fight me for this, you insolent impostor! Aha!—you waver, do you? I scarce thought your sword would match your tongue in keenness."

But the prisoner's hesitation—if hesitation it was —proved but momentary.

"Sir!" he returned haughtily, "your challenge shall not go unanswered. Perhaps a just God may permit me to avenge in part the fiendish cruelties you practised at Culloden!"

He heard the Duke curse him violently below his breath, before replying:

"It shall be a combat to the death then, you daredevil! For those of your presumptuous breed I have no mercy. If you be not the coward that I think you, make haste to show your boasted courage!"

With this closing taunt, the Duke, breathing hard with rage, began tugging off his outer garments in clumsy haste. His rival, following his example, removed rather reluctantly his tartan coat, unsheathed his claymore, and stood clad in a loose white blouse,

—secured by a leather sword-belt,—and a ragged philabeg of the MacNeil tartan. The Duke next rolled up his sleeves, and the Prince again complied, though with hesitation, conscious of arms somewhat too white and rounded for a man's. But the dungeon was dusky, and the Duke remained blind to these incongruities. He regarded the slender figure of his antagonist with contempt, and indeed the odds seemed to favour his own great bulk and powerful muscles.

"Now,—my bonnie vaunter!" cried Cumberland, wrenching out his sword, "you're as pretty as a woman;—can you fight like a man?"

He saw—to his intense exasperation—that his rival stood lightly balanced, calmly awaiting the signal for the start. It burst in venomous challenge from the Duke's lips; and like a panther, poised for leaping, the Prince sprang forward in response.

As in some weird, appalling dream, Agnes was conscious of her agile movements,—of the fierce darting of the old broadsword to meet Cumberland's,—of rapid thrusts given and parried;—yet all the while she felt as if a stronger hand than hers held the claymore, and another mind mastered hers, and that she was but the passive instrument in another's hands. She fought as Charles had taught her,—in every skilful stroke, in every lithe turn of the wrist, in every supple shift of place,—as if the duel itself had been only a pastime, and the Prince stood by, directing every motion. Nay more!—Charles himself might have fought there in her stead, so closely did she follow his teaching,—so perfectly did she imitate each trick of French or Italian swordsmanship which he had imparted to his apt scholar.

But it was not the courage and skill of the last Stuart, alone, which nerved her delicate body, and strengthened her slender hand. The men of the past were fighting *with* her, fighting *through* her, against this cruel tyrant;—the heart of the great Montrose, —that heart ever bravest in war, ever noblest in peace,—true, in the prison, and on the scaffold, and still revered and dreaded, when the earth had closed above it;—that heart throbbed in her own pulsebeats.

The proud blood of Dundee,—that fiery, fearless champion of his king, who scorned to name another, sovereign, and died,—loyal to the last, at Killiecrankie;—that hot blood burned and rioted in her own veins, and battled against pain and weakness, and filled her with a spirit mightier than her own, to save one cherished life!

From the beginning Agnes realised that in agility, if not in skill as well, she was the Duke's master. It was strength only that she lacked, a man's untiring strength, and that she needed sorely, for, in one of their rapid movements, she struck her injured arm against the wall, and the fiery pang of it racked her through and through. With an effort almost superhuman, she repressed the increasing pain, and forced herself to face the deadly task in hand. Cumberland was losing ground;—his girlish antagonist pressed him hard. The Duke was purple-faced and panting, but the "Prince," light and supple, betrayed no sign of exhaustion.

With unexpected swiftness came the climax. The Duke made a misstep,—failed somehow to parry his opponent's thrust; and the next moment the sword of Dundee, relentless, had leaped the space in a lightning flash of steel, and sank in Cumberland's shoulder. At this, the conqueror shrank back, shuddering, averse to look upon his handiwork, while the Duke, supported by the wall, called angrily for aid, and vainly tried to staunch the wound.

At length, loud footsteps were heard descending, and a number of guardsmen entered in headlong haste, to stare astounded at the scene;—an amazement greatly increased by the victor's shrinking attitude, and by Cumberland's repeated utterance: "Curse your tardy heels, you laggard villains!—This damned scoundrel has all but murdered me!" And then to the jailor: "Put him in irons, do you hear? He shall pay in full for this outrage! And you, knaves,—bind up my shoulder, and help me hence before I swoon from loss of blood!"

Thus supported by two of his guard, the Duke quitted the dungeon, in a somewhat different state of mind from that in which he had entered it. But he scarce had crossed the threshold when the victor, left alone, began to stagger dizzily,—flung out both hands in a vain attempt to save himself from falling, and sank—a senseless heap—upon the pile of straw.

• • • • •

As the ship *L'Heureux* crept stealthily through the mist-wrapped Irish Sea, a number of gentlemen upon her deck conversed in muffled tones with an English refugee, who had just arrived on board with startling news. Suddenly, one of them broke excitedly away from the group, crying distractedly:

"You say they do report the Prince a prisoner at Fort Augustus? My God! 'tis Mistress Leslie!—Command the captain instantly to steer for shore."

The Prince—for it was he—betrayed the utmost agitation;—and his desperate purpose was self-evident. His hearers stood dumfounded, powerless to combat this frantic impulse, when Murray, adroit as usual, caught the Prince's arm: "Your Majesty, I beg of you,—do nothing rashly!" he entreated. "These tidings are but half-correct; 'tis true that Mistress Leslie was apprehended for her part in your escape, but her release was soon obtained, and she is now in perfect safety among her relatives in Skye."

The Prince received this reassurance with relaxing brow, but he responded firmly:

"You may be right, my lord, yet I will first make sure, for should the Englishman's report be true, I would move heaven and earth to save one ringlet of her hair!"

"Your Majesty must yield in this," persisted Murray. "To turn the ship aside would be to court destruction for you and all these gallant gentlemen, whose fate is one with yours!" He turned to the priest standing near: "Your Reverence, will you convince his Highness of the truth regarding Mistress Leslie?"

The prelate, responding to the meaning glance, said quickly:

"Your Highness, I can only confirm Lord Murray's testimony, and assure you that I have absolute knowledge that the maid is safe!"

And with this perjury they sought to lay the Prince's fears.

Murray's conscience did, indeed, reproach him at thus abandoning Agnes to her fate; but he found himself again compelled to sacrifice her upon the altar of a supreme necessity. Yet he was by no means certain that Charles had been fully convinced, and at the first opportunity, he confided in his fellow-perjurer.

"The girl, in truth, lies prisoned in his stead at Fort Augustus, but, look you,—I'd not have him know it for twenty million pounds! He's gone stark mad over the lass, and for her sake he'd fling himself into the 'Butcher's' maw. Sooner than he should have his will, I'd bind him hand and foot and lock him safe within the hold! Make haste, then;—tell them to hoist all sail, and clear the Channel! We'll soon be beyond reach o' rumours."

· · · · ·

Whatever hour the clock might tell, it was black midnight in the dungeon when Agnes slowly struggled back to consciousness. Bewildered by pain and darkness, she imagined herself still wandering among the mountains, and, partly rising, whispered wildly: "Your Highness!—Dugald!—O God, where am I?" She started up, gazing frantically about her for the glimmering hearth that had always lit the gloom of their retreat. But all was utter blackness, and the girl sank back, distraught with fear, and shuddering like a frightened child.

But her trance of despair was mercifully shortened by the approaching flicker of the jailor's lantern, whose faint light, dimly illumining the dungeon, instantly recalled to her bewildered mind her present disconsolate state. Either out of respect to the beauty and high birth of the prisoner, or from admiration of his courage, the jailor had ventured to disobey the Duke's command to put the Prince in chains, rightly conjecturing that Cumberland, even if his condition permitted it, would not immediately revisit the scene of his humiliation.

The Duke, however, was abroad next morning, more injured in mind than body, and feeling most keenly the sting of shame that his conqueror should be the "Italian Prince," as he contemptuously called his handsome and courtly rival. It was owing, nevertheless, to the absence of that same despised Prince that Cumberland had escaped a death-blow to more than his pride; for had a stronger hand than Agnes's backed the agile thrust, the Duke would probably have ended his *humane* and illustrious career upon the spot.

By dint of bribing the guards, and intimidating the jailor, Cumberland kept within bounds the secret of his defeat. It was not till the fourth day after the duel that he made any attempt toward a second interview with his victorious captive; and even then he did not go alone, but took with him a most redoubtable ally.

CHAPTER XXXVIII

"NOW, WAE TO THEE, THOU CRUEL LORD!"

"Now wae to thee, thou cruel lord,
 A bluidy man I trow thou be;
For monie a heart thou hast made sair,
 That ne'er did wrang to thine or thee!"

THE Countess of Menteith had joined the company of noble Whigs at Fort Augustus—ostensibly for safety,—really for stratagem. Now, as his Grace entered the temporary drawing-room where his adherents gathered, the Countess came to meet him with that deep semblance of admiring zeal which she—of all sycophants—knew best how to assume.

"Ah, good-morning, your Grace!" she cried coquettishly, "so you have come hither, like the sun, to impart to us your radiance?"

The Duke, from whom flattery rebounded like a bullet from armour, quite ignored this winning speech, and proceeded straight to his purpose.

"You have, doubtless, heard, my lady, of the Pretender's capture, and how he lies in chains within this very fort? If you would kindly lend me your presence for a little while,—providing you object not to visiting the dungeon;—I believe you knew the Pretender at Holyrood?"

"I was detained there much against my will, your

Grace," replied the Countess with an excellent show of indignation, " and I was, perforce, obliged to attend that ridiculous court,—the most absurd travesty of royal state, I do assure you!—Such bare apartments, and such dreary furnishings!—it gave me quite a shiver!—And those dreadful Highlanders made my blood run cold with their outlandish dress and barbarous language! My joy at seeing English faces is truly inexpressible, my dear Duke!" she concluded with a languishing smile, while the onlookers exchanged meaning glances, for the tale of the Countess's doings at Holyrood, and her failure to win the Prince's favour, had travelled far beyond the Scottish border.

. . . . .

In terror at anything which might betray her secret, Agnes had not dared to send for a surgeon, but had bound up the throbbing arm as best she could, setting her teeth against the pain, for the unhealed wound had opened, and her cheeks burned with fever. Giddy with suffering and weakness, she was scarcely able to stand, but her heart still beat undaunted.

When Cumberland and the Countess entered, they were met by the same look of proud defiance which the Duke had encountered. But, at sight of her rival Agnes drew back, with a gesture of recoil,— of consternation,—yet one so swiftly past, so instantly controlled,—that it might have gone unheeded by any other eyes than the Countess's. But that dame,—her always keen perception intensified by malice,—saw the tell-tale gesture,—saw, indeed, the whole adroit imposture which the girl had hitherto maintained. The moment of vindictive triumph she had so long awaited, had come at last, and the heiress of Menteith was not one to neglect opportunities.

"Your Grace!" the Countess cried, "this is no man;—'tis a madcap maid, who lost her heart to the Pretender at Holyrood, and fled to join him after Culloden!"

The Countess was no advocate of truth, and now, in her malicious exultation, did not hesitate to assume the part of Sapphira. It was a question whether the Duke or his prisoner showed the more astonishment. Cumberland's face was a study in its wavering incredulity; but Agnes's wore a look of the most childlike amazement at this glaring falsehood.

"Your Grace!" cried the accuser, "this girl is a bold impostor, who has dared to play her tricks even upon your Royal Highness!" The Countess was with difficulty repressing her amusement at the Duke's beguilement, not daring to indulge it openly, for fear of offending her royal patron.

Cumberland, impelled by the slow dawning of conviction, yet muttering, "Impossible! Impossible!" strode across to Agnes, and laid a heavy hand upon her shoulder. The feminine gesture of shrinking with which she recoiled from him was sufficiently convincing.

"Man, woman,—devil,—whatever you are,—have done with your trickery! Do you know, mad deceiver, that it is William of Cumberland with whom you have to deal? Explain the meaning of this pre-

"Your Grace' the Countess cried, 'this is no man!"

"Now, Wae to Thee, Thou Cruel Lord!" 329

sumptuous imposture, or you will answer to the King on Tower Hill!"

But the exultant Countess readily assumed the office of avenger, and seizing Agnes by the arm which Cumberland had relinquished, poured out her long-fermenting fury. Unlimited by truth or reason, she showered on her defenceless foe a very flood of epithets and accusations, the heaped-up product of malignant rage.

Agnes endured it all in superb silence, her eyes disdaining to bestow a single glance upon her persecutor. She had torn herself from the Countess's grasp, and was standing in the centre of the room,— her body motionless as marble, her hands clenched instinctively; and only the hot colour, surging in crimson waves from throat to brow, betraying the intensity of outraged feeling.

At the very height of her frantic vituperation the Countess sprang forward, whispering venomously into Agnes's ear:

"'She bade good angels and saints defend her,
  And sank in the arms of the young Pretender.'

"You pretty madcap," hissed the fury, "do you flatter yourself the Prince ever valued you for aught but your beauty? If you hadn't had hair like Scottish cairngorms and cheeks like Scottish heather, he wouldn't have wasted a blink of the eye upon you, my fair Highlander!"

The Countess did not recollect that it was exactly a year since her bitter defeat at Holyrood, but she pursued her vengeance none the less zealously.

How much longer she would have continued her vehement flow of language must remain undecided, if the Duke, not out of pity for the victim, but from sheer impatience at the lengthened tirade, had not finally interposed, and himself assumed the office of inquisitor,—a right which the Countess did not again dare to usurp.

"And now, girl," he demanded, "I'd have you explain what you meant by feigning to be the Pretender?"

"In truth, your Grace," was Agnes's cool response, "I am surely the Pretender since I am not the Prince. I never claimed to be—*King Charles the Third!*"

The Duke turned upon her in a fury, his small blue eyes like angry beads.

"How dare you thus defy me?" thundered he, "how dare you speak such dire treason against my honoured father, George the Second?"

But the girl stood scornfully unmoved. Furthermore, her inherent sauciness leaped to the surface.

"He is doubtless ' your honoured father,' " she replied deliberately, "but he is *not* King of Scotland!"

Cumberland ground his teeth in futile rage. "Such a country!—Such a country!—Traitors! Rebels! Fiends! No reasonable being would choose to remain in it an hour!"

"I think your Grace is mistaken," said Agnes with sweet composure, "at least, all Englishmen do not share in your opinion." And then, leaping into taunting Scotch: "I'se tak' ye to a place nae far frae Stirling, whare thretty thousand o' your coun-

"Now, Wae to Thee, Thou Cruel Lord!" 331

trymen ha'e stayed for ower four hundred years, and there's nae sign o' their ganging hame yet!"

As the immensity of this insult began to permeate the Duke's mind, for the girl referred to the battlefield of Bannockburn, where, on June 24, 1314, Bruce defeated the army of Edward II., he faced about with the snort of an angry bull.

"You pretty Scottish vixen,—how dare you mock me?—You would scoff at Majesty itself! But you shall render me full tribute yet for all these merry gibes!—Beware that day,—sweet amazon,—beware that day!"

. . . . .

In spite of his wounded shoulder, and more deeply wounded pride, Cumberland was compelled to proclaim the deception which Agnes had practised upon him, since from the moment of her surrender he had given orders for the abandonment of the searching-parties dispersed over Scotland, as well as for the withdrawal of the war-ships in the Channel.

On the evening following the Duke's disillusion, Kenneth Campbell, returning to Fort Augustus with one of the scouting-parties, received the startling news of Agnes's imprisonment. Torn with conflicting feelings, he straightway sought permission to visit the lovely captive, and—it being granted—immediately bent his footsteps toward the dungeon.

It was close upon midnight, when, taking the key from the jailor's hand, he unlocked the door, and crossed the gloomy threshold. Holding the lantern high above his head, he advanced softly, fearing to startle the prisoner by too abrupt an entrance. Thus moving, his foot struck sharply upon something that lay within the shadow of the wall; and, as he stooped, his eyes caught a flash of steel. It was the sword of Dundee, which had fallen from Agnes's hand when she had fainted;—which she had vainly searched for, and thought lost. He raised it tenderly and hid it under his cloak. But he caught no glimpse of the girl,—no sound of stir or movement, and, half-alarmed, he searched with anxious eyes the dusky vault. There was a pile of straw in one corner, and, his gaze at last falling on it, fell also upon her he sought.

She was lying asleep on that rude couch, her hands crossed lightly on her breast, her calm and dreaming face just upturned, like some fair marble saint upon an ancient tomb. Kenneth, shading the lantern-rays with his hand, lest they should shine upon the sleeper, stole forward softly, holding his very breath for fear that she awaken. The dark folds of her tartan, torn and faded, wrapped her from head to foot like some plaided warrior, trailing its tattered fringes against her rounded cheek,—rounded still, though pale with want and suffering. There was that in its purity of outline and expression which sent to Kenneth's heart a strange, reproachful thrill,—as poignant as an arrow. He became vividly—cruelly—conscious of how vile a thing he had done in his accusations, and doubts of her. How had he dared mistrust her,—this maid of hero's mould, with face and heart as pure as any angel's!

Suddenly,—as if, somehow,—aware of the passionate self-abasement of his gaze, Agnes stirred ever so slightly, and a ring upon her hand,—a topaz rimmed with diamonds,—shot white and amber flame. Kenneth started violently. He had seen that ring a hundred times upon the Prince's finger,—on the day of Charles's entry into Edinburgh,—on the night of that bitterly-remembered ball, and on that grim, grey morning of the duel. But to see it thus—on Agnes's hand! The sight roused all the old mad jealousy that had poisoned his mind so long. But now he would not let it master him;—he fought it with a giant's strength, and conquered. She might wear the Prince's ring upon her finger;—she might even wear his image in her heart, and yet be not one whit less the Agnes he had loved—*loved* still—with all his soul.

He would not waken her to ask of her forgiveness, —that were cruelty;—he must reveal the depths of his contrition through the stronger medium of action. His should be the hand to rescue her from the clutches of this devil Cumberland. He would atone to the utmost for the grievous sin he had committed.

. . . .. .

Cumberland renewed his inquisition next day by demanding of Agnes the hiding-place of the real Prince, and, upon receiving an absolute refusal to comply with this slight request, burst into a storm of furious oaths and menaces.

"Withstand me in this,—my fair masquerader,— and I will wring the truth from you by force if need be! I'll have you lashed or starved into submission, —aye—by the gods!—if you persist in this obstinacy,—I'll send you to the gallows,—woman though you are!"

She lifted her lovely eyebrows with superb indifference, and shrugged her pretty shoulders lightly.

"I cannot blame your Grace for using any means within your power to secure so important a secret. I have never heard that the House of Hanover were noted for their chivalry toward women, nor that the Duke of Cumberland was an exception to his kinsmen. I had hardly looked for mercy from your Grace."

Then, with one of her startling changes of mood, she wheeled,—very tall, indeed, in her masculine dress, —and looked the Duke full in the face. And even Charles himself stood not more stately, nor more brave.

"Do what ye will!" she cried vibrantly, "try torture and starvation,—all ye've threatened,—perchance some fruit will come of it!—Ye may wring the secret from these *dead* lips o' mine, but, *living*, they shall utter not a word! Have done with idle speeches, or keep them for your subjects,—of which I am not one, my lord;—we Scots die not of empty threatenings!"

. . . . .

Not many days after, Agnes received a visit from Sir Duncan Forbes. The gentle old Whig, his kindly heart wrung by Cumberland's many cruelties, met this daughter of his boyhood friend, with tears of deep distress. In almost his first words he begged her to forego her stubborn silence, and confess the truth concerning Charles.

"Surely ye dinna think I'm like the 'fause Menteith,' the coward wha betrayed the noble Wallace?" cried Agnes, bitterly reproachful. "Death comes inevitably to us all. What does it matter how?—As died Montrose upon the scaffold,—as fell Dundee at Killiecrankie,—however swift it come, or slow, why, 'tis but death to face, as face it each one must!—*Death, but not disloyalty!*"

"Nay, ye maun be reasonable, Agnes," replied the old man, "I'm thinking 'twill be nae news to the Duke to tell him whare ye left the Prince. I mak' sure he kens the place a'ready, and so ye'll be nae traitress, an' ye tell him what he asks."

"Then why doesna he seize the Prince?" cried Agnes instantly, and Forbes, unprepared for the sudden thrust, stood answerless.

"Ye'll break my hairt, child," he exclaimed at length. "Do ye think I'll bear to see you throw your bonnie life awa, and I your father's friend? Ye dinna count the cost, lassie;—the Duke's cruel man, a sair cruel man!"

"And ye'd ha'e me deliver the Prince into his hands!" the girl rejoined, flushing angrily. "Ah, Sir Duncan, the blood o' Montrose and Dundee doesna flow in traitors' veins! Their very ghosts would rise to curse me, an' I betrayed *my King!*"

She came close to him and touched his arm. Her face was pale, but very brave; one slender hand was clenched against her bosom.

"Heaven give me strength!" she whispered, "Heaven give me strength to die,—like them,—*leal to the last!*"

CHAPTER XXXIX

"WHEN TYRANNY REVELLED IN BLOOD OF THE TRUE"

> "The hoof of the horse, and the foot of the proud,
>   Have trod o'er the plumes on the bonnet of blue;
> Why sleeps the red bolt in the breast of the cloud,
>   When tyranny revelled in blood of the true?"

FROM Agnes's prison Duncan Forbes went immediately to Cumberland, and began an ardent intercession in the girl's behalf. The Duke attended with scant courtesy and cut short the eloquent plea in mid-air.

"Save your breath, save your breath, Mr. Forbes," he growled. "The girl has had her choice; let her abide by it!—Either she shall tell me what she knows of this thrice-cursed Pretender, or she shall die. And I should advise *you*, sir, to cease succouring rebels!"

"Your Grace cannot mean to pursue such a course!" ejaculated Forbes, in horror. "This maid with the blood of Montrose in her veins,—what knoweth she of fear? With her threats avail not! These unfortunate Jacobites are utterly deluded, but they deserve not the calumnies that are heaped upon them nor all the sufferings they are enduring! And this unhappy girl, why, she is innocent of all save a mistaken passion,—a wild infatuation,—for this hapless Prince! For God's sake, spare her such a fate!"

"Spare her? By all the laws of vengeance,—*no!* Show me an edict from *Heaven*, and I'll not spare her!—She shall go to the block with her fellow-traitors,—for treason to the King's most august Majesty!"

"Beware, beware, your Grace," said Forbes, quietly. "There are some things that even the King cannot do with impunity!"

"Do you dare threaten?" snarled Cumberland. "Am I to be baffled by such so-called 'friends'? Oh, you Scots are bitter vipers, always ready to show the fangs of treason!"

Forbes still retained his masterful composure, but his face had grown pale with rage at the insult to his countrymen.

"I speak not treason, but truth," he answered. "The Stuarts lost their throne because they trampled on men's rights;—beware, my lord, lest *you* fall not beneath a greater condemnation. Remember, mercy is enjoined by God on those who sit in royal places; and he who violates divine commands must reap the harvest he has sown. If this maid dies by your mandate, you will have perpetrated a crime more foul than all you have committed. For if you know not mercy, you should at least know that respect which every man should feel toward woman. But if chivalry fail to move you, then I will have done with useless words!"

"Talk not to me of 'mercy' toward a rebel, of chivalry' toward a vixen like this maid!" cried his Grace contemptuously. "Traitor, or traitress—they shall suffer alike! As for this cursed country,

I have exacted speedy vengeance; Scotland is as Glencoe was, when William III., my namsake, had wrought his will on treason!"

"Aye," said Forbes, solemnly, "and upon you shall fall a greater curse than the curse of Glencoe!"

The Duke sprang up with a furious oath, but Forbes faced him calmly. "Nay, nay, my lord, hear me through! I shall not be long speaking, but hark to this: you have outraged every sense of mercy,—human or divine;—you have stained with black dishonour the name of Christian England! God shall punish you, man shall hate you; your name shall be breathed as a curse throughout Scotland, so long as men remember the days of 'the '45'!"

He paused, in cold contemplation of Cumberland's voiceless rage at a prophecy fulfilled to this day. Then he reached his cloak from the table, and turned to leave the room.

"I shall lodge to-night at the 'Wallace Arms' in Fort William. If a cell in the Tower awaits me, there will be no need of search. Your Grace will know where to find me!"

It was not till Agnes Leslie was brought to the Castle, a prisoner, that the news of her extraordinary part in Prince Charlie's deliverance became known in Edinburgh. The effect it produced on Sir Hugh was indescribable, and quite sufficient to fill his wife with utter consternation. He denounced Agnes fiercely, called her all the abusive names he could invent, and ended by declaring she deserved her fate and that he would not lift a hand to save her from the scaffold.

"And what's mair, there's nae respectable body that will, noo she's ended by forfeiting her guid name,—the limmer!"

"Then it's been left for you, Hugh Campbell, to speak a thing baith fause and foul!" cried Mistress Catherine, her latent courage leaping up in passionate defence, at this vile slander. "There's nae man in Edinbro' has breathed ane word against her bonny name; the hairt of her is white as snaw frae heaven. Shame on ye, Hugh, shame on ye, wi' sic thochts i' your soul!"

"'Tis the maist unwomanly performance I ha'e yet heard o', I rede ye, and that ye daurna deny!"

"But bethink ye, Hugh, how young she is;—only twa-and-twenty!"

"Twa-and-twenty! A bairn o' twelve wud ken better! A pretty piece o' wildness 'tis for a maid to wear a man's dress, and roam the kintry armed like a Highlander in company wi' that mad Pretender! She has played a man's part, noo let her pay the forfeit, and bear a man's punishment!"

"Oh, Hugh, dinna be sae hard! 'Twas a' for the young Prince's sake! And she's but a wee, bit lassie, when a's said, and the fairest thing the guid God ever made, and if they tak' her bonny life, I'll never wish to see the light o' morn!"

"Haith, ye loon!—awa wi' your idle talk. Dinna fash yoursel' wi' greetin'; ye needna gang to the Grassmarket to see the hizzy hanged!"

But his wife had been Catherine Graham before she

was Catherine Campbell, and thirty years of an unhappy married life had not wholly quenched in her the fire of that war-like race.

"Hugh," she cried, "have ye no hairt? The lass is bluid o' my bluid, and would ye ha'e me lift not a finger to save her young life? God forgi'e ye, ye're a cruel man, Hugh Campbell!"

But Sir Hugh was unshaken as stone. "Aye, ye speak truth," he retorted, "ye Grahams are mad bluid,—ane and a'! But hark ye, Mistress Campbell, to what I say. I ha'e harboured rebels beneath my roof-tree lang enough. Gang ye to this mad lass,—or lad,—whichever she ca's hersel',—since she's sae far forgot her sex,—but, an' ye gang, *never again step across my doorstane!* Ye'll likely fin' traitors enough to bear ye company, and ye'll mak' a merry court for the Pretender!"

. . . . .

That night, when darkness fell, a woman's shrinking figure stole, ghost-like, from the house beyond the Netherbow. It was poor Catherine Campbell pale and terrified, yet true, despite herself, to the bond of heroic blood which bound her to the maiden of Clan Leslie. Inspired by a courage not her own the trembling creature made her way to the Castle and there besought an interview with the hapless prisoner.

She was somewhat dismayed at sight of the forlorn young Highlander who advanced to greet her clad in a tattered philabeg, and a mud-bedraggled plaid in which he vainly sought to hide himself.

"May the guid God preserve us, lassie!" Mistress

Campbell cried, astounded; "dinna tell me ye've scampered roond amang sae mony men i' that short skirt, and wi' your knees bare!"

The young Highlander blushed vividly.

"Oh, Aunt Catherine! surely ye winna think I wore the dress because I liked it! But when 'twas a choice between wearing it, and saving a precious life, —the life of our Bonnie Prince Charlie,—ye wouldna ha'e had me hesitate?"

"Na, na, lassie, I'll no' be scoldin' ye. It will just be a wee bit unusual. I dinna recollect that lassies did the like i' my young day, but times ha'e maybe changed."

"I pray there was nae need i' your day!" cried the girl, "and that there'll ne'er be need again sae sair as this!"

She sank to a seat as she spoke, and attempted to hide the objectionable garments in the faded folds of her plaid.

"It isna very cheerfu' here, Aunt Catherine; perhaps ye'd best not stay."

"'Tis a fearfu' place for ye, lassie! Alas! that my ain sister's bairn should ha'e come to this!"

"The great Montrose was 'prisoned in a cell as grim," Agnes answered; "surely *I* shouldna murmur!"

"But he was a man grown, and a soldier at that, and ye are but a slender lass!" Mistress Campbell remonstrated, not a little perplexed by the girl's mode of reasoning, for Agnes had a way of regarding herself as a man, and scorned to claim immunity by favour of her sex.

"How did ye daur to ficht a duel wi' that bluidy Duke? Unco braw it was, forsooth, but will ye no' be thinkin' 'twas a wee bit *onladylike*, my dear?"

"I am afraid it was very *unladylike*," agreed Agnes mournfully, "but it just had to be done! 'Twas 'the sword of the Lord and of Claverhouse.' And it was God and Prince Charlie that conquered,—not I!"

Agnes had heard with great composure Sir Hugh's denunciation of herself; but her wrath blazed up at his cruel threats against Mistress Catherine.

"He's a wicked man, Sir Hugh," she declared emphatically; "he didna deserve a child, and 'twere not for *you*, Aunt Catherine, I'd be glad that God never sent him one!"

"Eh, lassie, lassie, these are dreadfu' times! One had best be baith blind and deaf.—Lassie,—I saw a fearfu' sicht the morn;—*there are heads aboon the north gate!*"

"O Heaven, I know it! There will be more ere the month is out. I would weep if I could, but all my tears were shed upon Drummossie Muir, and when I pairted from our Prince, and there are none remaining!"

"God's pity, lassie, ilka thing is changed;—the warld seems sairly different." And then, through piteous sobs:—"Ye ken the Stuart roses that ye lo'ed sae weel?—they're withered a',—they wouldna nod their bonnie heads for me nor Betty. And ye are like the posies, Agnes,—sae white and fair a' they, and now ye're plucked by cruel hands, and the wind o' death blaws fierce upon your head! I mind me o' the auld sweet sang ye used to sing: 'The flowers o' the forest are a' wede away!'"

* * * * *

Mistress Campbell's ardent affection for Agnes led her to the point of appealing in person to Cumberland, but an interview with the churlish Duke threw her into such a state of terror that Agnes finally persuaded her to leave Edinburgh and go to some of her Graham kinsmen at Stirling.

"Ye canna help me mair, Aunt Catherine," she said at their sorrowful parting. "My life is in God's hands; 'tis He that will decide."

* * * * *

Agnes heard without surprise that she was to be sent to London as a prisoner, for she had not expected Cumberland's resentment to sate itself upon so brief a vengeance. She knew nothing of Kenneth's desperate but futile efforts in her behalf;—indeed, she did not dream of his presence in Edinburgh, and, when she thought of him at all, wondered rather resentfully if he were still with Cumberland at Fort Augustus, as MacLeod had told her. For Kenneth, since that midnight in the dungeon, had zealously avoided a meeting with the woman he had once so deeply wronged, and now so remorsefully loved.

One afternoon, when Agnes was sitting disconsolately in a corner of her prison, gazing out through the close-barred window at a tiny vista of the town below, a woman opened the door of the cell, and paused in hesitation on the threshold.

Lady Mackenzie, wife of the third Earl of Cromarty, had been known in her girlhood throughout Scotland by the name of "Bonnie Bell Gordon," a name which still clung to her after marriage, because of her great and winning beauty. She was about thirty-five, in the full bloom of her exquisite womanhood,—with a tall, fine figure, the proudly poised head, characteristic of all the Gordons, large blue-grey eyes that hid both fire and tenderness, and a wealth of glowing auburn hair that fell, after the mode of the time, in rich curls about her shoulders. Over her simple dress of dark grey she wore the Gordon tartan, thrown loosely round her like a cloak, one corner of which she had drawn over her head, hood-fashion, but now allowed to fall back, leaving her face free, as she stepped across the threshold.

The figure that rose to meet her, though clad in plaid and philabeg and tartan jacket, was that of no man. To a discerning gaze, the form revealed feminine outlines, and the features girlish appeal. Bell Gordon descried a certain wild likeness to the Chevalier in the pale, proud face, the mournful hazel eyes, the despairing droop of the red lips.

"You are strangely like, yet so strangely different!" she exclaimed.

Agnes—upon her part—had never before met Lady Cromarty, though she had often heard of her beauty and charm, and, of late, had felt her heart go out in sympathy toward her unknown fellow-sufferer, for George, Earl of Cromarty, lay in the Tower, awaiting sentence for high treason.

"Mistress Leslie, I have come to tell you that you are the bravest lass in all Scotland, and that there's not a loyal heart that does not pray for your release!"

And her lovely, earnest eyes looked straight into Agnes's.

"Ah, but is Prince Charlie safe? It is for that I care! Yestre'en I heard that he was captured, and I could not sleep for thinking of it!"

"Set your heart at ease, dear lassie; he is far beyond his foemen's reach,—owing to your great courage. The ship on which he sailed arrived at France in safety, full ten days ago.

"And now, my dear," she continued softly, "we are fellow-victims in the hand of fate, for I, too, am virtually a prisoner, since George, alas! is one. We are bound on the same hard journey; shall we not go in company? 'Twould lighten the loneliness for me, and perhaps to you I might be some protection,—however slight."

Across the girl's mournful face there flashed a gleam of hope. "Oh, if you *would* take me with you, Lady Cromarty!" she cried gratefully. "I have been lonely unto death, with every earthly friend of mine in exile!" She put her hands in Lady Mackenzie's, and it was undoubtedly the Prince's ring,—that splendid topaz, rimmed with diamonds,—that flashed its Stuart white-and-gold upon her slender fingers. "The Duke," she cried, "I am afraid of him!—I care not for his threats, nor their fulfilment; but, of late, he has tried to make love to me, tried to win me with coaxing and caresses, and then I detest him a thousand-fold! But I have a dirk lying here,"—and she touched her breast,—"Prince

Charlie's own it is,—and if ever he offer me insult, he shall know if its steel be true!

"But if *you* bear me company, we will be brave together!" She paused, with a deepening colour. "But oh, my lady, will ye not find me some garments of woman's wearing? These were donned from duty,—not pleasure. Must I wear them the rest of my life?"

She was clear-eyed as a child, and she spoke with a child's directness.

"You shall have a gown of mine, dear lassie," Bell Gordon assured her. "Our day of silks and gems is past, until the King comes hame." And she sighed deeply. "There are reasons why I should not go to London," she whispered softly into Agnes's ear, "but go I must, upon the chance that my frail influence may save my husband's life!"

. . . . . .

A fortnight later, Agnes stood beside Bell Gordon on the frigate's deck, and watched the coast of Scotland fade from sight, as the *Bridgewater*, with all sails set, swung out into the current, bound for London.

CHAPTER XL

"BETTER LO'ED YE CANNA BE"

"Better lo'ed ye canna be,
Will ye no' come back again?"

AS the *Bridgewater* made slow progress up the stately Thames, a maze of wharves and shipping, Bell Gordon pointed out to Agnes the conspicuous features of this wonderful world-city: the splendid towers of Westminster Abbey, lifted beyond that fatal Hall where Charles the First had suffered sentence, and where the titled followers of his young descendant were soon to meet the same relentless doom. The sombre mass and clustering turrets of the Tower itself—where many a royal victim,—many a noble captive,—had languished in the dungeon of despair—rose grim against the lowering sky that seemed to touch the vessel's bow.

"Ah me, how clearly I remember the day when first I came to London," sighed Bell Gordon in mournful reminiscence. "Then the sun shone, and 'twas summer, and I, a care-free, joyous girl, was like to sing for mirth. And the happy days that followed;—oh, they were crowded full with pleasure and delight. On one bewildering evening I went with my father to a wonderful ball at St. James's, and there I danced—yes, *actually danced*—with the

Prince of Wales,—the Brunswick Prince of Wales, I mean, for our dear 'Jamie the Rover' was only King in name, and Bonnie Charlie was a boy in far-off Rome. Well, I danced with the Prince of Wales,—'twas that same year that he became the King;—but what he said to me I could never tell, being far too dazzled to remember. Alas!—how great a change! For I was 'Bonnie Bell,' eighteen and blithe of heart;—and as many years have passed as I was aged then. To-day,—O Heaven!—*to-day* I am Lady Mackenzie, an intercessor for my husband's life, and the man of whom I must entreat is that same Prince with whom I danced,—George Second, King of England!"

. . . . .

Meantime, Kenneth, whose duty had compelled him to accompany Cumberland to London, had vainly exhausted every mode of supplication upon the vindictive Duke.

"I have had little time to waste on women," said Cumberland at one of these fruitless interviews, "but this Scottish beauty seems worthy of my attention."

Kenneth set his teeth in the rage he might not speak, and clenched his hands in a mighty effort at repression.

"Your Grace must remember that this maiden comes of one of the noblest families in Scotland," he replied.

"Oh, indeed," sneered Cumberland, lifting his brows in careless scorn; "well, no matter,—all Scotland is but a conquered province."

"It is hardly magnanimous of your Grace to say so!" exclaimed Kenneth, unable to suppress this faint gleam of indignation which was all he could allow himself to show.

* * * * *

In that grey prison of the Tower, where loyalty to Charles had led her, Agnes watched the days creep grimly by. The only respite to her loneliness was the frequent presence of Lady Cromarty, who, ostensibly living in lodgings near the Tower, spent what time she could spare from her passionate intercession for the Earl with the forlorn and seemingly unfriended captive. Cumberland was a more fitful but not less frequent visitor; he would enter at any hour, either to pour out a flood of oaths and menaces, or to launch himself upon a clumsy attempt at love-making, which—as she had told Bell Gordon—Agnes dreaded immeasurably more. The Duke's frantic efforts in this direction—he was hardly a graceful lover—might indeed have been amply ludicrous under other circumstances, but Agnes was neither in the mood nor in the situation to feel amusement. But there finally befell an incident which ended these visitations.

The Duke had appeared, and the girl had risen as usual, to stand immovable with folded arms and high-flung head. Cumberland, advancing with an awkward bow, and with an air of mock humility,—which graced him but indifferently,—bent low, with the intention of kissing the dainty hand that rested outward on her arm, a purpose which an agile movement on her part completely frustrated.

"Oh, my pretty rebel," coaxed his Grace reproachfully, "how can you have the heart to deal so hardly with your most humble lover? 'Twas not alone my *shoulder* that you wounded, but my *heart* as well! Surely it were not bold in me to kiss your *hand* when you have granted others much greater favours. May I not presume to steal *one* kiss of your lips, or have you given them all to my *cousin Charles?*"

The next instant the Duke received a stinging blow across the mouth, delivered with anything but gentle force. Agnes had wielded her slender glove as dexterously as she had once wielded a more dangerous weapon; and the Duke fairly staggered,—less from the force of the blow than from its unexpectedness. Before he could recover his composure she turned on him with eyes aflame.

"Prince Charlie would never have offered me one thousandth part of such indignity! *He* was of royal birth,—a gentleman of honour; and *you*, with all your boasted power, with all your stolen name, are the vilest of scoundrels!"

An earlier sword-thrust of her dealing had gone fiercely home; so now with this. The Duke's face became distorted by baffled purpose and inflamed chagrin; his very tones were quivering with convulsive fury.

"Have done, you cursed vixen, with your insolence! So you have dared to spurn me, fair piece of sheer audacity!—Well, you have sealed your fate! For this, and for your obdurate resistance, your life shall pay the forfeit!"

She faced him with superb indifference. "Indeed, my lord, the scaffold would be sweet compared with what I have already borne! And now I pray

"Better Lo'ed Ye Canna Be"

you to be gone, and leave me to at least an hour's peace!"

. . . . .

On the evening of that same day, Agnes was roused from a desolate reverie by the entrance of an officer in the uniform of the Scots Fusiliers. Thinking him one of the guards, she barely glanced in his direction, and was turning away again, when the intruder advanced, exclaiming brokenly: "Agnes! Agnes! In God's name, speak to me!" *It was Kenneth Campbell!*

With a deeply startled gesture, Agnes turned, like one who faces a long-vanished friend across a mighty chasm. Each recognised the other with a sense of shock, a moment of unbroken silence which neither sought to break. Then Kenneth, coming forward, knelt beside her, lifted a fold of her gown from the floor, and kissed it.

"Oh, Agnes, Agnes!" he exclaimed remorsefully, "how have I sinned against you, in my *thought!* You, the loyal, the courageous, the unsullied! Oh, let me kneel here at your feet, to prove my penitence, —my longing to atone—if so I may—for my transgression,—my great transgression!"

The words were sobbed—not said—in a passionate outpouring of contrition. She listened in tremulous silence.

"Kenneth," she said gently, "do not kneel to me; but listen, for I, too, have something I would say. I know you speak of those last days in Edinburgh before you joined the Duke, and of the enmity that came between us. You thought I loved Prince

Charlie as I should not love,—since I was not his equal. That was a great mistake! 'Tis true that I adore him,—and that I soon shall die for him,—but as a patriot only! Call it a child's love,—a soldier's love,—what you will,—it was never a woman's love!"

Each seemed a revelation to the other,—so altered were they both from those old days of Edinburgh. The rigid dominance in Kenneth which had so often challenged Agnes to revolt had vanished utterly, and left instead a pleading penitence. And Agnes, —before, she had been simply sweet and gay and mischievous;—now, with her heart attuned to grief, the richer chords of courage and devotion sounded sublimely through her soul.

"It was the letter that persuaded me," began Kenneth. He had risen, and stood regarding her with an entreating gaze.

"Oh, the letter! Its mission was twofold! The Prince promised therein to restore to my uncle, Sir Norman, the old earldom of Rothes, and also entrusted me with the duty of informing Donald Cameron of his appointment to a lofty honour; but because of the jealousy in his army, his Royal Highness wished me to arrange an interview between them in secret, and so——"

"I saw but two sentences," Kenneth interrupted, "two sentences that burned themselves into my very soul:—'*the turn is to the left, and the door is unbarred,*' and '*the King can never repay for all.*'"

"Oh!" she cried, swept by a surge of understanding, "oh, I see how you erred,—you supposed,—I could very easily have explained it, but that would have been a betrayal of confidence. I thought you very cruel to watch me and suspect me so, when I had done no wrong,—I,—ever a creature of impulse, who never did aught in cold blood. The directions were given in order that Donald might meet the Prince alone, with none to know their meeting. The secret passage was the one I followed so blindly that day of the duel,—the turn *was* to the left, and the door *was* unbarred, but, oh, how wrongly you construed it!"

Kenneth buried his head in his hands, and groaned aloud.

"O Heaven, what a jealous fool I was! Had I but followed the Campbell motto: 'Trust Winneth Troth'! To think I threw away my dearest hope in life because of those blind suspicions I harboured in my heart! Oh, Agnes! Agnes! how I wronged you!—I *dare* not ask you to forgive!"

"There is much to forgive on both sides," she answered with pardoning sweetness. "I was very provoking in those days,—often thoughtless, and, I fear, unkind. I do not wonder you failed to read me right. If only you had trusted me a little;—I was not really so capricious! But I cannot blame you. If not my friend, be a generous foe! You must forgive me, Kenneth, for having wounded you, now I am near to death!"

"Near to death!" he cried, appalled. "Oh, Agnes, say not so! Never, while I draw breath, shall your sweet life be taken by this cruel tyrant! To-night I offered back my sword to Cumberland, as once I gave it back—ah, how unjustly—to Charles Stuart, —and said that as he knew not how to spare a noble foe,—that foe a maiden and a hero,—I would no longer render him allegiance! He is inexorable,— no prayer can move him!—but there are higher powers than he; to them will I appeal!"

With the light of old aspirations kindling his sad eyes, he stretched out his arms to her with a pleading gesture.

"Agnes! Can it be? *You* have asked of *me* forgiveness,—have uttered not one word in rage against me!—Can I dare to hope that my love—which has never altered—will ever be met by you——"

"Ah, Kenneth, you speak of things long dead,— of things as far away as another life;—those days are like sealed pages, never more to open. I am not the Agnes Leslie that you knew,—a gay creature, with all her faults. I am a changed being,—*since Culloden!*"

And Kenneth saw his flickering hope die in the socket.

. . . . .

By the light of a single candle, whose glimmer did not half dispel the darkness, Agnes sat alone. The gloomy room, its walls and floor and ceiling all of stone, was pervaded with a deep chill which little attempt had been made to overcome. The smouldering fragments of a tiny fire, flickering in a corner of the chimney, did not cast a perceptible warmth beyond the hearth, and at times she shivered unconsciously from the sepulchral dampness. The only furnishings of the place were a table and chair of the rudest material, and a bed of the same description. The sombre blackness of her gown and snood made a painful contrast to the warm colouring of her hair and the startling pallor of her face. Her cheeks had lost all their traitor bloom; they were whiter now than the whitest roses.

Her mother's prayer-book, with a picture of James VIII. on the fly-leaf, lay open on the table before her; but although she occasionally looked down at it, and sometimes even turned a page, it could hardly be said she was reading. For her eyes were oftener fixed on the shadow-thronged recesses of her prison beyond the narrow confines of the candle-light. Her fingers marked the place at two passages from the Psalms:—"My soul is full of troubles, and my life draweth nigh unto the grave.—I am afflicted and ready to die.—Lover and friend hast thou put far from me and mine acquaintance into darkness," and "Let the sighing of the prisoner come before thee; according to the greatness of thy power preserve thou those that are appointed to die."

Presently the jailor entered, tried the heavy window-bars, looked to the fastenings of the door, and, glancing sharply at the prisoner, retired with heavy tread. Agnes watched him, wondering bitterly if he thought her slender strength sufficient to overcome such obstacles.

When he had gone, she conquered her lethargy somewhat, and, rising, moved with a visible effort toward the fire. Kneeling down beside the hearth, she drew from her bosom a faded bit of tartan, and held the thing it folded to the feeble glow. The

Prince's ring blazed forth its diamond lustre and its topaz gold, and flashed and burned, exultant, in the gloom. But with the jewels in her sheltering fingers, lay something dearer yet,—*a tress of silken yellow hair*. A little sob escaped her lips, as reverently she kissed them,—the ring,—the lock of hair,—not with the passionate touch of youth that once she might have given, but with the lingering caress of final parting.

"Why died I not upon Drummossie Muir with those brave clansmen of my blood? Only six days sooner,—only six short days,—and I, too, might have slept—a peaceful, dreamless sleep—amid that crimson heather! Why could not I have died as valiantly for our sweet Prince's sake as any Scotsman there! May not a man's heart beat within my woman's breast! Ah, the fierce rapture of that glorious charge! that charge to hopeless doom,—it had been sweet to me! And sweet the death it brought, with those who died for *his* sake!"

Apparently the effort of moving had exhausted her, for after the dwindling fire had flickered out, she did not change her posture, but clasped her hands upon a chair, and bowed her head upon them.

Her birthnight and the Prince's glided slowly by, and kneeling there, in that damp, dark cell of the Tower, she heard the bells of London ringing to welcome the New Year.

CHAPTER XLI

"OUR HAND IS ON THE BROAD CLAYMORE"

> "Ochon, ochon, our glory's o'er,
>   Stole by a gay deceiver;
> Our hand is on the broad claymore,
>   But the might is broke for ever!"

CUMBERLAND sat, immovable, regarding with savage intensity a letter lying open before him. It was a remarkable letter, and had been brought that morning by a remarkable messenger,—none other than Angus MacDonald! The Duke, with a muttered oath, again perused the contents:

"If you dare so much as to touch this maid with your finger, William of Cumberland, you will know whether there be spirit left among the clans! You trod them down at Culloden like the heather beneath your bloody heel, but the heather will spring again out of the dust, and our vengeance yet lives to strike the tyrant. You have shattered our hopes, but not our courage, and our hands still grasp the claymore! By the ancient honour of the Celtic race, by the courage of the clansmen of Culloden, by the knowledge that God will avenge our wrongs, I swear to you,—William of Cumberland,—that on the day you free this captive maid, my life shall be offered for hers, and I will give myself into your hands to suffer all your tyranny ordains.

"DONALD CAMERON, Master of Locheil."

As he read, a fiendish smile curled the Duke's lips. He realised—with all the fierce delight of a cruel nature—that the vengeance which this letter proffered him would be a thousand-fold more satisfying to his vindictive rancour than any penalty he could inflict on Agnes herself. To secure the person of Donald Cameron—the son of a rebellious chieftain, and himself a rebel and an outlaw—would be the very height of triumph. Cumberland struck the table a heavy blow of hideous exultation. "Your advice is worth following, my good fellow," he soliloquised. "You shall suffer in her stead. Methinks that you will grace the scaffold nobly."

With this benignant comment he summoned Angus to his presence.

That dauntless rebel to King George appeared between two guards, in that same attitude of proud composure which characterised his countrymen. Angus, after having escaped a second time from his tormentors, had made his way to Lochaber, and there joined his youthful chieftain, who, with faithful Cluny MacPherson, had been left to guard the casks of French gold, buried near Loch Arkaig. Angus now encountered the Duke's stern gaze with the most exasperating indifference.

"I suppose you expect a pardon as reward for delivering up this outlaw," Cumberland said sneeringly to the Highlander.

"Our Hand is on the Broad Claymore" 359

Angus, infuriated, sprang upon him with a snarl.

"How dare you speak of it, foul Sassenach!— Wolf of a mongrel breed! Do you think I am as vile as you, that I would buy my freedom with my chieftain's life? Why, I tell you 'twere greater honour to die upon the gibbet at *his* side than sit beside your infamous sire on his stolen throne!"

"Hold your tongue, you insolent traitor!" roared the Duke. "If I release you, it is only that you may bear my answer to your damned rebel of a chief. Tell him from me that on the day he surrenders himself to justice, this cursed beauty of a vixen shall go free, but I scarce think he will marry her, unless the wedding be performed upon the scaffold!"

. . . . .

The House of Peers, convened in solemn council in Westminster Hall, had declared Lord Balmerino, and the Earls of Kilmarnock and Cromarty to be guilty of high treason. The titled prisoners were led back to the Tower, with the fatal edge of the axe turned towards them, an immemorial custom in the case of those condemned to die; and, four days later, the same august assembly pronounced upon their hapless heads the doom of death. Meanwhile, the surges of relentless vengeance had swept, unstayed, their red tide of destruction from Inverness to London. At York, at Penrith, and Carlisle, had scores of victims suffered death under the atrocious treason law of Edward III., a hideous relic of the Middle Ages.

Among the sufferers at London was gallant Edward Farrington, a victim from the hapless defence of Carlisle, the capture of which by Cumberland and the cruel fate of Prince Charlie's gallant little garrison, form in themselves a tragic drama.

Agnes had begged Kenneth to intercede in Edward's behalf. "It would be dreadful enough if he had joined the cause for love o' the Prince, but I fear 'twas for love o' me." And then, with an instinctive touch of Gaelic imagery, she added sorrowfully, "O that I should have had the weaving of his shroud!"

Edward Farrington went to his death, undaunted, with the same gay courage of his college days. He sent a last brave message to Agnes: "Tell Mistress Leslie 'tis reward enough to die in the cause that she has loved." And this gave Kenneth Campbell a bitter pang of remorse.

To Kenneth, each account of this fell work of axe and gibbet brought repeated shuddering. He realised with fearful vividness how deadly was Agnes's peril. Tower Hill, ere now, had seen many a fair head bowed in cruel death; would eighteenth-century England endure such a spectacle? There were times when he felt that Cumberland dared not commit so great a crime as to send this girl to the scaffold for her sublime devotion; there were other times when he thought him capable of any revenge, however fiendish, and then he shuddered with the icy chill of horror. If she should die he would be haunted always by the ghost of a girl with a white rose in her hair, and yellow cairngorms at her snowy throat,— the gay, exultant wraith of Holyrood.

He had ceased to sue for mercy, where mercy there was none, and had sought a more potent source of power in the unfortunate Frederick, eldest son of George II. Kenneth had contrived to let this Prince catch a sight of Agnes in her prison,—the girl herself being utterly unaware of it,—with the result that the Prince became straightway zealous in behalf of the beautiful Jacobite. Yet, even then, Kenneth trembled lest Cumberland's influence should prove supreme, and topple all his frail endeavours for Agnes's deliverance into the sheer abyss.

Meantime, Lady Cromarty, though half-distracted by the Earl's impending doom, consumed no time in futile weeping. To every peer in London, to every gentleman of high degree, she went, with passionate appeals for mercy; and, in her desperation, she even visited Cumberland himself.

On this last occasion she had taken Agnes with her, as an inspiration to her drooping courage; and the two entered reluctantly the presence of the dreaded Duke. Cumberland made no effort to relieve the tension of the scene; simply bestowed upon the suppliant a cold, contemptuous stare. Lady Cromarty sank to her knees before him, and laid a trembling hand upon his coat, which he, however, rudely pulled from her despairing grasp, and, as she still sought to detain him, repulsed her with such violence that in rising she staggered heavily, and was saved from falling only by Agnes's quick support.

"O your Grace, for God's sake, have pity!" she moaned distractedly; "have pity as you are a man of woman born, and do not turn a deaf ear to my pleading!"

The scene was so distressing that Agnes's tender heart could hardly endure it.

"Stop your foolish shrieking!" shouted Cumberland. "If any influence of mine can send your husband to the gallows, he will go there before another sunset! Save your breath to cry his coronach, or whatever barbarous name you call a dirge! —I'll make short work of these damned Scottish traitors!"

"You fiend!" cried Agnes, outraged beyond control. "You fiend! I will pray·God to punish you! And He *will* punish you," she added, with fierce conviction.

"Hold your tongue, my fair impertinence!" snarled Cumberland, "and beware of what you say. You will soon need to plead for yourself!"

"And plead I would not before such a judge, were blackest death before me!" cried the girl in molten fury. "I would sooner sue for mercy from the master-fiend himself than from you!"

And Agnes, supporting the fainting Lady Cromarty, glared indignantly at the Duke.

"Take her away!" snarled Cumberland to Agnes. "I am sick of these maudlin scenes! If *I* had my way, every soul in Scotland—men, women, babes—should hang for high treason!"

"Dear me," mocked Agnes maliciously, "'tis most fortunate 'your way' is not followed; the country would be somewhat depopulated!"

Cumberland, as usual, turned purple, and with

every sign of rage, ordered her to withdraw, and "be done with her audacity."

At first half-stupefied by Cumberland's brutal words, Lady Cromarty recovered somewhat as Agnes assisted her from the room. "What did he say?" she whispered, "what did he say?—That he would send George to the scaffold?—God help me! God show me how to foil his evil power! If only my strength fail not! Pray for me, dear Agnes, that it fail not!"

She swallowed convulsively. "God pity Scotland when that man becomes her king!"

"He never *will* be king!" cried Agnes fiercely. "God would not be so cruel!"

And these words were a prophecy; William of Cumberland's blood-stained footsteps never reached the throne.

. . . . .

Lady Cromarty, pausing upon the threshold of Agnes's prison, caught her breath at the sound of faint, sweet singing.

> "English bribes were a' in vain,
>   Tho' puir, and puirer, we maun be;
> Siller canna buy the heart
>   That beats for aye for thine and thee."

Bell Gordon entered, white and shrinking, and knelt beside the singer, whose song died suddenly at sight of her.

"Agnes, my poor child, pray to God for courage!—There is one within this Tower whom you know;—one dear to you,—young Donald Cameron!"

"Donald Cameron!" echoed Agnes in a haunting tone, "Donald Cameron here! My God! a prisoner!"

She had turned a deathly pallor, and looked as if about to faint, but, as Lady Cromarty slipped an arm about her, she straightened suddenly, with a mighty gathering of her strength; and she was none too soon, for Cumberland had entered.

He gazed at her a moment in fiendish exultation, and then began to read aloud from a document he held.

"'Forasmuch as Donald Cameron, Master of Locheil, by his most foul rebellion against his lawful sovereign, George the Second, hath forfeited his life, and, furthermore, as he, while yet at large, did solemnly swear to surrender himself to the royal mercy, in the event that Agnes Leslie, imprisoned in the Tower for treason to his Majesty, the King, should be released on his submission, I do herewith declare that sentence unto death is thus pronounced against him'!" . . .

Here Cumberland, unable longer to control his mounting sense of triumph, flung down the document and fixed his savage eyes upon the girl.

"He is condemned to die,—hear you that?—to die a traitor's death,—aye, for *high treason* by the English law;—you know, I think, what that means? Spoke I not truly, then, my lovely rebel, when I said you had best save your prayers for yourself,—and, I might add,—your lover? But you are of so bold a spirit, perchance you would prefer to look upon the sight, as did the valiant sweetheart of the traitor

"Our Hand is on the Broad Claymore" 365

Dawson?" Cumberland taunted fiendishly, recalling the dreadful incident that forms the subject of the pathetic ballad, "Jemmy Dawson."

Throughout this brutal speech, Agnes had remained seated, her hands lying clenched in her lap; at every sentence of the fearful doom she had shrunk, as if from a physical blow, nor did she once withdraw her eyes from his.

But the Duke had barely ceased to speak, when she swayed to her feet, and faced him in full defiance, her lovely face uplifted haughtily, her figure rigidly erect; and even Cumberland stood appalled at the weird intensity of her gaze. Suddenly, she began to sing, in tones whose ringing sweetness chilled the soul, so dreadful was their mockery of mirth:

> "*Hey, Johnnie Cope, are ye waukin' yet?*
> And are ye'r drums a-beating yet?
> If ye were a-waukin', I wad wait
> For to gang to the coals i' the morning!"

How strange a fate was hers, that even in this hour of her most poignant anguish she triumphed over her foe. For Cumberland's face turned grey at that defiant scorn, and his hands clenched violently, and his body trembled in a storm of baffled rage.

But now the sound of heavy footsteps grew audible without, the ponderous door was pushed aside, and there, in chains, between two guards, stood Donald Cameron.

CHAPTER XLII

"RED ROSES UNDER THE SUN"

"Red roses under the sun,
   For the King who is lord of lands,
But he dies when his day is done,
For his memory careth none
   When his glass runs empty of sands."

A SPLENDID and heroic figure, majestic still, he made in his once brilliant tartans, and yet dauntless mien. But Agnes only saw in him the wraith of that fair Donald of the garden, whose bonnet she had twined with fragrant tokens.

Brutally exultant, the Duke confronted the young Scot. "So you've come, my dashing Highland rebel, to greet your bonnie bride, ere you hie to your merry bridal with death to-morrow eve?"

But no mockery could shake the prisoner's lofty calm. His clear blue eyes were fixed upon the Duke in a superb disdain; then, with complete disregard of his captor, he turned to her he loved.

Agnes still remained where she had stood,—unmoving, one hand upon the table, the other pressed against her bosom,—like some fair, frozen thing, devoid of life. There seemed no quickening of her breath, no quivering of her lashes;—a marble incarnation of despair. But now, as Donald Cameron came toward her, the clashing of his fetters on the stones dispelled her torturing stupor, and she took a swaying step in his direction, repeating in a low, appalling voice, the fatal sentence of the vision: "*And the lad of the oak-leaves walks between armed men, with fetters on his hands.*"

Cumberland had the grace to withdraw, leaving the two victims of his cruelty to the utter anguish of their last meeting. For a moment they clung to each other in speechless woe, for neither dared to face the other's agony. Agnes's head was bowed upon Donald's shoulder, and, as he clasped her to him, his lips touched her loosened curls in a sad caress. At last she summoned strength enough to raise her head and meet his loving gaze with wide, unweeping eyes, the while her delicate body shook with fierce, convulsive sobs, and her lips grew pale as ashes, and her words forced their way in a piteous whisper.

"Donald, *you* in chains,—for my sake! O Son of God, have mercy! The rose, the thistle, and the heather I plucked that day of parting,—they had not power enough to baffle fate;—my prayers, my longing, and my love,—they were not strong enough to save you from this predestined doom! The wizard spoke too wisely; his prophecy is come to pass: '*For his fate sways your life as the moon sways the sea.*' O Christ, have pity!

"Why died you not upon Culloden, Donald? That had been mercy! That had been joy! Kind would have been the sword that took your life, my darling, for it would have given you a quiet grave beneath the heather, and not——"

She broke off, gasping sharply, stifling the cry that started to her lips, then turned in his clasp, and, with averted face, sobbed out: "I cannot bear it, Donald! I cannot bear so terrible a thing! That you should die that death for *me*, for *me*, who love you better than my soul; for me, who would have died in rapture, knowing *you* were spared! O God!—and such a fate!—'tis worthy of the fiends of hell! Donald, is there no land of peace, no valley of forgetfulness, wherein no memory enters? For even in the grave I could not rest, remembering *how you died!*"

"Ah, think not of it, sweetheart! 'Twill be quickly past! To die for you and for my King would hallow any doom. Let them mutilate my body as they will; they cannot touch my *soul*, and that will ever be with you, Agnes! See, here is the verse writ by the great Montrose the night before his execution." He drew a slip of paper from his breast. "'Tis graven on my heart as well!

"'Scatter my ashes, strew them in the air,—
 Lord, since Thou knowest where all those atoms are,
 I'm hopeful Thou'lt recover once my dust,
 And confident Thou'lt raise me with the just.'"

"Ah, Donald, you are brave as he was! Once I was brave, I think, but now—my strength is gone, and I can bear no more!"

A dreadful shuddering ran through her slender figure, and the nerves of her white throat quivered as in some fearful physical agony. Her face was colourless as marble, lips and cheeks alike of the same absolute pallor, and her eyes shone fixed and burning, like stars out of mist.

"The castle in the Highlands where we played; 'tis a blackened ruin now. Donald, 'tis like our lives;—yours on the awful brink,—and mine so marred with grief that none could know it! Oh, Donald, if my soul might pass with yours! if together we could journey to that other life where there is no more suffering,—no more woe!—no more days of slow, unending dread! I have long since ceased to number them; one day alone, I remember,—*April 16, Culloden!*"

And over the fatal name her voice trembled, as a mother's might have trembled in naming her dead son.

She let Donald kiss her hands and lips, and fold her again in his arms, without the terrible agitation she had shown at first. The violence of her grief seemed to have spent itself, as some mighty wave, hurled on the jagged rock, falls into shattered foam. She stood mute and passive,—conscious only through a dimness of agony that this was their last meeting upon earth.

Donald's face was of a deathly whiteness, as, with gentle urgence, he loosed the arms that clung about his neck.

"Farewell,—my love, my dear one,—my wife that should have been! This spray of heather shall not leave my breast till all is o'er! May Heaven's love enfold thee,—darling of my heart,—until we meet— to part no more—beyond the grave!"

. . . . .

When the fatal footsteps ceased to echo, Agnes flung her hands to her brow in a gesture of wild bewilderment, and staggering to a chair, burst suddenly into a violent storm of weird, unearthly laughter, a dreadful travesty of mirth.

Lady Cromarty, emerging from the deep embrasure where she had stood concealed, sprang to the girl, and caught the icy fingers in a restraining clasp.

"Agnes! Agnes! For God's sake, forbear! He may be pardoned even yet; I will seek the Prince of Wales,—the King!"

In her own breast she harboured no faintest shadow of hope, yet she saw this desperate comfort was absolutely needful to alleviate Agnes's suffering. But Agnes heeded not her protest. "Why, if every Scotsman's head were set on London Bridge, still we must be brave," she cried, and laughed again,—that eerie, haunting laughter.

Could it be that the girl's mind was beginning to give way beneath this agonising weight? She, who had borne every sorrow with the most undaunted courage? Yet had not the bound of endurance been reached at last? "She is either threatened with a fever," thought Bell Gordon, "or she is on the verge of madness. The wonder is she has not gone mad before!"

But when Lady Cromarty returned at night, after her weary quest through endless London streets, she found her unhappy ward composed and quiet, the feverish colour vanished. Agnes was sitting before the table, mute and motionless, the prayer-book lying open in her hands, with eyes that neither read nor saw.

"I shall go to Kensington to-morrow," said Lady Cromarty; "the King attends prayer in the chapel at 3 o'clock; 'tis then I shall offer my petition. May Heaven attend me in that hour!"

On being thus addressed, Agnes had turned her head in Lady Cromarty's direction, but she gave no appearance of listening, and made no attempt at response. Bell Gordon felt a fear at that unnatural calm; to her, wild woe and frantic weeping would have seemed less ominous.

The shadows of that dreadful night crept down about the Tower, enfolding it completely, as in some sable shroud. In that encompassing despair all objects took upon themselves a weird significance; the candle, quivering in the heavy draught, the dying ashes on the hearth, were both the tragic symbols of a fleeting life, whose wavering flame would soon be quenched in death.

Agnes sat against the wall, enveloped in her plaid, and beside her lay Bell Gordon, her head pillowed in Agnes's lap. Physically exhausted, Lady Cromarty quickly sank into a dreamless sleep; but the girl sat rigidly erect, her eyes fixed on the black, barred squares of the window, as on some ghastly vision. Agnes grew numb and cold in her constrained position; yet she would not move for fear of disturbing the sleeper. To her, sleep was a horror, a dreadful demon waiting to devour her, as soon as she should cross the boundary of his realm. For weeks her slumber had been tortured by fearful dreams,—grotesque, distorted things,—the offspring of a sorrow-haunted brain; and she had fought desire for sleep with all her force of will, knowing too well what host of goblins sleep would bring. She had banished them hitherto from her waking hours, but to-night the barriers of resistance were laid low, and over them swarmed the demons to people and possess the chambers of her brain. And thus she sat, a statue for stillness and for pallor, with that dread fixedness of gaze, that neither changed nor wavered, until the grey mid-winter dawn awoke upon that fatal day.

Lady Mackenzie, whispering words of vague consolement, made hurried preparations for her mission, but Agnes spoke no word until the other, upon leaving, bent to kiss her. Then Agnes, without change of posture, murmured low: "There is no hope on earth! 'Tis a fatal day for all who love the Stuart line!" And Lady Cromarty remembered that it was the 30th of January, the day on which Charles I. had died a martyr,—and thus remembering, shuddered.

. . . . .

A little group were gathering, expectant, about the chapel door at Kensington, for it was known that King George was coming hither to prayers that afternoon. Among them, mantled in her sombre cloak, stood Lady Cromarty, clutching wildly to her breast the paper which was to determine the fate of Lord Cromarty and the young Master of Locheil. After an agonising interval of waiting, the royal company was seen approaching from the Palace, the King—protected from the cold by a rich mantle, faced with ermine—walking in their midst. With whitening face, Bell Gordon scanned his features, for likeness of that Prince with whom she had tripped a measure nineteen years before; and wondered sadly if he, in turn, could have recognised in this grief-stricken woman the gay Bell Gordon of his youth. To enter the chapel, the King was obliged to pass closely by her, and, seizing this opportune moment, Lady Cromarty glided forward, and sank on her knees in his path, clutching his trailing cloak in one imploring hand, while with the other she proffered the petition. With frantic supplication she raised her eyes to his, crying faintly: "Mercy,—my lord, the King!"—felt blackness rush upon her, and sank, insensible, at his feet.

When she recovered consciousness, she found herself in a shadowy apartment of the Palace, with her companion, Lady Stair, bending anxiously over her. "With his own hand the King raised you up, and gave you into my keeping," she told Bell Gordon. "He is now considering the petition, and Lord Stair and his Grace of Hamilton are with him, pleading in the Earl's behalf. By sunset we shall know the King's decision."

"By sunset!" echoed Lady Cromarty; and, to herself, "O God! there is no time to spare!" for, by torchlight that same evening, Donald Cameron would meet his doom. Aloud she said: "There is yet an hour to pass. Will you not go, my lady, and see that a coach be in waiting to bear me straightway to the Tower, when his Majesty's decision is made known?"

When Lady Stair had gone upon her errand, Bell Gordon leaned back, faint and languid, in the elbow-chair, her delicate hands clenched tightly upon the massive arms. In her unnerved condition, each slightest sound came freighted with foreboding. The heavy moments dragged themselves interminably on; without, the dreary winter twilight spread its dim, grey pall; and still she sat thus, listening, her fingers clenched upon the chair, and the tortured muscles quivering in her slender throat. Once she spoke aloud, "Could even death be worse than this suspense?"

At last she heard a footstep in the adjoining chamber, and Lord Stair himself parted the sombre curtains. Even amid the dusk, Bell Gordon read upon his face a look of anxious hesitation. Somehow she rose, and steadied herself against the wall; and speechless, gazed at him with eyes of piteous entreaty. He gently took her hands before he spoke

"My lady, have no dread!—I only fear to startle you with news too joyful!—The King has granted pardons to them both;—*your husband and the young Locheil!*"

The room was mist to Lady Mackenzie's eyes; for a moment she was forced to lean against Lord Stair. And she murmured to herself: "This, too, is pain!"

In a joy as sharp as anguish, she made her way to where the coach was standing outside the Palace gates. "To the Tower!" she cried. "For God's sake, hasten!" and sank back, almost fainting, upon the cushioned seat. While the horses clattered noisily along the streets, she saw in a dreamful maze the myriad blur of faces, the lights that glimmered out amid the murk. And dreaming still, she reached

 "And the lad of the oak-leaves walks between armed men;—"

her journey's end; the coach drew up; and she alighted at the Tower.

As she glided swiftly through the gloomy corridors, she encountered Cumberland himself; and, drawing her skirts aside, as if his very touch contaminated, she swept past him with all a woman's splendid scorn. On the threshold of her husband's prison she paused, elated by her triumph, to give into the jailor's hand a paper with the royal seal. "A pardon for Lord Cromarty!" she cried, and then, "*Release the Master of Locheil!*"

CHAPTER XLIII

"MONY A HEART WILL BREAK IN TWA"

"Bonnie Charlie's noo awa,
   Safely owre the friendly main;
Mony a heart will break in twa
   Should he ne'er come back again."

LADY CROMARTY entered, to find Agnes kneeling by the open window, with her bowed head resting upon her clasped hands. At Bell Gordon's entrance she slowly turned and met her gaze with one of wild distraction; and with the dreadful appearance of looking past her at some appalling spectacle.

"He is dead," Agnes whispered, still gazing intently at Bell Gordon, and her face wore a strange, unnatural calm that chilled her companion's blood. "Donald Cameron is dead; he died an hour ago. Did you not hear the bell?—But no!—you had gone away, you could not hear it. They led him yonder through the courtyard. See how their footsteps stained the snow,—as if—*with blood!* He was fast bound with chains,—the guard on every side,—yet he raised his eyes to the window,—one last look of farewell,—O God! one last, last look! and the bell was tolling! tolling! Hark! I hear it now!"

She sprang to her feet, shuddering in every nerve, pressing her hands to her ears, as if indeed shutting out the dreaded sound.

"The bell!" she cried, "the bell! It is killing me! O God! will it never stop!"

Lady Cromarty stood motionless, frozen speechless by this new horror. Before she could make any wild attempt at explanation, Agnes had thrown herself at Bell Gordon's feet, and clung to her, sobbing piteously:

"O your Majesty, save him! save him! 'Tis only this one life I ask,—one life, out of all we gave you! We ne'er asked aught of thee or thine before; we gave you all we had, and spared not one! Oh, you will not in mercy refuse my only prayer! Save Donald Cameron, your Majesty,—save him, or let *me* die in his stead!"

Her voice rose to a wail of bitter anguish. Bell Gordon, herself almost frantic, bent above the frenzied girl, uttering wild words of reassurance, but in vain. She was unheeded,—unheard. Agnes again sprang to her feet, crying distractedly:

"No, no, you are not the Prince! If you were, you would not reject my petition! And what avails my pleading? Prince Charlie is not here;—he is far away across the sea!—he cannot help me now! And it is all too late, *too late*, for Donald Cameron is dead! *And the bell is tolling,—tolling!*"

And again, with a low, shuddering sob, she pressed her fingers to her ears.

Roused at last from her distraction, Bell Gordon seized Agnes's hands in hers, holding her fast, while she strove desperately to pour relief upon a heart so broken that hope could find no lodging.

"Agnes, Agnes, listen to me!—It is the truth I

speak!—Donald Cameron is not dead; this very day the King pardoned him! See, here is the paper commanding his release;—the death-sentence is changed to exile!—Look, Agnes, look, if you will not believe me!"

But the girl covered her eyes, and turned away, shuddering.

"No, no!" she moaned, "it is you who seek to deceive me! He is dead, he is dead, and you come too late to save him! O Donald! Donald!"

And with another deep, heart-rending sob, she fell senseless into Bell Gordon's arms.

She awoke, indeed, but only to the frenzied speech and wild delirium of fever. For days she lay, tossing ceaselessly, with bright, unseeing eyes; and from her lips flowed incoherent phrases, distorted, meaningless, cast, like broken driftwood, upon the shores of reason. It was as if her memory wandered through the ruined temple of past hopes, pausing beside each shattered column, stooping above each lovely fragment, searching down long vistas of despair, and crying ever one beloved name.

Through those long dreadful weeks Bell Gordon watched with an unfailing tenderness, an almost motherly affection, beside this pitiable victim of a monstrous tyranny. Agnes had grown dear to her as her own, and she saw with a sinking heart the cruel progress of the malady. But Bell Gordon had not kept this faithful vigil without the seeming sacrifice of her most cherished hope; now that her husband had been snatched from death, her most intense desire was that her child should be born in Scotland.

But when, at the end of three weeks, Agnes's fever

continued unabated, Lady Cromarty summoned the surgeon who was permitted to visit the hapless inmates of the Tower, and asked of him a question. For a moment he bent, pityingly, over the unconscious girl, then he turned to Lady Cromarty.

"I see not how the journey could alter her condition,—save for better,—for worse she could not be, and live. Perhaps, too, the change from this prison atmosphere to a purer air,—above all to that of her own country, may rouse her from this strange delirium. By all means, go, my lady, if such be your desire!"

The exiled Earl had already sought refuge in France, when Lady Cromarty set out upon her painful journey to Scotland. Enough physical hardships, alone, beset her path to have turned back one a single whit less dauntless; and to these were added the distressing condition of her fellow-traveller. It was late in February, and in England the spring rains had already begun, making travel both difficult and dangerous.

On the eve of her departure, Kenneth Campbell came to Agnes's bedside and, kneeling, kissed the frail, unconscious hand. Then, in a broken voice, he entrusted to Bell Gordon's care the ancient sword which he had found that fateful midnight in the dungeon.

"She gave for it all that was hers,—perhaps her life. Her touch has hallowed it! 'Tis not for me to keep!"

As the heavy coach jolted northward over the miry roads, Bell Gordon sat with Agnes's head in her lap, and shivered at the distracted speech that flowed continually from the girl's lips;—wild appeals to the courage of the clans, frantic pleading for Donald's pardon, broken stanzas of that scornful song which she had hurled at Cumberland;—repeated over and over, till the heart recoiled, in aching pity, from such depths of suffering and despair. Agnes had so long enacted the Prince that her personality seemed actually merged in his, and she thought as he would have thought,—spoke as he would have spoken. And Lady Cromarty began to fear lest this pitiful delusion should never end,—save in death.

At length, upon a bright spring day, the bold mass of the Cheviots rose before Bell Gordon's longing gaze, and her heart beat with rapture as she realised that she had reached her native land,—that Scottish soil lay firm beneath her feet. On the evening of the 5th of March they arrived at the little village of Melrose, and there, in the shadow of the ancient Abbey and the magic Eildon Hills, Bell Gordon's child was born,—the little child upon whose rosy neck was marked the semblance of a tiny axe,—the dreadful symbol of her father's over-shadowing doom, and who, as Lady Augusta, became the wife of Sir William Murray of Ochtertyre.

Lady Cromarty's indomitable spirit seemed to lend her bodily strength, and so great was her desire to reach the Castle in Ross, that ten days later she resumed her journey northward. All this while Agnes had lain insensible, sunk in a baffling lethargy, which no effort of Lady Cromarty's could dispel. The wild delirium had left her, but the overpowering languor which had followed was yet more ominous.

So alarming became Agnes's condition that Bell Gordon stopped the coach one afternoon near a wretched cluster of huts, and herself alighted to seek aid. Fortunately, she found, in one of the better dwellings, a physician from the neighbouring town, who immediately accompanied her to Agnes.

On a heap of straw in one corner of the hut the girl lay, an old military cloak thrown around her, and her hand still grasping the broadsword of Dundee. Her tangled yellow hair fell in a shower of gold about her shoulders, painfully intensifying the startling pallor of her face. Her great brown eyes, larger and darker now, by contrast with their marble setting, were fixed in a motionless gaze, wide and inscrutable, as if her mind were far removed from the actual time and place. She neither stirred nor spoke when the surgeon entered; indeed, she seemed unconscious of his presence till he bent over her and took her hand. Then, only, did her gaze leave the distance to rest with a startled look upon his face.

"You are not a friend to the King," she murmured, in a faint, dreaming voice, "yet I think you would not do us injury."

Lady Cromarty had entered with the surgeon, and, presently, she touched his sleeve, and, drawing him apart, related Agnes's tragic story. At its close she turned to him, whispering anxiously: "Tell me, sir, what will be the end of it? This infant in my arms is scarcely dearer than is she,—sweet, dauntless girl!—For God's sake, lighten my anxiety!— Tell me she will recover!"

"She has youth in her favour,—that is all!" he said gravely, in answer to the terrified appeal, "but even youth may be helpless in such an extremity! She has borne all,—body and soul,—that any mortal can endure;—enough to kill the strongest man,—how much more a delicate woman, and 'twill be little less than a miracle if she recovers."

And as he left the hut he murmured bitterly, "Another martyr to the Stuarts!"

. . . . .

In the ancient Castle of Ballone, the sea-girt fortress of Lord Cromarty, Agnes lay, in that strange deathlike trance from which no sound could wake her. Her cheeks had the delicate pallor of white petals, and her long brown lashes lay upon their rose-pure softness like shadows upon snow. Her lips showed a faint scarlet line, and the yellow shimmer of the hair that brushed her face had the luminance of gold on marble. She had lain there, in hushed unconsciousness, for well-nigh twenty days; it was mid-April now.

It seemed to Lady Cromarty while she watched beside the silent figure that even death itself could never be more still. Yet dreadful as it was to have her lie so like a lifeless image wrought of marble, it was a hundred-fold more merciful than those fearful days when she had tossed incessantly, sobbing out wild entreaties and imploring prayers that forced their utterance from the very heart-throbs of despair.

Once a priest came, and knelt and prayed beside the still, white figure, while Lady Cromarty kept guard at the chamber-door. The other clergy of the neighbourhood were all of the Whig persuasion, and Bell Gordon would have none of them here.

To-night,—it was the fatal eve of red Culloden,—she realised with sudden desolation how hopeless was this battle with despair. Agnes was growing hourly weaker; in a few days more this sublime self-sacrifice would be fully consummated, and the last of the loyal Leslies would have passed to a martyr's grave. She bent with stifled sobs and kissed the smooth, pure brow, and it was cold to her lips as death.

At daybreak of that sad 16th of April, Bell Gordon wakened, with a woeful heart. A rosy light was stealing up the heavens, and strewing crimson petals on the sea. But Bell Gordon shrank from its beauty and drew her child the closer.

"Were she to waken now," she murmured,—"were she to waken and remember,—she would die of grief!—I am glad she cannot waken,—better that death should take her sleeping."

A faint stir in the chamber made her turn from the window. There, in the rosy dawn-light, stood Agnes, calm and stately, a faint, sweet smile upon her lips, and one hand holding to her breast a slender spray of heather.

"I dreamt a wonderful dream last night," the girl said very softly. "I thought I strove to walk upon the sea, and sank as Peter did who went to meet Our Lord. And suddenly, as the waves were closing o'er my head, Christ came to me upon the water, and took my hand, and raised me up, saying: 'Sink no more into these waves of grief. Those who died are happy; thou shalt weep for them no more! And he, whom thou hast mourned as dead, yet liveth!' And with these words, He laid His hand upon my bosom, and the pain that throbbed there ceased; and the face of the Christ, so beautiful and tender, seemed to bless me, and straightway I awoke, and felt myself made well.—Save that I am weak, there is no illness left."

She pressed the spray of heather to her bosom. "The weight has passed away," she murmured softly, "*and Donald Cameron lives!*"

CHAPTER XLIV

"THE SUN SHINES SWEET ON THE HEATHER"

> "The sun shines sweet on the heather,
> When tempests are over and gane."

IT was ripe mid-summer of the year 1749. The purple glory of the heather lay upon Scotland's hills like a royal mantle. The undulating vastness of the moor, unbounded as the sky, was spread with hue of amethyst,—or so it seemed afar; but when the feet had crossed its confines, this glowing carpet changed its kingly colour, and purple melted into rose, and lifted nodding sprays and elfin clusters, and set to rocking in the whispering wind the sunset-tinted spires of the heather,—the fairest flower ever made by God,—till myriads of dancing bells rang out their fairy melodies.

On all the violet reaches of Drummossie Muir no creature stirred, no being breathed, save for one solitary figure,—a girlish figure, in a tartan plaid, with brightly flowing hair, a-glimmer in the sun. Yet though the figure moved in seeming solitude, the eyes held not a trace of loneliness within their sunny calm. There was a wistful peace in the uplifted face, that blent in perfect concord with the tender reverie of the scene. She trod the heath as lightly as a fay; the trailing fringes of her tartan brushed the tinted bloom, and the faint, exquisite fragrance of the heather rose like subtile incense.

Along her pathway ran the low, uneven ridges, canopied with purple, which marked the resting-place of heroes. A moment before she had knelt and touched those hallowed mounds with soft, caressing fingers; now she paused, and looked back at them, not with woe nor shrinking, simply with tenderness and deep homage.

"If Donald were but here!" The whisper did not break the stillness, but the fingers twined above the cairngorm at her breast grew tense with fervent longing. Her gaze, which had sought the distance, pursuing a swallow's flight to seaward, had fallen to the blossoms at her feet. Suddenly, a light, compelling thrill ran through her, fraught with portent, and, looking up, she saw him coming toward her through the heather.

Unchanged he seemed,—the Donald of her dreams, —the Donald of the days of Holyrood,—from the fair head, uncovered in the sunlight, to the plumed bonnet by his side. Motionless, mute with transport, she stood and gazed upon him, as if her very soul poured through the gates of vision. Transformed from wistfulness to wonder,—from longing to the rapture of reality, she felt no need for speech or movement,—no wish save to let the blissful truth sink deep into her being.

Slowly he drew near, his blue eyes shining with their changeless splendour, the splendour of his love. Then, suddenly, the spell was lifted that held the two apart; a moment more, and they were clasped in each

"And looking up, she saw him coming toward her through the heather."

other's arms. Agnes was whispering broken words of ecstasy, that forced their way in mighty overflow from the unsealed fountains of her soul.

"O Donald, my darling;—when I remember the fearful shadow over you,—when I think of the lives that went out around you on every side,—I can never cease to think of that deliverance,—to bless the God Who in mercy gave you back to me!—Donald, with every breath I draw, so long as I shall live, I will bless the love that saved your life;—the love in Heaven and the love on earth!"

And Donald answered by a tender tightening of the arms that clasped her, and by the gentle kisses he pressed upon her brow.

"But Donald, tell me,"—and her eyes were widening with the old-time fear,—"how have you dared to venture hither,—*you*, an exile still,—and,—in the forbidden dress?" And she touched with a sad caress the folds of his belted plaid, for in 1747 the cruel law was passed by Parliament depriving the Highlanders of the right to wear the tartan, or even to dress in their own manner, under pain of imprisonment or transportation.

"Agnes, it is to Colonel Campbell, our mutual friend and benefactor, that I owe the privilege of treading, unharmed, upon my native soil, and of wearing the forbidden costume of the conquered Scot!" The words were spoken fervently, with mingled gratitude and bitterness, and, presently, he murmured mournfully:

"O my hapless country,—doomed to suffer such a fate! O land of mine, wherein the tartan, loved of all our ancient race, may nevermore be worn by their descendants!"

The tears of passionate resentment were sparkling in his bright blue eyes, but he dashed them away, exclaiming: "Nay, Agnes, I am coward now, and 'tis no time to weep, for grief avails us nothing! In the town yonder Angus waits us;—when I took ship for France, I found him,—faithful comrade,—by my side. For one day only I am free to walk on Scottish heath, and that day wanes full swiftly." He pointed to the westward-dipping sun. "Agnes, Scotland is no longer ours;—the tyrant rules, and we are powerless. Whither shall we flee, then, sweetheart? To France?"

"O Donald, not to France, where the brave Locheil died an exile;—'tis the country of broken hearts!"

"Then to America," he answered, "'tis a land of freedom, that welcomes and befriends the fugitive. Thither have thousands of our countrymen, rent from their native land, already found a refuge!

"'The Lady of Locheil,' they called you once in Edinbro'," continued Donald softly. "Will you be in truth 'the Lady of Locheil,'—will you be my wife forever, beloved Agnes Leslie?"

She turned and looked in his with sweet unwavering eyes. "Forever, Donald Cameron, in this world and the next, so long as love abides, and God is King!"

A solemn silence like a benediction attended on her answer. Then Agnes spoke in mournful reminiscence:

"This is the 19th of August, Donald. Four years

ago to-day the standard was unfurled upon Glenfinnan, and from you there came to me that slip of bark I welcomed with such rapture. Four short years, and yet,—O Heaven,—what an age of anguish!"

"Think not of them, Agnes," whispered Donald. "God only knows the reason for that abyss of suffering,—for that vast company of broken hearts! For us,—the shadows and the tears;—for them,"— his speaking gestures swept the lonely moor,—"for them,—*the glory of the dead!*"

"O Donald,—all our shattered hopes! The closed gate at Auchnacarry that nevermore shall open; the prayers like withered rose-buds that never shall unfold!—The dreams that thronged my soul at Holyrood, when Prince Charlie led the ball with me!—If you had but been there, Donald,—through all the splendour I longed for you,—lover of mine!—And Lydia Leslie's gown,—it was fashioned of dreams, I think,—shall never again be worn by me, nor shall a child of mine ever wear it—until the King comes hame!"

"Ah, sweetheart, we must go," said Donald gently. "The sun is setting fast."

Beside one hallowed mound they knelt together, and Agnes pressed upon it a tender reverent kiss. "Laddie, farewell," she whispered. "And you,— brave heart,—who lie at rest beyond the sea,—from Heaven send a blessing on your children!"

They rose, and stood looking westward across the tragic heath. The sun had reached the horizon's brim, and lo!—a miracle! The hills of Ross were purple islands in a sea of gold; the river Ness was a bow of jasper, shot with arrowy flame; and the sombre towers of Inverness were lifted through the amber glow, as in some mystical mirage. All things were touched and sanctified by that transfiguring light; even the desolate moor where Scotland's hope lay buried was glorified by the hallowing splendour.

The exiles stood in silence and watched the mystic radiance creep up and flood the heavens, and fade in tender tints of twilight. Donald's face was lighted with a splendid peace, and Agnes, as he clasped her to him, could feel the fervent beating of his heart.

Death had been so near to him that its dank breath had touched his forehead, and yet he had survived that ghastly contact, and the shadowy pathway, shunned of all men, had not been his to tread. But life,—that rapturous, transfigured life, to which he was restored,—had that wherein the past could claim no part;—an ecstasy,—a glory,—a something whereon God had breathed, as on a crystal,—effacing Death's fell stain,—and hallowed it forever!

. . . . .

The sunset-fire grew faint,—was quenched in mist of twilight; not so the glory in their hearts, for that no earthly mist could dim. They turned their faces whither,—a beacon of hope to guide them,—a star burned above Inverness.

In the Highland town they found an aged minister of the Scottish-Episcopal denomination, who had served the Stuarts in two wars, and, because of his fidelity to his church and king, was now a hunted outcast, forbidden even to read prayers without perjuring himself. He received the fugitives with an eager welcome, for there is no fellowship so strong as suffering, save that of love itself. There, in the tiny chapel, denied to worshippers because its minister had refused to take the oath of perjury—that of swearing that James VIII. was not his father's child—the solemn words were spoken that bound them in holy union,—a union indissoluble, till God Himself should part them for a little space.

In the first sacred hours of their marriage, they stood upon the vessel's bow, and gazed at the bright host of stars embosomed in the placid Moray Firth, and at the heaven of stars that shone above them. And, as they listened to the rising tide, so soon to bear them free, Agnes remembered pityingly another ship that had sailed at midnight. And so the hour came, the sails were lifted, and the stately ship weighed anchor outward bound.

CHAPTER XLV.

"WHO FOUGHT AND DIED FOR CHARLIE!"

"No more we'll see such deeds again,
   Deserted is each Highland glen,
   And lonely cairns are o'er the men
     Who fought and died for Charlie!"

ON a certain stormy April evening of the year 1754, a figure shrouded in a sable cloak entered with faltering footsteps a little tavern at Avignon. Having ordered a room, and dismissed the servant, he cast aside the enveloping cloak, and sank dejectedly beside the hearth, revealing to the firelight the features of the once blithe "Bonnie Prince," now, alas! how sadly altered, how marred by misfortune and sorrow! With a deep-drawn, shuddering sigh,—the echo of a sob,—he lapsed into woeful reverie.

"To what fearful depths have I fallen when the memory of the only heart I ever truly loved kindles in me such shame! . . . And Agnes!—she is safe within your keeping, Donald, who alone were worthy of her! Does she ever think, I wonder, what suffering she escaped when she refused to link her fate with mine? Does she ever think with a shudder of the homeless wanderer across the seas, for whose life she risked her own, and who, degraded and despised, drags out a miserable existence? What can a bird do that has found no nest?—He must flit from bough to bough!——

"And yet she loved me, call it by what name ye will! The splendour of that love,—once it inspired me to hope,—to venture;—now,—O Heaven!—that love will haunt me all my ruined life!—From the moment that she left me, I have known no hour of peace, no hour of honour; and, losing her, I passed to utter darkness!"

He took the flickering candle from the table, and, holding it to the mirror, gazed for a little while at the face it shone upon. Then, with a despairing groan, he turned away.

"It is still more changed than I had thought!—Even *you*, Agnes, would never know me now!"

Suddenly, he started up again,—a momentary radiance in his eyes,—those eyes, as yet unchanged,—the bright, melancholy brown eyes that had charmed so many hearts with their winning glances;—he started up,—drew toward him pen and paper.

"I will write and ask it,—ask one word of sympathy and hope!—*She* will not withhold it!—Even in this hour,—lost being that I am,—*she* will not condemn me, for her heart is tender as 'tis pure, and angels are the readiest to forgive!"

He wrote for some time in silence,—the quill pen moving slowly over the paper; then, suddenly, he paused, and held the letter to the light, a strange decision kindling in his mournful eyes.

"No! No!" he reiterated, rising in agitation, "it shall never be! Shall I play the coward to the only soul I reverence?—Has she not suffered enough through me, that I should call her thoughts to scenes of wretchedness!——

"Of the priceless debt I owe, can I not pay this much, that no voice out of Hades shall ever disturb her peace,—that no shadow from my outer darkness shall ever fall across her life!"

And over his features, changed as they were by suffering and woe, there flashed the light of sacrifice that touched them to transfiguring beauty, as, with calm determination, he held the unfinished letter to the candle's flame, and watched it burn to ashes!

When this was done, he sank once more on the seat by the fire, and communed with his own sad spirit.

"O Scotland!—my beloved country!—land of such loyal hearts!—I, who love you,—for whom you endured such affliction, must never again behold your beauty;—never again gaze upon your glorious mountains, clad in heather!—I, whom you called the 'Bonnie Prince,' must live and die,—a wretched exile,—beholding you nevermore!

"Yet I once had my triumph,—my fleeting dream of glory,—that still throws its splendour across my darkened years!—O Agnes! Agnes!—if I had but set before me your ideal;—had only suffered you—my loved, lost star,—to guide my troubled way!—But I have wandered far,—O Heaven! how far!—from that pure beacon,—and I have paid the penalty of wanderers!—*To live, and not to live!* Even my deadliest enemy might pity me to-night!

"To the last my heart will be with Scotland!—O my gallant Highlanders, *you* would never have forsaken me, like these false friends of mine! And Murray—he sacrificed the woman I love to save my worthless life.—I will not look upon his face again!—Eight years ago this day—eight endless years—O God!—Drummossie Muir! Again, in dreams of anguish, I see the wild, waste moorland,—Culloden's fatal heath;—and again the clans charge onward to their death;—Camerons here, MacLeans yonder, gallant Gordons and loyal Stuarts breast to breast,—pouring their blood for me like water upon those English bayonets;—again they rally, again they are swept down, like dying leaves before that hurricane of flame, and death and desolation drop their ghastly curtain over that dread day! Yet even then,—when the star of the Stuarts,—that fated race of kings,—doomed throughout all the centuries, from woeful Mary to *me*, last and most wretched of all their hapless line,—even then,—when that star set forever on Culloden,—I might have worn my sorrow nobly;—might at least have breasted the surges of despair, not sunken beneath their engulfing waves!—And instead!—To what abyss of misery have I fallen! —What heritage of shame is mine!—Death is all I can look for now, and even death may not end—*remorse!* O God, it is *too late! too late!*"

. . . . .

A few years after the tragic "'45," Kenneth sailed to America, to serve with the King's forces in the war with Canada. But Fate was kind to him; the New World was wide, and the path of his life never crossed that of the woman he loved and had lost forever. Kenneth attained the highest military honours; he rose to the rank of general, and made the name of Campbell renowned throughout the army. For some, time might have come with consolation to set another image in the heart; but Kenneth lived and died, unforgetting, holding forever the memory of one face;—a strange fulfilment of the curse of Glencoe.

. . . . .

To Donald and Agnes, although exiles, Fate was gracious; the home they found in the New World enshrined in it the memories of the old. Agnes's loyal love for Prince Charlie never waned,—never lost that spirit of devotion which had made it a thing sublime. It was a love which Agnes herself could not have analysed,—could not have told wherein it resembled the love that is one with loyalty, wherein it differed from the love of a maid for a man.

"The Bible bids us 'fear God,' and 'honour the King,'" she was wont to declare. "Could I honour the King too much?"

She had been known to strike anyone who dared to call Charles the Pretender; and, to the end of her life, she never failed to rise in indignant protest when the prayers were read in church for the royal family. "The Elector of Hanover released him," she would say of Donald's deliverance. No power on earth could have made her say, "The King pardoned him." George II. was never king to her; her heart owned allegiance only to the unhappy Prince across the water, whose sceptre was of shadows, whose kingdom was of dreams. The rumours of his darkened life she passionately denied; her love for him throve with the delicate strength of the pink morning-glories that bloom to this day on the little isle of Eriska, off the west coast of Scotland,—where the Prince planted

"Who Fought and Died For Charlie!"

them upon disembarking. Of her, as of him, it might be truly said: "Scotland cannot judge thee, for she loves thee!"

. . . . .

In the year 1784, almost half-a-century after their confiscation, the forfeited estates of Scotland were finally restored; and the country of Locheil came again into the possession of the Camerons. Donald and Agnes returned to Auchnacarry,—nevermore to wander;—and built beside the hallowed ruins of the ancient castle the stately mansion which still shelters their descendants.

Of their sons, the eldest,—Donald,—bore his father's title of Locheil; the second,—Charles Stuart,—took his mother's name of Leslie, and succeeded to the earldom and estate of Rothes; and the third, called Norman, after him who slumbered on Drummossie Muir, won for himself a record,—he and his sons' sons,—on many a battle field, and one of his descendants,—a lad with the name and face of "the gentle Locheil," took part in the glorious charge of the Scots Greys at Waterloo. And there was, besides, a daughter,—a fair but not a fairer Agnes than she of whom Charles dreamed at Holyrood.

. . . . .

Certain priceless tokens were treasured by the Camerons:—a curl of golden hair; a silken breast-knot that had once been white; a splendid topaz ring; and an old Highland claymore, with the letter S in its twisted hilt and a faded bit of blood-stained ribbon. The curl had been cut from the head of "Bonnie Prince Charlie"; the breast-knot had been worn by

Agnes Leslie on that fateful autumn day of "the '45," when Holyrood welcomed back the last of the Stuart Kings; the ring had flashed in the midnight gloom of a dungeon, and gleamed in the dying embers of an Old Year's Night; and the sword was the sword which "Bonnie Dundee" wore to his death at Killiecrankie, and which a girl—his kinswoman— had drawn for a Prince's honour. Sacred they were held by those who loved the fallen cause, and sacred indeed they were,—if love and loyalty can hallow earthly things,—for they were relics of the bravest men that glorious Scotland ever knew;—the gallant Highlanders, who gave their lives in a vain but splendid heroism,—a sublime last attempt to recover the throne of the Stuarts, and, all unseeking, won for themselves imperishable fame—a fame that shall live forever, enduring as Ben Lomond, as long as the Highland heather,—once dyed crimson with their blood,—enfolds their hallowed graves!

"Dark though the day be, its clouds will blaw past,
  An' a morrow will come wi' the sun shining fairly;
Up the red steep we will struggle at last,
  An' place the auld crown on your head, Royal Charlie!"

HESTER OF THE GRANTS

A ROMANCE OF OLD BENNINGTON

By THEODORA PECK

A CHARMING story of Vermont in early days, when it was part of the so-called Hampshire Grants. The little Green Mountain villages know a wealth of stirring romance, hitherto untold, marked by the flavor of the forest, and the rugged strength of sturdy mountaineers. This tale takes one back to the days of a race that won its living from the soil, and loved and hated, fought and died with the intensity of primal people.

Frontispiece by Thomas Mitchell Peirce. Cloth $1.50. For the special Vermont Edition, see last page.

ADMIRAL GEORGE DEWEY, U. S. N.:

" 'Hester of the Grants' is a most stirring historical novel, and I have read it with additional interest because of my state pride. A noteworthy achievement which promises still more for the future."

U. S. SENATOR REDFIELD PROCTOR:

"I have read 'Hester of the Grants' and so have my wife and children and grandchildren, with very great interest. An interesting story, touching with the hand of romance a very interesting period of our early history."

HON. CHARLES H. DARLING, Asst. Secretary of the Navy:

" 'Hester of the Grants' is a faithful and interesting portrayal of the struggles of those who were perplexed in the extreme, and in addition to the historical allusions it has the merit of being a most readable and delightful story."

CORPORAL JAMES TANNER, Commander-in-Chief, Grand Army of the Republic:

"To say that I was very much interested in 'Hester of the Grants' but faintly expresses it. I took it up at a quarter past ten P.M. and became so absorbed in it that I simply could not quit it until I reached the end, which was a little after three A. M."

MAJOR-GENERAL F. C. AINSWORTH, Military Secretary, U. S. A.:

"I have read 'Hester of the Grants' with interest and pleasure. It is a good story well told, and is well worth reading not only by the sons and daughters of

Vermont, but by all who are interested in the lives and times of those who helped to build that commonwealth and to defend it in its infancy."

PROF. J. E. GOODRICH, University of Vermont:

"I could not but note the authoress' careful study of the topography of Bennington, as also the extent to which she had reproduced the tone and atmosphere of the time. The book will quicken local patriotism and should prove to younger readers an appetizing introduction to the history of the Republic of Vermont."

GOV. C. J. BELL:

"'Hester of the Grants' should be read by every New Englander."

PROF. EDWARD H. GRIFFIN (Dean), Johns Hopkins University:

"A distinctly successful attempt to reproduce the life of the Revolutionary period. I am delighted to know that the book is meeting with so much recognition."

NEW YORK TRIBUNE:

"Most of all to be praised for its atmosphere of truth, an atmosphere which envelops the substance of the narrative as though with the light and air and color of old Bennington in its most picturesque and exciting days."

ARMY AND NAVY JOURNAL:

"A spirited and wholesome story of love and war in Vermont during the Revolution. Miss Peck has treated her theme with womanly feeling, grace, and dramatic art of a high order. The whole story abounds in the Green Mountain atmosphere."

JOURNAL OF COMMERCE AND COMMERCIAL BULLETIN:

"The spirit of the time has been very cleverly caught and sustained, and, to select one instance from many, the chapter describing the battle of Bennington is a most vivid piece of writing. The book will be read by all Vermonters, young and old, and many for whom the state itself has no special attractions will find the story irresistible from its innate truth and naturalness."

BOSTON TRANSCRIPT:

"So exceedingly well written as to blend history and fiction cleverly. The author has interwoven a complicated plot and a strong love interest that places the romance far above the many of its kind."

THE VERMONT EDITION

OF

"HESTER OF THE GRANTS"

BY THEODORA PECK,

deserves a place in your library, especially if you are a Vermonter, and interested in Vermont history and Vermont authors. The story has made a place for itself in literature, and the new edition makes a very desirable book. Handsomely printed on fine paper and profusely illustrated from photographs of the beautiful and historic scenes in which the story is laid.

$2.50 net, by mail $2.68.